NORTHLAND

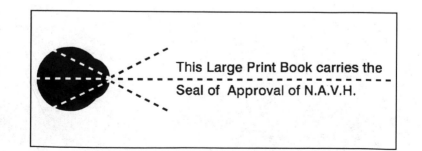

This Large Print Book carries the
Seal of Approval of N.A.V.H.

NORTHLAND

A 4,000-MILE JOURNEY ALONG
AMERICA'S FORGOTTEN BORDER

PORTER FOX

THORNDIKE PRESS
A part of Gale, a Cengage Company

Farmington Hills, Mich • San Francisco • New York • Waterville, Maine
Meriden, Conn • Mason, Ohio • Chicago

Copyright © 2018 by Porter Fox.
Maps by David Lindroth.
Thorndike Press, a part of Gale, a Cengage Company.

ALL RIGHTS RESERVED
Thorndike Press® Large Print Popular and Narrative Nonfiction.
The text of this Large Print edition is unabridged.
Other aspects of the book may vary from the original edition.
Set in 16 pt. Plantin.

LIBRARY OF CONGRESS CIP DATA ON FILE.
CATALOGUING IN PUBLICATION FOR THIS BOOK
IS AVAILABLE FROM THE LIBRARY OF CONGRESS

ISBN-13: 978-1-4328-5748-6 (hardcover)

Published in 2018 by arrangement with W.W. Norton & Company, Inc.

Printed in Mexico
1 2 3 4 5 6 7 22 21 20 19 18

for Sara

The Northland

PACIFIC OCEAN

ROCKY

BRITISH
COLUMBIA

ALBERTA

NORTHERN ROCKIES

SASKATCHEWAN

Banff

Calgary

Medicine Hat

"Medicine Line"

Great Northern

Vancouver

Bellingham

WASHINGTON

Coeur d'Alene

Columbia River

MONTANA   Glasgow   RR

Little Bighorn
Battlefield National
Monument

Missouri R.

The Medicine Line

ROCKY   MOUNTAINS

ROCKY MOUNTAIN FRONT

IDAHO

Oregon Trail

Bozeman Trail

MANITOBA

Lake
Winnipeg

Regina

Winnipeg

PLAINS

NORTH
DAKOTA
Bismarck

Fargo

Standing Rock
Sioux Reservation

Dakota Access Pipeline

GREAT

SOUTH
DAKOTA

Seven Fires

PLAINS

Oregon Trail

Denver

PLAINS

UNITED

E   D

100   MILES

1000 KILOMETERS

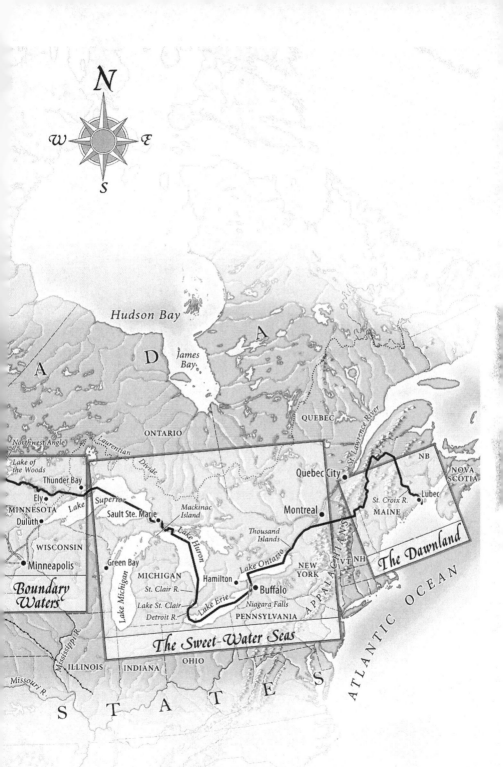

CONTENTS

INTRODUCTION

No one knows where America's northern border begins. It is somewhere near Machias Seal Island, twenty-five miles off Jonesport, Maine. Most know where it goes: six hundred miles around Maine's panhandle; across New Hampshire, Vermont, and New York; west along the Saint Lawrence River; through four of the five Great Lakes; into Minnesota's Boundary Waters; and straight across North Dakota, Montana, Idaho, and Washington on the forty-ninth parallel.

On paper, the boundary looks like a discarded thread — twisted and kinked in parts, tight as a bowstring in others. Much of the line was drawn before modern surveying technology was invented, so it follows things you can see on a map: rivers, lakes, latitude, longitude. Where the boundary tracks a waterway, the rule is to follow the deep-water mark, making it look like a very drunk or very old man drew it freehand — which, in some cases, is very close to the truth. The only indication that two of the world's most powerful nations meet on these stretches is a procession of faded American and Canadian flags on either side, planted in yards, on porches, and on telephone poles.

The northern border looks like an accident in many places. It runs along the forty-fifth parallel straight through the Haskell Free Library and Opera House in Derby Line, Vermont. Near Cornwall, Ontario, it splits the Akwesasne Mohawk Indian reservation in half, and in Niagara it bisects the largest waterfall on the continent. Homes, businesses, families, golf courses, wood pulp factories, and a natural-gas plant straddle the line. Taverns were purposely built directly on the borderline during Prohibition to welcome Americans on one side and sell them booze on the other. Where the boundary follows the forty-ninth parallel in the West, it cuts straight through obstacles like valleys, watersheds, and eight-thousand-foot peaks — necessitating a chaotic system of rules and easements to determine sovereignty and access. Pan out 50,000 feet above the line and you see the shape of America. Zoom in and you recognize the timber yards, kettle lakes, table-lands, and two-lane asphalt roads of what locals call the "northland."

Northlanders have little interest in the rest of the Union, and the rest of the Union has little interest in its northern fringe. There are other names for it: northern tier, Hi-Line, north country. Academics who study borders call either side of a new boundary where the line is vague and where the populations on both sides are still intercon-nected a "borderland." As the border be-comes more defined and enforced, the borderland evolves into "bordered lands" — where movement and commerce are re-stricted. What was once a singular region becomes two, and both sides develop indi-vidual identities, economies, and cultures. Land on either side of the US-Canada border exists somewhere between these two.

At 5,525 miles, including Alaska, the northern border is the longest international boundary in the world. Without Alaska, the 3,987-mile line capping the Lower 48 is the third-longest. Politicians, federal agents, pundits, and most Americans focus on the line with Mexico, even though its northern cousin is more than twice its length and many times more porous. The only known terrorists to cross overland into the US came from the north. Fifty-six billion dollars in smuggled drugs and ten thousand illegal aliens cross the US-Canada border every year. Two thousand agents watch the line. Nine times that number patrol the southern boundary. According to a 2010 Congressional Research Service report, US Customs and Border Protection maintains "operational control" over just sixty-nine miles of the northern border.

For two hundred years, the northern border *was* America's principal boundary. The history of the continent played out along the line, chronologically from east to west: the Age of Discovery; the first colonies; the fishing, timber, and fur trades; the French and Indian Wars; the British Empire; the American Revolution; Lewis and Clark's Corps of Discovery; the War of 1812; the Indian Wars; and westward expansion.

An old friend once described the northland as "a place that didn't change between the American Revolution and 1970." It is true. Bands of Scandinavians, Russians, French, Scottish, Dutch, and German Americans — descended from original settlers — still live there in an archipelago of ethnic islands. Some of the largest remaining American Indian tribes — the continent's actual first settlers — live there too, most on exploited and tyrannized reservations. Auto maintenance, home maintenance, knowledge of weather, fishing, and hunting are essential skills because there is often no one there to do it for you. You can still put groceries on an account in the northland, run up a weekly tab at the bar, or take out your neighbor's fence after one too many as long as you fix it within the month. The landscape there represents "nature" to people who visit for a long weekend and then race home. To northlanders, nature is not a thing you go see; it is the place you live.

It is not all quaint. There are problems like teen pregnancy, domestic violence, drugs, poverty, obesity, bigotry. Unless there's oil or gas to drill for, the economy is typically slow. In many places, there isn't much to do in the winter except work, watch TV, go to church, get drunk, get mad, or all of the above. The winter is long. It gets dark at four in the afternoon and stays that way until eight in the morning. It gets so cold that streetlights shine straight up through airborne frost instead of down. Towns smell of woodsmoke, and windstorms sweeping south from Canada make the forest groan.

When modern civilization finally arrived,

the northland changed quickly. Silvery highways now cut across the backcountry, and high-voltage power lines slice through remote mountain passes. Tourists wearing safari vests have overrun centuries-old fishing and mill towns in the Northeast, while developers have made a killing selling luxury mountain homes in former western ranching and mining towns. Before September 11, 2001, half of the 119 border crossings between the US and Canada were unguarded at night. Since then, the Department of Homeland Security has increased the number of agents by 500 percent and installed sensors, security cameras, military-grade radar, and drones — cutting off northland families, businesses, church congregations, hospitals, and Indian nations from their Canadian counterparts.

The northland's fragile environment has taken a hit as well. In a warming world, temperatures in northern latitudes are rising faster than southern temps, threatening snowpacks, rivers, forests, habitats, wetlands, and freshwater reservoirs from Washington's North Cascades to the Great Lakes to Maine's North Woods. Overfishing and warming waters in the North Atlantic have left the fishery on the brink of extinction, while pollution and erratic water levels in the Great Lakes threaten America's primary supply of surface freshwater. In North Dakota, a historic oil boom has transformed the state — and America's effort to lower greenhouse gas emissions — in a mad dash to pump as much oil as possible before the end of the fossil fuel era.

I grew up in the northland, on an island in northern Maine. I saw how living close to America's northern border shapes communities there. There are river valleys near the boundary where everyone speaks French, others that fly the British flag. Locals speak with a Scottish-Acadian-Massachusetts brogue that inverts *a*'s and *r*'s — distorting the word "karma" into *kah-mer*. General stores in the North sell poutine and rappie pie. Markets on the coast stack their counters with the same salted cod sticks and pickled hogs' feet that British colonists once preserved.

My father was a boat builder, and we spent half the year in the North Atlantic, close to where the line begins. It was an exotic place to come of age. Fog bends the light in the morning and turns seawater green black. Wisps of it curl through the streets and strafe thick stands of pine and spruce. In the winter, nor'easter gales make the rain gutters sing and blow the front door in. In the summer, the ocean is a wide, blue basin, in constant motion and brushed by the wind.

We drove three hours farther north every summer to a hunting lodge that my great-great-grandfather built in 1909. It is seven miles from the Canadian border. Half the town is from Canada, half from America. People there rarely agree with one another, but they are quick to laugh. They tell stories in the old style, rooted in dark, underlying irony. (Mother-in-law falls off a lobster boat. Lobsterman hauls her in with twenty lobsters hanging off her dress. Lobsterman's wife yells, "Set her again!") They are quicker to talk about you when you leave the room. It is a small room, the northeastern corner pocket of the country.

When I was old enough to leave home, I wandered west — first to Vermont, then Wyoming. I inadvertently moved along the line, always above the fortieth parallel, and found something familiar there: ethnic communities with centuries-old histories, small towns that modern America skipped over, forgotten industries and Old World professions that rely on hands, not machines. There are fewer houses and longer stretches of nothing in between. Some of America's last herds of wild game live in the northland. Predators roam the centerline of empty highways. Forests of old-growth hemlock, fir, birch, and rock maple; wild rivers; unnamed mountain ranges; and some of the largest roadless areas in the US cluster along the northern border like dust gathers against a wall.

Every news report I heard about pipelines, border walls, droughts, and security crackdowns along the northern boundary made me want to visit the northland again, before it changed for good. I wasn't sure how I would get there or how long it would take to cross the country. I didn't even know if my arcadian concept of the northland existed across the continental US. I knew I wanted to follow the Hi-Line from Maine to Washington. The border would be my guide, but I planned to tour all of the northland, ranging within a couple hundred miles on the US side. I didn't make an itinerary. There was no timeline. I started the way every other northland explorer had for the last four hundred years: I packed a canoe, tent, maps, and books and headed for the line.

■ ■ ■ ■

PART I
THE DAWNLAND

■ ■ ■ ■

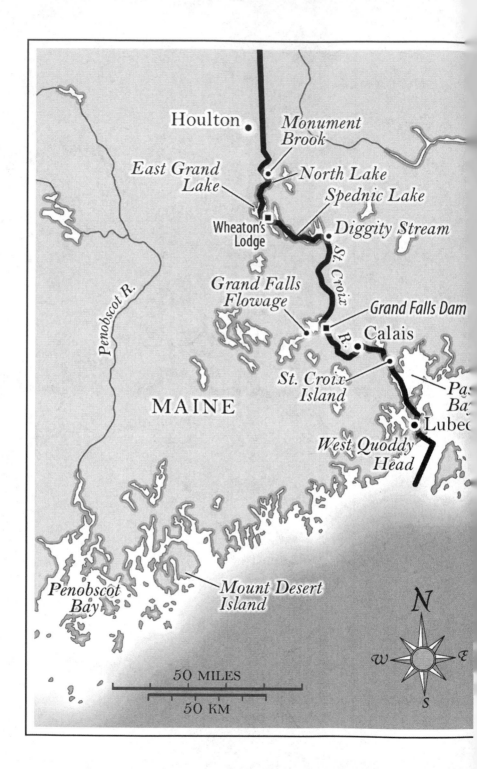

Houlton

Monument
Brook

East Grand
Lake

North Lake

Spednic Lake

Wheaton's
Lodge

Diggity Stream

St. Croix

Grand Falls
Flowage

Grand Falls Dam

Calais

St. Croix R.

St. Croix
Island

Pa͏
Ba͏

Lubec

MAINE

West Quoddy
Head

Penobscot R.

Penobscot
Bay

Mount Desert
Island

N

W   E

S

50 MILES

50 KM

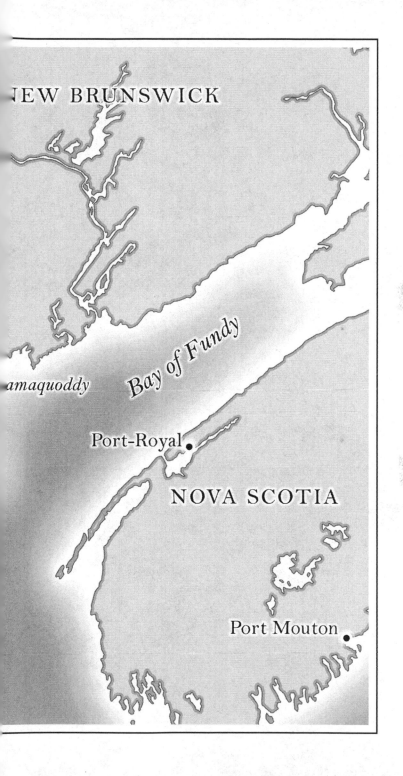

1

The line emerges from a cloud of light. It is invisible. Nothing distinguishes either side. It runs across the Gulf of Maine before cutting west around the gabbro bluffs of America's easternmost shoreline. From there, it passes into Passamaquoddy Bay and the Saint Croix River watershed before vanishing into the woodlands of northern Maine.

The wind blows constantly on the coast. It smells of pine, salt, decomposing fish, sea lavender, clam flats, seaweed. The tides are so powerful that they create the largest whirlpool in the Western Hemisphere. One hundred days of fog a year — not so much a mist as a permeable ocean above the ocean — and five-story sea cliffs make the coastline an ironbound dead end. The sound of trees and grasses hissing, swells hitting rock, is so constant you stop noticing after a while. The rumble blocks everything out. It envelops you, cuts the edges off the scene, and transforms it into a photograph. What you see in the picture is the edge of America and the beginning of Canada. A few trawlers motored along the line my first day there: one to the north, two in the south. Winds were out of the west at twelve knots. Seas two to four feet.

Three clapboard wharves, two rotting piers, and the Lubec town dock form a rickety barrier between America's easternmost town and Canada. Lubec occupies a rocky peninsula that divides Johnson Bay from Lubec Channel. Nearly every direction you look from the eastern tip, there is water.

At 4:45 a.m. in early October, a layer of ice coated the town dock. The air temperature was twenty degrees Fahrenheit, sea temperature forty-two. Across Quoddy Narrows, Canada's southern shore was a charcoal sketch. There were no lights, but I could hear voices. At the bottom of the ramp, a hand came toward me. "Milton Chute," a large man said. Milton had white hair and a white goatee and was wearing a baseball cap that read "Captain" across the crown. I shook his hand, and his sternman announced himself: "Roger."

An awkward moment passed. No one seemed to know why I was standing there.

I'd met Maine Department of Marine Resources Sergeant Russell Wright the day before. He suggested that Milton might guide me along the first few miles of the border. Milton worked in one of the northland's dying trades. He was a fifth-generation fisherman who had purse-seined, fish-dragged, urchin-dragged, clammed, and scalloped in Passamaquoddy Bay for fifty years. After four centuries of overfishing, the North Atlantic fishery was nearing extinction, and many of Maine's iconic fishing communities were dying with it. I had called Milton at 6:25 p.m. to ask if I could drag for sea urchins with him the next day. "If you'd called five minutes later," he said, "I would have been asleep."

Fishing in the northland had always been hard, Russell told me. Something about northern latitudes spins nature's forces out of control. The Bay of Fundy has the largest tides on the planet, rising and falling up to fifty vertical feet twice a day. Storms in the North Atlantic are among the most violent in the world, and the average water temperature around Lubec is forty-five degrees. Lobstermen tie mooring balls, rated to hold twenty-thousand-pound vessels, to weighted traps to keep currents from dragging them away. Every year, a trawler or two goes down, taking with it several Lubec fishermen. At the end of Water Street, next to a double-wide concrete boat ramp, a blue sign reads, "Future Site of Lost Fisherman's Memorial Park."

Lubec had been a border town since the beginning, Russell said, populated by bootleggers, businessmen, snake-oil salesmen, fishing families, smugglers, shipbuilders, and frontiersmen. Half the town looked like it had been built in the 1700s, the other half in the 1970s. Clapboard Georgians and colonial saltboxes sidle up against mobile homes and vinyl-sided shacks. Three-story Victorians overlook work lots packed with RVs, ATVs, skiffs, dories, lobster traps, and giant spools of yellow nylon rope. Something about living with your back against an invisible wall makes people think they're invincible. Smuggling got so bad in 1791 that George Washington dispatched one of his best men from the Continental navy, Hopley Yeaton, to bust smugglers and enforce tariffs around Passamaquoddy Bay.

Creating a new border out of thin air was not an easy task. Founding a new nation wasn't either. The US government depended almost solely on tariffs its first few years to keep the country afloat. Congress created a new division of floating tax men called the Revenue Marine — later renamed the Revenue Cutter Service — and authorized ten new cutters to serve between Georgia and Maine. The slender, two-masted sloops were about fifty feet long and were fast enough to overtake any loaded merchant vessel. Still, Yeaton failed to convince locals in Passamaquoddy Bay that the line they fought for now divided them from their friends, family, and business partners in British Canada — and that any goods crossing the line had to go through a customs house.

The northland was an interwoven patchwork of commerce at the time. Trees were cut in Canada and milled in America. Fish were caught in America, processed in Canada, and then shipped from facilities back in the US. Two centuries of intermarrying among French, Loyalist, Acadian, Indian, German, Scottish, Dutch, and American settlers created families and a borderland that straddled the line. Around Lubec, smuggling continued unabated until Yeaton received more cutters and troops, enabling him to establish a fragile authority over the bay.

The Revenue Service became America's only armed maritime force after the Continental navy was disbanded following the

Revolutionary War. Cutters patrolled the coast and blocked slavers from reaching US ports after the Slave Trade Act was passed in 1794. Congress revived the navy that year, and cutters were enlisted to fight alongside frigates for the next century. In 1915, President Woodrow Wilson merged the Revenue Cutter Service with the US Life-Saving Service to form the US Coast Guard.

The Coast Guard doesn't forget its own, and in 1974, five cadets, a handful of officers, and two undertakers unceremoniously appeared in the backyard of a private Lubec home. Their mission was to exhume the "Father of the Coast Guard." The home was set on what was once Yeaton's farm, and he was supposedly buried in the backyard. The cadets dug until they found his remains. The following August, the USCGC *Eagle* arrived to transport Yeaton to a memorial tomb at the Coast Guard Academy in New London, Connecticut.

Milton Chute had no use for the Coast Guard, Marine Resources, Customs, Border Patrol, or anyone else who wanted to tell him where he could fish or how much he could catch. It was a small miracle that the urchin market had found Maine fishermen in the first place. The fishing industry was struggling in the late 1980s, when Japanese buyers arrived looking for the thorny crustaceans that northland fishermen had cursed most of their lives. In Japan, the buttery inner roe of the green urchin is a favorite among blue-collar diners. Japanese buyers driving refrigerated box trucks along the Maine coast offered twenty-five cents per urchin at first, then a dollar a pound, then two dollars. When the price hit seven dollars a pound, Milton said, urchin draggers could net up to $8,000 a day for much of the thirty-eight-day season. Milton bought a new pickup truck and a second boat. Then, in a self-defeating cycle all too familiar to northland fishermen, the urchins started running out. Marine Resources stepped in. New regulations cut Milton's limit from more than twenty crates a day to seven. Now it was getting harder to break even.

Milton sat on the dock, swung his legs into a skiff, and shimmied onto the seat. He was sixty-nine years old and needed things to get easier, not harder. He was just under six feet and not as limber as he once had been. He had a substantial belly and moved with the slow, powerful precision of a black bear: one foot in front of the other, head bowed, one hand on the railing to steady him. He steered like a bear too, with the palm of his right paw resting on the skiff's tiller.

Milton was seventeen when he dropped out of high school to work on a seiner. He hadn't stopped fishing since. His grandfather taught him the trade. The old man rowed a wooden dory along the border six days a week for sixty years to set his nets — the same way Chute men had since the 1800s. At sunset he hauled his catch and the eight-hundred-pound boat a hundred yards up the beach. "He was a hard man," Milton said.

Milton drove the skiff at full throttle against a ten-mile-an-hour ebbing tide. A few feet from the *Captain's Lady,* Roger grabbed the gunwale and held up a hand to help Milton off. Milton swatted it away and hoisted his giant haunches onto the rail. He had owned too many boats to count and spent too much money on them to tally. He didn't know why he'd named his last two *Captain's Lady,* he said. He just liked the sound of the words together.

Roger tossed the mooring line into the sea, and Milton steered us out of the harbor. One of Milton's kids had rigged up a coffee-stained IBM laptop to his GPS so that Milton could see his track on a bigger screen. A greenish blip moved across the chart as we steamed north along the border. The boundary was a green line. On the water, it was nothing. There were no flashing lights or border patrol. No sign that two nations converged there.

I asked Milton if he had any contact with Canadian fishermen. "None," he said. "They're allowed to do whatever they want." The spirit of sharing along the world's friendliest border had not been going well recently. The sovereignty of nearby Machias Seal Island had been disputed for more than two hundred years. The island is set in one of a half-dozen "gray zones" along the northern border that are claimed by both the US and Canada. Conflicting language in the 1783 Treaty of Paris, which ended the Revolutionary War and drew the first miles of the northern boundary from Maine to Minnesota, created the confusion. Bad maps and bad information produced a line that ran along imaginary rivers and mountain features. It took more than a dozen treaties and agreements over the next two centuries to iron it out.

Machias Seal Island wasn't a problem until the price of lobster spiked in 2015 and Nova Scotia fishermen started setting traps there. Death threats, cut lines, and close calls between American and Canadian fishermen followed. An American lobster-man lost his thumb while jostling with a Canadian boat. An American captain threatened to ram and sink a Canadian government ship after the ship hauled away his traps. (The Canadians returned them.) The dispute was never resolved, nor were several others in gray zones along the line.

Fishermen at Dixon Entrance, between Alaska and British Columbia, have been battling for fishing rights for years. US and Canadian companies began vying for oil-drilling rights in the Beaufort Sea, near the Arctic Ocean, in 2016. In 2012, a border conflict erupted over albacore fishing grounds off Vancouver, and a thirty-year battle to regulate the salmon fishery in shared waters off the Pacific Northwest was finally settled in 2016. One of the most public feuds along the northern border is playing out in the Northwest Passage — the fabled water route to China that only recently thawed enough to allow boats through — where American ships are claiming navigational rights on water that Canadians say is theirs.

The Western Hemisphere was crisscrossed with overlapping borders when Samuel de Champlain sailed into Passamaquoddy Bay on June 26, 1604. Pope Alexander VI had issued a papal bull two months to the day after Christopher Columbus returned from his 1492 voyage, creating a north–south "line of demarcation" one hundred leagues west of the Azores. Everything east and south was the domain of Portugal; territory to the west answered to Spain. The Portuguese moved the line twelve hundred miles toward South America to protect their claim to Brazil. Marie de Médicis, queen regent of France, drew an east–west boundary years later along the Tropic of Cancer to preserve North America for French exploration. As for undiscovered lands on America's Eastern Seaboard, she said, "The strongest in those quarters are masters there."

France was far from a master in North America when the father of the northland arrived on what is now the US-Canada border. Forty years of religious wars — some of the most brutal fighting in human history — followed by two international wars, had emptied royal coffers. A quarter of the population was dead. King Henri IV was humbled and broke. The French navy possessed only a handful of ships, and the people's spirit was broken. Westward from the flattened villages of Brittany at the turn of the seventeenth century, North America was France's best chance for a new start, and the window to get a foothold there was closing.

France wasn't the only nation looking for a clean slate. Kings, noblemen, and businessmen across Europe had already claimed massive — and conflicting — swaths of America. Within fifty years of Columbus's discovery, the Spanish conquered Mexico, crossed the Mississippi, settled Florida, discovered the Grand Canyon, and claimed California. Basque ships had been fishing the waters off of Newfoundland for years before Columbus arrived, and Norse ships had landed in Nova Scotia long before them. The English also explored Newfoundland and Nova Scotia, claimed California, and attempted a settlement in North Carolina.

Competition between kings, treaties signed in Europe, accidents, misinformation, and luck divided up most of America's northland. No one knew what was at stake. Most early explorers thought North America was about three hundred miles wide, and few had any idea what natural resources the northern tier held. Gold, silver, pearls, slaves, molasses, and rum were available in the south. In the north, there looked to be only trees, fish, a few copper veins, and rocky soil that was difficult to farm.

Champlain and the 1604 expedition's financier, Pierre Dugua, Sieur de Mons, had explored the Saint Lawrence River the previous spring and found the climate and landscape promising for a settlement. They assumed, incorrectly, that since the Bay of Fundy was at a lower latitude than France, it would enjoy milder winters. The *Don de Dieu* and *La Bonne-Renommée* headed for the bay from Le Havre, France, on April 7. They got lucky with the wind and made the crossing to Nova Scotia in four weeks.

Each boat was about a hundred feet long, and both were outfitted like self-sufficient forts, with provisions, defenses, and building supplies for a year. Holds were packed with dried vegetables, fruit, sheep, pigs, salt pork, wine, hard cider, herring, cod, and grain. Houses for noblemen were prefabricated in France, including roofing, glass windows, and solid oak doors. Shipwrights built complete kits for a fleet of small vessels to be assembled and launched on American shores.

There were about 150 crew, all hand-picked by de Mons and Champlain. Officers and noblemen held the top posts. Professional sailors, some with experience in America, captained and operated the ships. Swiss soldiers were hired to man the arquebuses — handheld cannons that preceded the musket. The bulk of the passengers were skilled artisans and laborers, including a shipwright, apothecary, surgeons, blacksmiths, carpenters, masons, armorers, gunners, miners, and locksmiths — the latter with experience repairing firing mechanisms. There were no women on the journey, just men and boys.

Champlain was thirty-seven years old in 1604. His official title was navigator, but his skills on the sea and at war made him the expedition's default leader. He was not born a nobleman. He was a Breton from a sailing family who had had fourteen years of elite military schooling by the time he was twenty-four. He had gotten along well with Indians around the Saint Lawrence in 1603 and learned about the coast and inland waterways from them.

After making landfall in Nova Scotia in early May 1604, and searching for a settlement site for a few weeks, de Mons and Champlain spotted a "most advantageous" island in a narrow passage, about fifteen miles northwest of present-day Lubec. The island was "eight or nine hundred paces [in circumference], with rocky sides three or four fathoms high all around." It was a classic Maine island, thick with fir, birch, maple, and oak trees. Two rivers emptied into the passage — one from the west, the other from the east. De Mons saw the cross-like confluence as a sign. He named the island Saint Croix and decided to plant France's new colony there.

By September, the basic layout of the colony was complete. Champlain had a battery of cannons installed on the southern shore. The British — who had explored Penobscot Bay 130 miles to the south the year before — would have to pass by their iron barrels to dislodge New France from America. He had most of the trees on the island cut down for firewood and planking, save some that were close to the water and one in the middle of what would be a town square. De Mons's home was built with casement windows packed in one of the ships and finished with a mansard roof, a brick fireplace, and a large French flag that flew overhead.

Some of the buildings were still unfinished when temperatures plummeted in November, and skim ice crept across the passage. When the ice thickened, the tides turned it into an impassable jumble, cutting the colony off from the mainland. The well the settlers tried to dig turned up dry, and the crops they planted didn't produce. Champlain had vastly overestimated the amount of firewood the island's trees could provide, and the group nearly froze as winter winds blew straight through their buildings. De Mons was right that Maine and France sit on a similar latitude, but ocean and atmospheric currents keep Europe far warmer. A global cooling phenomenon known as the Little Ice Age was also pushing Arctic air down on America's northeastern coast that winter, adding to the deep freeze. By January, three feet of snow covered the ground and the only food left was the salted stores the crew had brought from France.

A mysterious disease spread through the colony in January, and a few weeks later several settlers died. A surgeon cut into the corpses but could not discern the cause. Champlain's explanation was a lack of fresh food, which we now know was close to the truth. He wrote in his journal about Flemish sailors who brought citrus on voyages to the East Indies to stave off disease. Since he was trapped on the icebound island, there was nothing he could do about it. The few settlers on Saint Croix who were immune to scurvy were hunters who ate fresh meat. Most of the others, who sat by the fire or lay in bed all day, eventually fell ill. By

March, thirty-five of the original seventy-nine settlers were dead.

Champlain and de Mons had studied other island settlements, such as the doomed French colony on nearby Sable Island, that had also been cut off. They were stunned that they had walked into a similar trap. There was more than pride and money at stake. In the Frenchmen's eyes, and those of their king, America's northland represented the best chance for their motherland to remake itself. New France would be a social experiment in liberty and religious freedom — a chance to correct some mistakes. Saint Croix Island was the first cell of a great body that would grow westward, discovering and occupying a new world. It would save the souls of native Indians; supply France with timber, fish, and minerals; and keep the British Empire to the south in check by drawing a border across the continent. It was worth suffering for. All they needed to do was make it to spring and hold the line.

Four hours and thirty minutes into our journey, Milton asked why I wanted to see the border. I told him I was traversing it from Maine to Washington. He asked why, and I said I wanted to see whether there were more places like this across the country.

"Where you going next?" he asked.

"Saint Croix River," I said.

"What kind of boat you on?"

"Canoe."

"You'll make it."

Milton drove into Cobscook Bay and let the boat drift as we waited for sunrise. Regulations prohibit fishing before dawn. He had been fined a few months before for lowering his rig too early. "They will know if you drop it five minutes too soon," he said. "The warden posts up on that point over there with binoculars — or someone else does and tells him." He could lose his urchin permit if he was caught again, and there was a long line of applicants waiting to take it.

Fifteen minutes later, sunlight touched the tip of the dredging tower, and a great whine erupted from the cable spool as Milton dropped the rig. The water was thirty feet deep. He let the net out five hundred feet behind the boat, and the *Captain's Lady* shuddered as it got purchase. Milton throttled up for the first run, then he and Roger commenced a routine they had performed a few thousand times: drive straight for half a mile, haul in the gear, dump the net, pick out the urchins, pack the crate, sweep the deck, turn the boat around, drop the gear, and do it again.

The first two drags were nearly empty. Milton repositioned a few hundred yards south, and Roger started pulling urchins from the net and packing them in crates. He sat on the rail and shucked scallops between runs. He ate them quickly — it wasn't scallop season — then handed me one on the tip of his knife. The meat was sweet and salty, but it didn't sit well at six in the morning, rolling in the waves. I spat it overboard when Roger wasn't looking, just in time for him to sneak me another. "This business is a screw on both sides of the deal," he said. "It's the biggest screw in any business I know. No one is getting away with anything."

Light spooled across the water from Canada and turned the underside of the clouds yellow and pink. We were about fifteen miles south of Saint Croix Island, a dot in the tideland that surrounds Lubec. The matrix of bays, basins, inlets, coves, and straits extends more than a hundred square miles. Milton spent the next hour chatting about prices on the VHF. The first boat to market the day before had sold seven crates at $2.80 a pound. An hour later, the last fisherman in had gotten $3.50.

When the crates were full, we headed home. A nearly full moon was setting behind Dennys Bay. Milton had seen a blood moon a few days before. "It was like an eclipse," he said. "The shadow blacked it out just like that, left that little ring." He said it was dark red, that it was just something that happened. Like a lot of magical things that happen on the water most people never see.

We rounded Moose Island, and Milton watched a small plastic clock on his console. He ranked other fishermen's pedigrees as we passed them. He knew most of their fathers and some of their grandfathers. A mile from the pier, he noticed a red trawler angling in front of him. He nudged the throttle, and the *Captain's Lady* hit nine knots. The red boat accelerated, and Milton dipped into an eddy behind Treat Island and slingshotted into the lead.

Milton got to the dock first, but his truck wouldn't start. He cursed as Roger tried to turn it over. With no other way to get his urchins to the landing, he ended up pushing the truck downhill to jumpstart it. It didn't work, and he and Roger tinkered under the hood while I watched the captain of the red boat sell his catch. The arrangement was surprisingly informal. A middle-aged Japanese man wearing a windbreaker wandered over and looked at the crates. The fisherman muttered something about how good the roe was. The buyer cracked a few urchins open and made an offer. The fisherman shook his head. The buyer made another offer. The fisherman nodded. The buyer handed him a wad of cash and carried the crates to his truck. That night they would be flown to Japan, and the following day the roe would appear on *kaiten-zushi* conveyor belts at restaurants throughout the country.

It was past noon, and I planned to start paddling the Saint Croix River early the next morning. I said goodbye to Roger and Milton, who were still fussing with the truck, and drove three miles to West Quoddy Head. The battered volcanic cliffs of America's easternmost point rise a hundred feet off the ocean, lean back, and push the forest inland. The water is green blue, and the confluence of wind and current knocks waves in every direction. The silhouetted walls of Grand Manan Island stand to the east and the rocky outline of the Wolves archipelago rises up to the north.

Even on a calm day, three-foot swells smashed into Sail Rock and the ebbing tide left a V of whitewater around lobster buoys.

A hundred yards from the cliffs, a candy-striped lighthouse flashed a white beam out to sea. Hopley Yeaton helped establish the original light there, financed by Congress in 1806.

It felt odd that the entirety of America was at my back. And even stranger that an international border passed by here. There was no sign of it on the water or land, no way to tell what was Canada and what was the US. The air smelled like algae and clam flats. The sound of waves crashing drowned out a dozen shrieking gulls. The sun dropped and the temperature fell. Two lobster boats motored out of Quoddy Narrows, both abiding the invisible line.

2

It was twenty-eight degrees the morning I strapped a canoe to the roof of my car and followed Route 1 north to the Saint Croix River. The Saint Croix has marked the boundary between New England and Canada since the day Samuel de Champlain landed there. The official line was drawn along the river at the 1783 Treaty of Paris. Both parties agreed that the border should follow the Saint Croix, but US emissaries Benjamin Franklin, John Adams, and John Jay tried to move the line northeast by claiming that a different river, the Magaguadavic, was, in fact, the Saint Croix — adding about eight thousand square miles to the US.

Such haggling over the border was common in America's early years. Several land grabs by the US and British Canada came close to war. The Saint Croix dispute continued for more than a decade, until the

1794 Jay Treaty, written by Secretary of the Treasury Alexander Hamilton and negotiated by John Jay, assigned a commission to locate the real Saint Croix.

British and American agents sailed and walked the area, interviewing families and local Passamaquoddy tribal members about who lived where, when. Conflicting reports poured in until commission member and British Loyalist judge Robert Pagan sourced copies of Champlain's drawings and writings from 1604. He then took the papers to Saint Croix Island and found the ruins of Champlain's buildings there — plus stoneware, a spoon, and a musket ball — settling the matter.

Passamaquoddy Bay appeared in flashes of cut blue light as I drove north on Route 1. I passed Saint Croix Island a few miles beyond Eastport and pulled over to take a look. The island sits a half mile offshore from the Saint Croix Island International Historic Site. It is layered in granite, seaweed, woodbine, and sedge. There is a small boathouse on the northern tip and a granite outcropping to the south, where Champlain built the cannon battery. A bald eagle flew over the river, and for a moment it seemed odd that so much in the world had changed while the island remained exactly the same.

I wanted to start my journey at the head of tide in Calais, Maine, but two hydroelectric dams blocked the way. I continued thirty miles north instead and put in upstream of the Grand Falls dam. An older man with silver hair and a blue work jacket was cleaning a sluice door when I arrived at the dam. He stood on a ribbon of concrete spanning the river, holding a long aluminum pole. I called to him over the roaring water a few times, pointed to my canoe, the car, the river, myself — trying to ask permission to launch the boat and park my car there. He looked up once and went back to what he was doing. I called out a few more times, and eventually he put down the pole and walked over.

"It's smaller than I expected," I said.

"This ain't the dam," he answered.

"What is it?"

"Auxiliary canal," he said. "Over that hill you'll see the real thing."

I told him that I wasn't looking for the dam, that I wanted to canoe the Saint Croix to Loon Bay.

"Loon Bay is ten miles north," he said.

"Can I get there by dark?" I asked.

"River goes south."

I pointed to the canoe again.

"So you'll be going upstream," he said.

He was right. Maine is shaped like a guillotine blade, pitched a few degrees toward the ocean. Nearly every major river in the state — the Kennebec, Penobscot, Androscoggin, and Saint Croix — spills from highlands in the west, east to the sea. Inland commerce followed gravity in colonial America, and Maine's rivers were conveyor belts that floated commodities downstream. Timber, pelts, minerals, and grain trickled down the fifteen-hundred-square-mile Saint Croix watershed. Shipwrights, tar gangs, riggers, and sailmakers worked Calais's shoreline, prepping oceangoing ships bound for Europe, Africa, and Asia.

Explorers, trappers, and log drivers used ten-foot black cedar shafts, harvested from bogs, to pole up the Saint Croix almost as fast as they could make it down. I had known I'd be traveling upstream and considered poling the way it used to be done, until a short, barrel-chested salesman at the Old Town Canoe factory told me: "They had muscles we don't have." Mainers have a way of making a point in few words, and that afternoon I bought a used five-horsepower outboard to mount on the back of the canoe.

I pulled the motor out of the trunk and showed it to the dam worker. He seemed amused. "No problem about the car," he said. It took a half hour to unload a ridiculous amount of gear: three dry bags, groceries, cooler, computer, GPS, map, life jacket, two paddles, tent, sleeping bag, cookware. From Loon Bay, I wanted to canoe twenty miles to a small outpost called Vanceboro. From there I would continue thirty miles across Spednic, East Grand, and North Lakes to the Saint Croix's headwaters at Monument Brook. The entire trip would be on the border. It would also pass through some of the most remote wilderness in the Northeast.

The man watched me mount the engine on the stern, push off, and spin in a complete circle. He didn't move as the canoe drifted toward the sluice door. I finally got the engine started, and the canoe shot forward out of the canal. It was surprisingly stable under power. It was a sixteen-foot "square stern," with a hard chine and a flat bottom to prevent tipping. The first square-stern canoe was built in the 1930s sixty miles upstream on East Grand Lake, though its exact origin continues to be debated. A fishing guide there took a saw to the stern of his canoe, fit it with a transom, attached one of the first outboard engines ever made, and — I am postulating here — vowed never to pick up a paddle again.

My GPS read seven miles per hour as I crossed Grand Falls Flowage. Five minutes later I was on the boundary. There wasn't a person or border station in sight. One foot to the east was Canada, one to the west was America. I scanned both shores for patrollers, cameras, sensors, drones. There was nothing but flat, dark water under a pale-blue October sky. The leaves were changing, burned red and gold, and a few floated on the surface. The sun was so bright and clear that it lit up the shoreline like a spotlight.

I had visited the St. Croix International Waterway Commission two days before in Saint Stephen to ask advice about canoeing the border. The commission is a bilateral partnership between the US and Canada responsible for "planning and facilitating management of the Saint Croix boundary water system." Former executive director Abby Pond acted as a liaison between border authorities and civilians. When I set up the meeting a week before, she told me that paddling the border might not be as easy as I thought.

Abby's desk took up a third of the commission's three-hundred-square-foot office. She shared the space with a secretary, who answered approximately seventy-five phone calls in the twenty minutes I was there. "In the old days," Abby said, "everyone treated both shores of the river the same." The border patrol didn't mind boaters visiting, picnicking, or spending the night on either side. Since 9/11, though, drifting across the boundary could land you in jail. "No one really knows what they're supposed to do," she said.

Maine shares the second-longest border with Canada — six hundred miles — of any state in the Lower 48, after Michigan. One hundred eighty US Customs and Border Protection agents watch the line from twenty-four crossings, using pickup trucks, ATVs, snowmobiles, planes, boats, and helicopters. There are still plenty of ways to slip across, though. Agents on the northern border apprehended three thousand people in 2016, including a thirty-nine-year-old Quebec man who was charging $8,000 per person to walk them across the line. That same year the *New York Times* reported that two parties near Swanton, Vermont, were caught on video sneaking over the boundary. One of the groups was dressed in camo and appeared to be armed. Customs and Border Protection (CBP) didn't get to the location in time and never found either group.

CBP is the largest federal agency in the US, commanding sixty thousand agents and a $12-billion budget. It states that its primary function is "keeping terrorists and their weapons out of the U.S.," though, statistically, there is no significant terrorist threat on either border. Drugs and human trafficking make up nearly all of the arrests along America's northern and southern perimeters. In its effort to "keep terrorists out," CBP sends most of its resources south to the Mexican border, even though the only known terrorists who *did* sneak across a US border came from Canada. One had illegally crossed at Ross Lake in Washington State, in June of 1996. He was shot by the NYPD months later, while preparing a bomb to detonate on the New York City subway. Three years after that, an Algerian man was stopped at the northern border; he later confessed to having been on his way to blow up LAX airport in the "Millennium Plot."

CBP and the Canada Border Services Agency work together on the Saint Croix River, Abby said. Crossing illegally can get you jail time on either side of the line. A man who paddled across the river on an inflatable mattress in 2016, to see his pregnant fiancée in Saint Stephen, was sentenced to two months in prison. A month later, two men were arrested after helping an Ecuadorian woman use a paddleboat to cross the Saint Croix. "The real problem on the river is that there is no border," Abby said. "It is unmarked. So you don't know what side you are on unless you are on land and you are really familiar with it."

Having spent years paddling canoes against headwinds and currents, I felt like the outboard engine was an invisible hand pushing the boat along. It was so easy to drive that I started looking for things to do. I checked the map and aligned it with the compass. I played with the time-lapse settings on my camera. If there was an obstacle ahead, I nudged the tiller an inch or two and the canoe turned around it.

The boat zipped east over the flowage, and I put my feet up on a thwart. It was impossible to know which side of the border I was on. It runs along the deep-water mark, but deep-water marks are carved by nature, not humans, and they shift constantly. I was trying to follow the line north toward the American shore when the engine hit a rock so hard that the propeller kicked out of the water and the motor stalled.

I hadn't noticed how much the wind had picked up until the canoe glided to a stop. Heavy chop slapped the gunwales and pushed it toward Canada. The engine started again, but the propeller wouldn't turn. I tilted the engine up and reached back to free whatever was caught, but the blades were clean. The shore was only a hundred feet away, and I tried to paddle back into the flowage. The wind and waves were too much, though, so I turned around and paddled toward a small dock in Canada.

A Canadian flag hung from a cabin just behind the dock. I tied up and, though there was seemingly no reason to sneak, I sneaked across the tiny front lawn and knocked on the door. No one answered. No boats or patrol cars pulled up. It was five in the afternoon and already getting dark. The temperature had dropped to around freezing. The waves on the lake were too big to safely paddle a loaded canoe, but I couldn't stay where I was. An hour into my cross-country adventure, it looked like my trip was about to come to a sudden, humiliating end.

I pulled the engine off the canoe and unscrewed the propeller. Three severed sections of a shear pin fell onto the dock. Growing up in the northland, you get to know shear pins. They act as a clutch between the propeller and the driveshaft and shear if the prop hits something hard. Every outboard carries a few spares under the engine cover. The used motor I bought did not.

I looked through my gear for a bolt or screw that would suffice, but there was nothing. I tried to paddle away from the dock again, but the overloaded canoe was so low in the water that the waves pushed me back after fifty feet. Back on the dock, I gathered the broken pieces of the pin and jammed them between the shaft and the propeller. I figured if I kept the engine in forward, the pressure would hold them in place. Miraculously, it did, and the canoe lurched off the dock.

The Saint Croix was a dark shadow by the time I made it off the flowage and back into the river. The wilderness around it was dense and primitive. A beaver waddled to the shoreline and swam around the canoe like it had never seen a human before. A few stars appeared, and the channel narrowed. The current was more powerful than I'd expected, especially for October, when water levels are typically low. The engine struggled, and the current knocked the bow sideways every few seconds.

A set of rapids broke over the gunwale, and freezing water poured into the canoe. The map said Loon Bay was seven miles away. It was too far. I tilted the engine halfway up and made better headway. When it got too dark to see rocks, I steered blind — using muscle memory to react to subtle movements of the bow. I don't know how long I drove like that or how far. I was lost in the effort, frozen, inching forward. At some point, the roar of the river died down, and the canoe slid into a wide eddy.

I spotted a campsite in the woods. I wasn't as far north as I wanted to get, but the site was perfect. A three-foot pile of dry cord-wood sat next to a fire ring. There were two tent sites and an outhouse. I tied up the canoe and lit a fire. A beaver whacked its tail; the report sounded like a gunshot. It got so dark I couldn't see the canoe or the river. The canopy blocked the stars. I stayed close to the fire and kept my headlamp on. It was spooky to be alone so far from civilization. On a map the boundary is a line. On land, it passes through impossible places — ravines, cliff bands, bogs, water-falls, rocky summits, whitewater — that few people ever see. Ninety percent of Canadians live within a hundred miles of their southern border. Twelve percent of Americans live in the northland, and most of them in cities like Seattle, Detroit, Chicago, Milwaukee, and Cleveland.

Camping thirty feet from an international border was unsettling as well. It struck me that if someone was trying to sneak across, their greatest find would be an unarmed solo camper, with a boat and enough gear and food to survive for a month. No matter what CBP and Abby had said, no one was watching this section of the boundary.

An hour later, a beam of light shot through the trees. The glare was too bright to be a flashlight. I thought it might be a vehicle, and I crept to the riverbank to see. The beam came from the opposite shore. I walked upstream a hundred yards and looked again. Across the river I saw that the light was coming from the crest of a full moon, rising over the treetops.

Silvery light filled the forest. My hands were silver. The Saint Croix was silver. I saw my shadow on the forest floor. It was unnatural. The glow was too bright to be the moon. Astronomers call the edge of sun- or moonlight passing over the Earth a terminator. Or a twilight zone. The zone moves a thousand miles an hour on the equator. It travels at half that speed in the northland. At the North Pole, you can walk faster than the terminator, creating your own sunrises and sunsets.

An otter slipped between my feet and disappeared into the river. I watched it for a moment, then walked back to my tent and stared at the changing light until I fell asleep. The emptiness of the northland was unfamiliar to me. It was devoid of light, cars, people, trails, and roads. Clouds of stars glowed through gaps in the tree cover. The forest was pure black where the moonlight was shaded. I grew up in this country, had explored it for thirty years, and thought I knew it. But this was different. The closer I got to the line, the more primal the terrain became.

Champlain survived until the spring of 1605 and traded for fresh meat with an encampment of Passamaquoddy Indians. By June, just forty-four of the original colonists were alive. Champlain was undeterred. He sailed the coast as far south as Cape Cod, mapping it and making alliances with Indian chiefs. He was a natural emissary and approached Indians confidently, without being threatening. He performed rituals with them, smoked with them, danced, and compared maps of the region. He followed messengers blindly upriver for days to meet with their headmen. He was an anthropologist as much as an explorer. His desire for discovery, knowledge, and salvation gave him a higher purpose, as well as incredible drive and endurance.

De Mons was not as inspired. He was so put off by the *sauvages* — especially after a conflict in 1605 near Cape Cod that left one Frenchman and two Nauset Indians dead — that he decided to move the French colony not south, but east to Nova Scotia. The lack of French presence in the Northeast over the next few decades encouraged the English to establish settlements from Massachusetts to Maine. One small skirmish in the summer of 1605 — that took no more than a few hours to unfold — moved the line between New England and New France more than four hundred miles north, leaving it almost exactly where it stands today.

The Nova Scotia settlement fared far better that winter, but de Mons's investors back in Paris did not. They wanted to move the colony out of the forbidding northland and south to the Caribbean. Champlain and the settlers were recalled to France, and for a moment, the dream of New France was dead. Two events brought it back to life and extended the colony's boundary farther west. The first was a renewed British effort to establish permanent settlements in America, beginning with Jamestown in 1607. The second was a fashion trend gaining momentum on the streets of Paris. Felt and feathers were out. Animal fur was in. Beaver pelts were most in demand. They were used to make cavalier hats popular with nobility, and later for Puritan capotains and top hats. The supply of beaver in northern Russia and Scandinavia was nearly exhausted, driving demand and prices up. Thicker furs like white fox, lynx, marten, and otter also fetched a higher price, and animals with thick furs live in the north.

Fur traders were already sailing to the northland, and Champlain and his sponsors proposed a monopoly to Henri IV. The promise of large profits swayed the king, and he supported another effort. Three ships set sail from the Seine on April 13, 1608. This time Champlain sailed with the title "Lieutenant for the Country of New France." He sent one ship to the Nova Scotia settlement and took the other two to the Saint Lawrence River. At sixty thousand square miles, the mouth of the river is the planet's largest estuary. It drains 350,000 cubic feet of water per second, mostly from the Great Lakes, and produced more pelts in the seventeenth and eighteenth centuries than anywhere else in the world. Champlain founded Quebec on high ground southwest of Île d'Orléans. His crew built a fortification quickly but were again unprepared for winter. The first snow came November 18, and by January, signs of scurvy and dysentery had appeared. Men died. Champlain ordered autopsies. The surgeon dutifully carried them out until he, too, fell ill and passed away.

News traveled across the Atlantic with surprising speed for the time, on fishing and trading boats. The hard winter did not go over well with investors, and that spring, orders arrived for Champlain to return once again to France. He wrote back that he would comply after he completed a mission of "certain explorations in the interior." His ambition all along had been to continue exploring America, and he had no intention of returning home before getting a chance to follow the great river farther inland. Instead of packing up, he gathered a team and sailed in the opposite direction.

Champlain wanted to extend French control as far west across the northland as possible. Constant war among Indian tribes made establishing allies, and colonizing New France, nearly impossible. The Mohawk Indians of the Iroquois Confederacy — Mohawk, Oneida, Onondaga, Cayuga, Seneca, and, later, the Tuscarora — were at war with almost every other tribe in the Northeast. Champlain thought that a sudden and decisive defeat might forge a lasting truce. Since his first trip up the Saint Lawrence in 1603, he had spoken to local tribes about inland rivers and the far-reaching "sweet-water seas" that the Saint Lawrence flowed from. The Huron Indians suggested that there was an even greater body of water to the west, which Champlain thought might be the Pacific. Legends of a Northwest Passage across America — and a route to the riches of China — had beckoned explorers to the Northeast for two centuries. If Champlain could find it, the future of New France would be sealed.

Champlain's first expedition deep into America's northland headed upstream on June 18, 1609. He and a crew of twenty sailed a shallop with a leadsman sounding for depth against a strong spring current. A crew of Montagnais Indians followed in canoes, and a few days in, the group met three hundred Algonquin and Huron Indians. Several chiefs considered joining

Champlain but wanted to know more about him. Specifically, they were curious about his fighting spirit, his *orenda*. Iroquet of the Algonquin Petite Nation and Ochasteguin of the Arendarhonon Huron met with him first. The two chiefs then spoke at length with each other, smoked tobacco, and paddled from the shore to Champlain's shallop. There they smoked more, meditated, and suddenly declared the mission worthy, signaling to their warriors onshore to prepare to move.

By the time the expedition started paddling upstream for Mohawk country again, it included two French shallops loaded with men and more than four hundred Indian warriors. It took a week to reach the Richelieu River, the eastern border of Iroquois country, thirty miles downstream from present-day Montréal. The first leg was longer than Champlain had anticipated, and, worried about a British attack while he was gone, he sent some of his soldiers back to Quebec. Seeing the diminished force, many more headed home as well.

Terrifying stories of what the Mohawk did to captives didn't help morale. The Mohawk numbered about eight thousand and guarded the eastern expanse of Iroquoia, which included most of the northland south of the Great Lakes to the Hudson River. They rarely lost a battle, and those they defeated were heinously tortured. Many northland tribes considered torture a way to commune with the gods. Some war parties mutilated victims after they died; some took care to keep them alive as long as possible. Male and female torturers pulled out captives' fingernails and burned their genitals with hot coals. They cut open arms and pulled the muscles out, scalped victims' heads and poured boiling tree sap on them. When a prisoner finally died, they often cut off his arms and legs, threw his entrails in the water, and forced his fellow tribesmen to eat his heart.

When Champlain paddled up the Richelieu River to Chambly Basin, he had just two soldiers left and a few dozen Indians. One soldier was de Mons's former bodyguard, who had been with Champlain since his first voyage to New France. Champlain carried a small, brass astrolabe and recorded his latitude daily. He was entering terrain that no European had ever seen. The Richelieu had been difficult to navigate in the shallop. Champlain studied how the Indians paddled whitewater and "tracked" canoes upstream by hauling them with a long cord. The crew took turns rowing, then left the ship for canoes and portaged around the rapids at Chambly.

The war party was well into Mohawk territory at that point, on what was beginning to look like a suicide mission. Champlain wrote extensively in his journal about how his Indian friends felled trees at night to build barricades around their campsite and waited for the full moon to pass before advancing. When the group finally reached Lake Champlain, the Frenchman gazed at the scene in awe. He could see the Adirondacks and Green Mountains. He drew sketches and studied minerals, rocks, and soil along the shoreline. He wrote about prodigious game wandering through the forest and the diversity of the environment. The lake was the only site he ever named after himself.

From there, the group stopped using fires and consulted medicine men to determine when and where they should attack. Champlain wrote about how the remaining chiefs used sticks to model a battle plan: "All the savages watch carefully this proceeding, observing attentively the outline which their chief has made with the sticks. Then they go away, and set to placing themselves in such order as the sticks were in." Warriors spoke about their dreams and considered them portents of how the battle would go. They continually asked Champlain about his dreams, but he didn't have any to share. When he finally dreamed about Mohawk braves drowning in front of a large mountain, the warriors rejoiced, saying that they knew the place and could now attack.

The mountain in Champlain's dream was in the south, near the falls at Ticonderoga. The expedition met the Mohawk there the next night. Both sides were in canoes and let out with battle cries when they spotted each other. It was a confusing moment. The Frenchmen and their allies paddled into the middle of the lake to regroup while the Mohawk took up a defensive position onshore. Champlain documented in detail what happened next. The chiefs sent two canoes to ask the Mohawk if they wanted to fight. The Mohawk said yes. The two sides decided to fight at dawn, when they would be able to distinguish each other. The Mohawk built a barricade around their camp. The Montagnais, Algonquin, and Huron paddled ashore to prepare. They kept Champlain and his soldiers hidden in the bottom of the canoes until they landed. At dawn, they formed ranks to march on the Mohawk, keeping Champlain hidden in the middle of the formation. Champlain's two soldiers crept through the woods around the Mohawk's flank. The Frenchmen carried short-barreled arquebuses, good for short-range fighting, and packed four balls at a time in the muzzle for a more devastating shot.

Champlain's allies fired first, killing a Mohawk scout near the barricade with an arrow. Mohawk warriors appeared moments later, clad in wooden armor. The two sides marched through the forest at each other until they were fifty yards apart. Champlain's group then parted into two columns, allowing the Frenchman to emerge. He walked fifty feet in front of them. The Mohawk stopped. It was likely the first time they had seen a European. One of three Mohawk chiefs raised his bow and aimed it at Champlain. Champlain fired, killing two of the chiefs at once and wounding a warrior. The Montagnais, Algonquin, and Huron let out a cry, and the two sides exchanged a volley of arrows. The two French soldiers then fired into the Mohawk's flanks and killed a third chief, along with several warriors. Confused and afraid, the Mohawk force disassembled and ran for cover.

Within a few hours the Mohawk fort had been ransacked, a dozen prisoners were taken captive, and shrieks from those being tortured filled the forest. The trip downstream to Quebec was fast. The boats averaged sixty miles a day and made it home in just over a week. There, Champlain was celebrated as a hero among the Indians. There was no time to celebrate, though. He transferred his command to a young nobleman and boarded a ship bound for France. He arrived in October, bringing to the king remarkable tales of New France, a pair of scarlet tanagers, and a porcupine quill belt.

Henri and de Mons were pleased with the news and sent Champlain back to Quebec to continue his campaign. Montagnais and Huron chiefs were waiting for him when he arrived in June 1610. They wanted to make another assault on the Mohawk. Champlain agreed, but on two conditions. The first was to have the Indians' assistance with extending New France's fur trade to Hudson Bay. The second was to receive help with extending the border of New France farther west, past Iroquoia, all the way to the sweet-water seas.

3

Frost circled the cuff of my sleeping bag. Sunlight moved through the trees and lit a curl of smoke rising from the fire pit. I could see the river now, the opposite shore, ripple lines, rocks, and eddies. Looking at the whitewater rushing down the middle, I realized the current was too strong for my engine to fight.

I decided to use the car to portage twenty miles to Spednic and East Grand Lakes instead. The river and border run through the lakes, and I could make better headway there. I tossed pine needles and kindling in the fire ring and made coffee. Watching the river was mesmerizing, the same way that watching a fire is mesmerizing. The current never stops. At night when you fall asleep, in the morning when you wake up. Summer, fall, winter, spring. The clouds stop, the wind stops, light from the sun and moon stops, but the river keeps going.

An osprey strafed the treetops, and golden maple and oak leaves spun south. The air temperature was thirty-five degrees. No wind. Sea smoke on the water. Bubbles rising from springs near the canoe erupted into tiny columns of vapor. The mist downstream was so thick I could barely see the next bend.

I packed the canoe and let the current swing the bow around. It felt good to use a paddle instead of the engine. The hull slipped between rocks and accelerated through the channels. The boat seemed to know where to go, naturally following the path of least resistance.

Nature in the northland carves its own path as well. An invisible wall along the northern border has kept it pristine, and species survive where they would have otherwise been wiped out. Entomologists considered the Tomah mayfly extinct in the 1930s, until a University of Maine student found one buzzing on the Saint Croix. Nine other endangered species live on the river: the rufa red knot, black tern, Canada lynx, common nighthawk, chimney swift, pygmy snaketail dragonfly, Saint Croix snaketail, winged maple-leaf mussel, and the deadly eastern cougar.

The Saint Croix sustains members of an

ancient Indian tribe as well, Donald Socto-mah told me. I'd met Donald my first day in Lubec, in a small building marked by a hand-painted sign that read, "Indian Town-ship Museum 93." His official title is Tribal Historic Preservation Officer of the Passa-maquoddy tribe, but his contributions to the tribe transcend office. Over the last forty years, Donald helped lead the effort to document and rebuild Passamaquoddy language, sovereignty, culture, landholdings, civil rights, tradition, and history. He is a modern-day wampum keeper, a title his great-great-grandfather once held.

Donald told me that the Passamaquoddy tribe was born from the Saint Croix and has always lived on it. Origin stories set in the watershed describe how the Great Spirit mixed clay with his own blood to mold people. Another says he shot an arrow into a tree, and out stepped man and woman. "Everything about our creation comes from the earth, comes from right here," he said.

The tribe has lived on the Saint Croix for more than twelve thousand years. Borders in the early days were rivers and watersheds. The Passamaquoddy portaged from river to river in the Penobscot, Machias, Saint Croix and Saint John River systems — covering as much as forty thousand square miles of territory between Bath, Maine, and Saint John, New Brunswick. In the summer, they took thirty-foot birchbark canoes into Passama-quoddy Bay to spear porpoises and pollack. They wove nets to catch spawning alewife and blueback herring in the estuary and at Salmon Falls. They ate bird eggs, clams, oysters, eels, fish, and game and lived in dome- and triangle-shaped wigwams. Women made maple syrup from sap in the spring and steamed lobsters by dropping hot stones into watertight birchbark baskets.

The Passamaquoddy had no written language until fifty years ago, so place names acted as signposts, describing river features and landmarks. *Matawamkiyak* (Mattawamkeag) means the "raised gravel bar" at the confluence of the Penobscot and Mattawamkeag Rivers. *Meqtoqek* translates as "where the river is red," and *sakotiyamkiyak* indicates a long, straight sandbar. The Passamaquoddy left pictographs on birchbark near Prince Edward Island to guide lost fishermen. Some petroglyph road signs in the watershed are three thousand years old and depict canoes, river contour lines, and the vector of the current.

Donald led me through a maze of mismatched tables in the museum's showroom, pointing to centuries-old Passamaquoddy wampum, delicate alder bows, and knives carved from deer antlers. It was late afternoon and already getting dark. There were no other guests. No staff. The only light came from a row of windows facing the road. A dozen handwoven baskets hung from a back wall, and a stack of antique photos of Passamaquoddy men and women wearing robes, wampum, headdresses, and top hats sat on top of a table.

Donald stepped among paddles, blankets, and display cases, then pulled out a chair in a back room and sat down. He had salt-and-pepper hair and the guarded demeanor of a man who had seen a lot of things that didn't make sense. The day we spoke, he wore a camouflage baseball hat and steel-rimmed glasses perched on his nose.

Most of Donald's sixty-three years have been spent convincing federal and state officials that his tribe has existed in the northland for thousands of years, and that that history — in addition to agreements made with the government — affords his people certain rights. The Passamaquoddy tribe once controlled three million acres — half east of the Saint Croix, and half to the west. After the Revolutionary War, the US and Canada handed out two-hundred-acre parcels of Passamaquoddy land along the

Saint Croix to veterans — ostensibly, to protect the border. State officials, back when Maine was a district of Massachusetts, set aside two plots for the tribe to live on. In the 1800s, the newly formed state of Maine forbade the Passamaquoddy from cutting trees or hunting on their land — so that non-Indians could. Industry and mill dams on the rivers wiped out fish populations, forcing tribal members to rely on government rations. In the 1900s, state Indian agents took control of food, medical care, heating oil, housing, and family services on the reservations.

Donald was taken from his family in 1964, when he was nine. Maine encouraged adoption on reservations at the time, a not-so-subtle effort to depopulate tribal land. Donald's sister and her husband, who was in the military, became his guardians. He attended thirty schools between Maine and Hawaii over the next decade. He thought about his home on Passamaquoddy Bay every day, and when he was nineteen, he pointed a one-hundred-dollar car east from Wisconsin, where the family was living, and never returned.

Donald has since stood two four-year terms in the Maine House of Representatives as a tribal representative, served on the

St. Croix International Waterway Commission, managed 120,000 acres of land for the tribe, worked on the tribal estate commission that manages land claims in Maine, and sat on the board of the national Intertribal Timber Council, in addition to a dozen others. In the 1980s, he was a key advocate in a lawsuit that returned a hundred thousand acres of trust land — that had been illegally seized by the government — to the Passamaquoddy tribe. He has written five books about his ancestors, collaborated on movies and TV shows, and personally preserved hundreds of hours of Passamaquoddy songs and language on tape.

Light faded outside and an overhead fluorescent light hummed as Donald spoke. Indian Township is a silent place in October. I didn't see a store, a person, or even a pet when I drove through. Most of the homes are one story. Many are placed on identical squares of land. The reservation is close enough to the ocean that you can smell the sweet scent of tidewater on a southern breeze. Outside the museum, gulls circled above red-tailed hawks, turkey vultures, and barn swallows.

Reservations that hug the US-Canada border have particularly difficult relations with both governments. Until 2001, US Customs and Border Protection and the US Coast Guard allowed Passamaquoddy tribal members to travel by boat between Canada and the US — as they had been doing for thousands of years. The Jay Treaty explicitly states that Indians have the right "freely to pass and repass by land or inland navigation, into the respective territories and countries of the two parties." But since 9/11, border authorities have hindered water travel and mandated that tribal members carry a US passport — a document that is, unsurprisingly, difficult and expensive to get for a member of a sovereign nation.

As with forty other tribes across America, and twelve reservations that straddle the northern border, the US-Canada boundary divides the Passamaquoddy tribe, stranding some two hundred members east of the line. Until recently, in a bizarre act of diplomacy, Canadian officials refused to recognize the tribe's existence. Travel restrictions by both countries, Donald said, have limited access to cultural and sacred sites. "If you had a boat out there, they would probably end up stopping you," he said. "If you try to cross the border and they don't think you're all-white, then you are going to get pulled over and get checked."

By 2002, every Indian traveling to Canada or back was searched, in both directions. Some were detained, others harassed or turned away. "So we did a peaceful march starting in Calais," Donald said. "We had about fifteen native people and a few non-native supporters. We marched right across the international border without stopping, holding up all the traffic, to say this is our land. And we don't like this racial harassment. Anybody with tribal plates would be stopped. So we marched back across. We didn't stop at the border again. We stopped in the middle of the international bridge and we stayed there for thirty minutes. Just to make a point. We don't recognize the boundary. And once we do recognize the boundary, we are losing half of ourselves. Because our ancestors say this is all our land. That border, we don't recognize it. It's there for these two powers."

Water bugs and lilies, plus a few submerged logs left over from the timber industry, floated in the flowage that morning. A hunter in a matching Grand Laker square stern motored in the opposite direction. The boat had almost the exact dimensions as mine but was fatter in the middle, with wooden ribs. A pile of duck decoys filled the bow, and a double-barrel shotgun leaned on the middle thwart. The hunter was supersized. His beard reached halfway down his chest, and his belly erupted from a pair of green wool pants. He made the canoe look tiny and greeted me with a flick of his index finger when we passed twenty feet from each other.

It took less than ten minutes to load the canoe onto the car and an hour on Route 1 to reach Spednic Lake. The landscape along the way was desolate: empty roads, empty trampolines, frozen kiddie pools, and gray skies. This was the northland that I knew: tobacco-stained beards, junkyard trucks, chainsaws, a weald of dense woodlands broken only by an occasional general store selling pickled eggs and whoopee pies.

As the land climbs the western edge of the state, the population thins from 114 people per square mile to 4. Maine was the third poorest state in the Union in 2011 — it recently rose to nineteenth — and the northland is its poorest region. One in five houses was either falling down or for sale. The Esso station near Topsfield had been closed since gas was $1.04 a gallon. I stopped at a general store and asked a middle-aged man surrounded by a sphere of frizzy gray hair where I was. "Wait," he said. Trucker hats in the general store spelled it "Waite." A blaze-orange sign outside read, "Welcome Hunters Miller Light." The place first opened in 1911, when William Howard Taft was president and World War I was still three years off. The store was the only business around for miles back then, and it still is today.

An hour later, after a quick stop to buy shear pins, I followed a one-lane road past a chain-link fence and the Vanceboro border crossing. A patrol agent followed me in a green-and-white SUV and drove a loop around the town boat launch after I pulled in. He parked and watched while I took the canoe off the roof and launched it into the flat water where the Saint Croix meets Spednic Lake. He was expressionless. Military buzz cut, aviator glasses. A faded Canadian flag flapped on the opposite shore, beside an exact duplicate of the American boat ramp.

The agent drove away, and I loaded the canoe and pushed off. The river was flat calm and, beyond the narrow eastern neck, opened into the lake. A wide, blue sheet of basins, coves, passages, and channels branched off in every direction. Spednic Lake Provincial Park spans the entire Canadian shore. The American side is a mix of private and state-owned land, nearly all of which has been conserved. The lake is seventeen miles long and covers seventeen thousand acres, roughly in the shape of a boomerang. Dozens of tiny islands, many with houses, crowd the borderline. On a summer day with bass fisherman and canoe-ists tooling across it, Spednic is a postcard of northern Maine. It is also famously shal-low and can see ocean-sized waves in a big wind.

I followed the border through Horse and Mollie Coves. A fire on a rocky headland a mile west could have been an Indian en-campment a thousand years ago. Donald had told me about an old Passamaquoddy rendezvous on Diggity Stream. It was in Canada, so I would have to slip across the border to camp there. I thought about skip-ping it after the agent circled me at the boat landing, but looking north, it seemed like an easy jump across the line.

Ten minutes after I zipped over the border, a small boat carrying two men dressed in black crossed my wake. They were a half mile behind me. The driver stood up. The passenger looked straight ahead. They were headed for Vanceboro. I shut off the engine, crouched down, and hoped that, from a distance, the canoe looked like one of the many rocks in Spednic. The boat slowed and stopped. My canoe drifted toward a small island. The men took off again, and I headed for Diggity.

You can't see Diggity Stream from the lake. Rocks, beaches, and forest blend into what looks like unbroken shoreline. I was a hundred feet away from it, on my third approach, when I finally spotted the outflow. The stream is framed by sand and alder. Golden light reflected off pondweed and pipewort growing at the mouth. The stream runs to First Lake, then Eagle Lake, which connects to Third Lake, Maudsley Lake, and ten more lakes before reaching a portage that connects to the Saint John River. The Passamaquoddy portaged the entire chain in the spring and fall when traveling between winter and summer camps. Diggity was the halfway point and had been a tribal haven for thousands of years.

Donald had shown me where the campsite was on a map. When disease tore through the northland in the 1600s, killing most of the tribe, he'd told me, they retreated to Diggity to heal. The epidemic came from Jamestown, Quebec, Plymouth, and Fort Orange. It followed European trade lines on rivers across the northland, spreading measles, chickenpox, smallpox, diphtheria, and influenza. Half of a village typically died within days or weeks of initial contact. Shamans attempted traditional remedies, and warriors shoved arrows down their throats and burned themselves alive to exorcise the plague. They believed it was caused by the gods. Europeans did as well, albeit a different god. Governor Bradford of the Plymouth Colony said the "hand of God" was responsible and that His purpose was to clear room for the newcomers. Cotton Mather performed an exorcism in the Massachusett language to see whether Indian magic, and sickness, affected white people. He reported, happily, that it did not.

The epidemic worsened, and New England tribes waged mourning wars. Warriors attacked neighboring tribes to avenge the dead and repopulate their clan, mostly with women and children. Men were often tortured and killed. Animal trapping grounds and pelts were essential to trade for European weapons, with which tribes could kill more Indian neighbors in what became a vicious cycle. The Iroquois eradicated entire populations from upstate New York to the Ohio Valley as they gained more trapping territory. From 1616 to 1619, disease killed 75–90 percent of coastal Indians living in the Northeast. About two million Indians lived east of the Mississippi when Champlain arrived on Saint Croix Island in 1604. By 1750, that number was 250,000. "Our people went deep into the woods, to this place, for protection," Donald said. "We've been going there for three thousand years."

A stone monument at the Diggity campsite commemorates the place as a historic stopover. The plaque, placed by Canadian officials, does not mention the Passamaquoddy by name. Donald had spent much of his life fighting to protect that name, he said. Eradicating Passamaquoddy history was another way that governments on both sides of the border avoided land claims and other obligations. Archaeologists in the early 1900s helped their case, theorizing that ancient ancestors of some of Maine's tribes were a different tribe altogether. They dubbed the first people to occupy the state "Red Paint People." The Paleo-Indians, they said, were Eastern Woodlands Indians who called the Maine Coast "The Dawnland," for the first rays of light to hit the continent every morning. They buried their dead with offerings of tools, animal bones, carved animal effigies, and small quartz pebbles painted with red ochre. Tool kits recovered by archaeologists contained woodworking implements for building dwellings and watercraft; finely wrought bone and ivory fishhooks, harpoons, and bone foreshafts; and long, narrow, slate lances for hunting whale and swordfish.

For half a century, history books explained how the Red Paint People walked off the glaciers, then vanished — making way for the Passamaquoddy and other tribes to move in. Donald and his peers pointed out that the language and culture of Maine's Wabanaki Confederacy — Micmac, Maliseet, Passamaquoddy, Abenaki, and Penobscot — were very similar to those of the Red Paint People. Academics and state officials told them they were wrong. Similar to the Passamaquoddy situation in Canada, if tribes are not officially linked to an ancient culture, they can't claim burial sites, land rights, or any of the thousands of exhumed corpses lying in Smithsonian Institution warehouses.

Recent linguistic and archaeological evidence revealed a new time line in the prehistoric northland. A dig site thirty miles from the Passamaquoddy reservation dated relics connected to the tribe at 12,500 years old. A similar site with Passamaquoddy artifacts had been excavated once before by archaeologists who supported the Red Paint People theory. Looking at spearheads and stone tools a few weeks later with one of the archaeologists who had been on the new dig, I asked how they had made the find. "We dug deeper," he said.

Every year, Donald leads a canoe trip down the Saint Croix from Spednic Lake to Calais. The first time he did it, he said, he didn't know where he was going. The group ended up at one of the hydro dams. They lowered their canoes around the massive structure, then scrambled down and continued paddling. "It's a lot more fun if you're going downstream," he said.

That night, I pitched my tent in a small clearing in the trees and watched the sunset from the beach. Foliage on the lakeshore reflected every color in the spectrum. Islands in Spednic looked like a Winslow Homer painting — bristling tall pines, rocky shores. It was a forest of water. It was the Dawnland that Donald's ancestors had called home, and the next day I would try to cross it all.

4

The wind started at two in the morning. Branches and leaves ricocheted off the tent, and the trees around Diggity Stream groaned. I barely slept, listening to gusts of wind burst off the lake. When I finally got up it was 5:30 a.m.

Fog flowed from the mountains into Spednic. The eastern sky was an arc of amber light. I heard wind roaring up the lake and smelled the dank scent of lake water turning over. It had been cold all night under clear skies and a swirl of stars. The Milky Way ran exactly over the middle of the campsite, perpendicular to the stream. Every constellation I knew was visible. The last thing I saw before falling asleep was a shooting star that split the sky in two.

This was the life that Champlain and most early explorers lived in the northland: cold, wet, slightly lost. They relied on Indians to survive, find their way, and export resources.

Tribes taught the Europeans how to fish, hunt, navigate, and stay warm at night. They showed them which plants were medicinal and which were poisonous. They demonstrated how to paddle a birchbark canoe, a vastly more efficient vessel than what explorers brought with them. They told their European friends oral histories of the continent: the end of the Ice Age, the migration of tribes, Indian cities in the West, floods, plagues.

I could have used some guidance. Spednic's main channel runs west–east for ten miles, and a northwesterly wind shooting through the gap had built up a wall of waves overnight. I saw whitecaps forming near Lindsay Island two miles away. The temperature was twenty-five degrees, and my hands were numb after breaking down the tent. The crossing would be nearly twenty miles. The odds of someone seeing me in the middle of the channel if something went wrong were slim. I doubted that even the border patrol would notice.

It was Columbus Day, not the best time to illegally squat a sacred Indian retreat. If I were a better seaman, I would have waited for the wind to calm down. But I was anxious to get going and get out of Canada. I warmed my hands over the fire and made a mug of hot tea. Then I pushed off and motored toward a line of waves that looked like they had rolled in from the ocean.

The wind blew twenty miles per hour through Diggity Cove and Green Bay. The swells were about two feet, and the canoe handled them well. The flat bottom and chine were incredibly stable and surfed down the backs of the swells. The waves died down in the lee of the Narrows but picked up again in Sandy Bay. Halfway across, I could barely see through the spray blowing over the bow. In a lapse of judgment, I took my hand off the tiller for a half second and reached forward for my raincoat. A blast of wind knocked the canoe sideways and the engine whipped to the side. A wave hit the boat at the same instant, tipping it violently. Freezing water poured into the canoe, and I jumped to the opposite gunwale to counterbalance.

Another wave hit. Three inches of water sloshed in the bottom of the hull. I shifted from one side to the other, trying to keep the canoe from flipping. The waves were so tall that I couldn't see over them from the trough. Whitecaps broke along the crests, and wind blew spray into my face. I managed to balance the canoe by holding on to both gunwales, but I couldn't turn the bow into the waves without crawling back to the motor.

I was exactly in the middle of Sandy Bay. A mariner's rule I learned growing up is that you have a 50 percent chance of swimming 50 yards in 50-degree water. My best chance was to get back to the engine. During a moment between waves, I scrambled to the stern and grabbed the tiller. The wind blew the bow around again, and the canoe lurched to the side. Another wave hit, and I twisted the throttle. The boat spun around and rode up and over the next swell.

The waves built for another hour. I was soaking wet and couldn't feel my hands. The lee of Birch Island looked calm, and I aimed for it. A half hour later, I pulled up on a sandy point, dragged the canoe ashore and lay down on a flat boulder.

The sun was warm, and it was a relief to be out of the waves for a moment. I peeled off my wet clothes and put on a shirt and sweater from the dry bag. I was somewhere between terrified and elated that I was halfway across the lake. The rest of the way was mostly in the lee of the mainland and looked like it would be calmer. I thought about Champlain's many hairy moments in a canoe and finished off a half bottle of merlot in honor of him. The deep-blue water off the western tip of Birch Island was etched by frothy whitecaps. There were no houses on either shore, no boats or roads or radio towers. Clouds moved through the sky at what looked like a hundred miles per hour. For the moment, the lake was as it had always been, wild and untouched.

I launched the canoe again and angled for the American shore. I couldn't steer broadside to the waves, so I had to cross in and out of Canada a dozen times over the next hour. I wasn't worried about border patrol anymore. Donald had convinced me that the line was not a real thing. I also hadn't seen a patroller since Vanceboro.

I ran the Canadian side of the border in the lee of Norway and Hinkley Points, then headed up the final stretch of Spednic. The wind finally died there, and I looked for the Forest City boat landing. The water was flat, and the nightmare of that morning eased away as I pointed the canoe toward a gravel boat ramp emerging from the woods.

The assassination of Henri IV in 1610 shifted the balance of power in the northland. Champlain's longtime supporter was gone, and Henri's wife, Marie de Médicis, had little interest in New France. Champlain spent years in Paris trying to appease investors and influence the royal court. He married the twelve-year-old daughter of a court secretary to gain access to Marie's inner circle, and he lobbied noblemen to rally behind his creation. Back in Quebec, Champlain paddled the Ottawa River, Lake Nipissing, and the French River; crossed the rocky Canadian Shield; and saw the vast expanse of Lake Huron. He met Otaguottouemin, High Hair, Petite, Putun, and Madawaska Indians, among many others, and kept a promise to his Indian allies in 1615 by attacking a central Onondaga village in Iroquoia — near present-day Syracuse, New York.

The battle did not go as well as the first. Champlain was wounded by two arrows in his leg and had to retreat. He convalesced with the Huron Indians over the winter and wrote extensively about their walled cities and elaborate farming complexes. When he could walk again, he hunted deer with the tribe and explored the surrounding territory. In the spring he paddled back to Quebec and sailed for home, again, to save New France from squabbling aristocrats.

While the French argued about the value of a North American colony, the English moved quickly to control the coast and, ultimately, cross the line that Champlain had drawn. In the end, the difference wasn't ships, weapons, or Indian alliances. It was people.

The "peopling" of British America began a year after Jamestown was founded and became one of the largest migrations in human history. Emigrating from England to the New World was not always a voluntary act. The lord mayor of London, who was an investor in the Virginia Company, rounded up hundreds of orphans from the streets and hospitals to be sent as "apprentices" to Jamestown. Most of them died, and constables were told to ship more urchins to the English port of Bridewell to be transported across the Atlantic. Churchwardens visited the poor and urged them to send family members overseas. One of the Virginia Company's founders, Sir Edwin Sandys, introduced a law to Parliament to force every parish in England to send its destitute to his colony, at the parish's expense. (It didn't pass.) By 1624, more than four thousand outcasts had been shipped across the Atlantic.

The Plymouth Colony and fishing ships along the coast of New England spread the English population north into Massachusetts, New Hampshire, and Maine. In the 1630s and '40s, twenty thousand Puritans, either displaced by or dissatisfied with the tyranny of England's Charles I, arrived on the shores of New England. They, too, spread to islands and coastal fishing villages in the northland, overlapping French settlers who had ranged south from New France's easternmost colony, Acadia. By 1650, the population of New England was fifty thousand. Settlers in New France numbered seven hundred.

Champlain saw the coming conflict and had his men dig ditches and erect fortifications around Quebec. It was not enough. Captain Samuel Argall, former governor of Virginia, sacked the French Jesuit colony of Saint-Sauveur on Mount Desert Island in 1613, then burned the structures that Champlain had built on Saint Croix Island. English and Scottish traders during the Thirty Years' War forced Champlain to surrender Quebec in 1629. England returned it after the 1632 Treaty of Saint-Germain-en-Laye, and Champlain sailed for the city he had built for the last time that spring.

New France's founder rarely left Quebec in his final years. He suffered a stroke in October 1635 that paralyzed him from the waist down. His condition worsened over the next month, and he lost feeling in his arms as well. He continued with official business from his bed and spent his last months conferring with and confessing to a Jesuit priest. Champlain's spirituality had carried him across the ocean into the deepest wilds of North America, and he did not question it in his final days. He recounted his successes and failures to the priest and a small coterie of noblemen from his deathbed. His last day in this world was Christmas 1635.

Within six years, New France was consumed by the Beaver Wars, a series of battles with the Iroquois over trapping territory. Thirty years later, the first of six bloody conflicts, collectively known as the French and Indian Wars, devastated communities on both sides of the New France–New England border. The wars raged for almost a century and destroyed nearly every town along the Maine coast. When peace was finally made in 1763, France ceded all of its territory east of the Mississippi to the British, and for a moment the line disappeared.

The fall of New France gave rise to the world's first global empire. The British were not charitable with their newfound hegemony. They had been trying to erase the French presence from North America since the 1600s, and in 1730 they forced residents of Acadia living between Maine and Nova

Scotia to sign a declaration of loyalty. Twenty-five years later, they deported them instead, no matter their allegiance.

The *Grand Dérangement* (Great Upheaval) deported 11,500 of the 14,000 Acadians living in New France. Most were shipped to the British colonies or England. Many later resettled in Louisiana, creating the Acadian culture that still exists there. Thousands died in transit, and only a few hundred escaped. Some of the escapees headed to Maine's Upper Saint John Valley, out of reach of British ships. Two hundred years later, the valley still holds a thriving Acadian community.

"Don't let the name fool you," Abby Pond said of Forest City. There was no city, just a boat launch and a single-lane dirt road that ran two miles to town. I walked for an hour down the road without seeing anyone. Orange leaves helicoptered from the sky. I eventually found East Grand Lake Road and followed it north toward Wheaton's Lodge, where I had reserved a room for the night.

It was surprising that a middle-aged man with dark hair and a dark complexion, wearing a black down parka and carrying a laptop computer, could illegally sleep in

Canada, cross the border thirty-five times, and then walk, unobstructed, into an American town. There was no law enforcement at the boat landing or on the outskirts of Forest City. "You can cross wherever you want," Pond told me. "But they have a saying up here: There aren't any local papers because everyone knows the news before it could go to press."

An elderly woman with a gray bouffant pulled up behind me a hundred yards down East Grand Lake Road. She was driving a four-wheeler and wearing a tracksuit. She didn't say anything at first, just stared at me and scowled.

"Where you coming from?" she finally asked.

"The boat launch," I said.

"What boat launch?"

"Forest City. On Spednic Lake."

"But where did you *come* from?"

"Vanceboro," I said.

"How did you get here?"

"I canoed. From Vanceboro. To here."

"But where are you *coming* from?" she asked again.

We stared at each other for a long moment, then I walked away. She followed me for a minute, then took off in the opposite direction. That night at Wheaton's Lodge, the owner, Patrick Patterson said, "That would be Georgie." Georgie had called the lodge after confronting me to report that someone she didn't recognize was walking through town. Patrick's wife, Sandy, had left the front desk to join the hunt. The two women drove around town — Sandy in a John Deere 4×4, Georgie on the four-wheeler — but didn't find anything. Sandy and I must have just missed each other, because I spent the entire episode waiting at the front desk beside a hand-scrawled note that read, "Writer guy arrives today."

I told Patrick that small-town, grapevine security was apparently more effective than the border patrol. "I guarantee you the patrol knows exactly where you are," he said. Patrick is just under six feet tall and north of two hundred pounds. His presence is channeled through a voice two octaves deeper than anything I've heard come out of a human. He used his gift in a previous life as a radio DJ and only recently reinvented himself as a guide. He and Sandy bought Wheaton's Lodge in 2012, and Patrick was still getting his head around the idea of driving skinny canoes through rough waters five days a week.

It is hard to imagine Patrick nervous about anything when he's wearing his northland business suit — duck pants, suspenders, flannel, wraparound sunglasses. He is the reincarnation of Paul Bunyan, with an affection for military terms and a seemingly endless supply of one-liners. He is the kind of northlander who knows a lot about the woods but also how to tell a good story. When I asked him how the border patrol knew exactly where I was, he unfolded five meaty fingers, one at a time, and said, "Cameras. Drones. Satellites. Sensors. Air surveillance. One way or another, they've got eyes on you."

The patrol had eyes on him one night when he was ice fishing with friends. "Ice drinking, we call it," he said. One of his friends loosed a couple of rounds from his 9-millimeter pistol at a beer can, and four snowmobiles approached "in formation." The snowmobiles stopped a hundred yards away and watched the crew. Eventually, four border agents walked over and asked if anyone had firearms or narcotics. "Every one of us has a firearm," Patrick told them. They asked what kind, and Patrick and his friends produced their weapons. "Does it bother you that your buddy's gun is bigger than yours?" one agent asked.

Sandy showed me my cabin, and Patrick offered to pick up my canoe at the landing.

His demeanor changed the moment we pulled onto East Grand Lake Road in his pickup truck. He had more pressing problems than the border. He had unknowingly joined another of the northland's dying tribes when he bought the lodge. A shift away from remote wilderness getaways among American travelers was cutting into his margins. Wheaton's Lodge has no TVs and limited cell phone service. Internet speed is dependent on meteorological conditions. The lodge is two hours from the nearest airport and is the perfect destination for anyone looking to unplug in one of the last untrammeled regions of America. The problem was, most Americans didn't want to unplug.

Maine's northland was once an exotic destination in America. Wilderness lodges in Aroostook and Washington Counties helped create the idea of domestic destination travel in the late 1800s. Wealthy tycoons of the Gilded Age rode the trains they built to Augusta and Bangor. "Sports" spent weeks in hand-hewn lodges hunting caribou, deer, and bear and drinking whiskey with rugged Maine guides. Many of the men who shaped modern America cut their teeth in the Maine woods. Henry David Thoreau's first naturalist essay was published after an expedition to nearby Mount Katahdin in 1848, six years before *Walden* was published. Teddy Roosevelt's first hunting trip was in Maine in 1878. He was nineteen, asthmatic, and skinny. He walked hundreds of miles with his guides, became lifelong friends with them, and took them with him years later to run his cattle ranch in North Dakota.

When Woodie Wheaton built his lodge in 1951, many of his guests were wealthy businessmen and celebrities from the coasts. East Grand Lake was featured in national magazines for its trophy smallmouth-bass fishing, and Wheaton's became one of the top fishing lodges in America. Rooms were booked May through October, a year in advance. Generation after generation of Wheaton's diehards arrived for their annual dose of blueberry pancakes, guide's coffee, and steak-and-fried-potato shore lunches. Things had changed, though, Patrick said. People these days wanted easy, not hard, and bookings were down during shoulder seasons. "It's getting hard to keep it open this late," Patrick said. "Ain't worth it after a certain point."

Patrick waited for me to empty the canoe and haul it onshore before loading it onto the trailer. We didn't talk on the drive back and repeated the routine in reverse at the lodge. Patrick drove away, and I looked for a place to keep the canoe. There was a small dock nearby, protected by a homemade dike. I tied it up there next to three cedar Grand Laker square sterns.

That night, East Grand Lake transformed into a cauldron of orange-blue light. The sky lit the water, and the water reflected it back up in an infinite loop. River flies buzzed through the twilight, and a commercial jet etched a magenta streak across the clouds. The northwest wind was gone, and glassy swells left over from the gale rolled through the water. The weather report said that the front had blown through. The next day was supposed be seventy degrees with southwest winds at five to ten miles per hour. If it held, I'd be able to reach the headwaters of the Saint Croix by afternoon.

Sea smoke swirled over the lake the next morning. There was no wind. The water was a mirror. Sandy packed two sandwiches, a wedge of pie, and a Stanley thermos full of guide's coffee in a wooden picnic basket, and at seven o'clock I headed out. Border commission surveyors had paddled near here two centuries before to resolve other disputes with the 1783 Treaty of Paris. One was the location of the "highlands" that the agreement named as the northern extent of the Maine border. The highlands had been a well-known portage east of the Saint Lawrence River since before European contact. When it came time to enforce the border, though, the British claimed that the ridge was located two hundred miles south, putting twenty thousand square miles of the northland in question.

Maine planted settlers in the contested region. Canada dispatched timber operations to cut forests there. On July 4, 1827, a logger named John Baker and his wife, Sophia, attempted to secede from what was deemed Lower Canada by the British. Baker raised a white flag with an eagle and a semicircle of red stars on it that Sophia had sewn and declared the region the "American Republic of Madawaska." That night, the Bakers' American neighbors, and one Frenchman hired to play music, threw a house party to celebrate. The following morning, likely a bit hungover, Baker wrote out the framework of the new republic, and a dozen families signed the document.

Baker ended up in a British jail a month later, and the Republic of Madawaska disappeared quietly. The border dispute did not. The Aroostook War broke out in 1838 between Maine and British Canada. US President Martin Van Buren authorized $10 million to raise a militia to fight the Canadians. Nova Scotia raised just $100,000. The war ended the following year without a shot fired.

Such border skirmishes weren't all bad for the United States. America instigated many of them to spark rebellion in Canada against the British. The Founding Fathers' ambition to include their northern neighbor in the Union was no secret. Benjamin Franklin demanded that the British cede all of Canada at the end of the Revolutionary War. Written into the Articles of Confederation was the line, "Canada acceding to this confederation, and adjoining in the measures of the United States, shall be admitted into, and entitled to all the advantages of this Union."

The Continental army attempted to invade Canada in 1775 to convince French-speaking citizens to fight alongside them. The campaign failed, and they soon retreated. US forces tried again in 1812 with a similar result. As late as the 1920s and '30s, the US Joint Planning Committee drew up plans to seize Canada. "War Plan Red" would commence with bombing raids on port cities like Halifax and Quebec. In

1934, chemical weapons were approved for the attack, and a year later, $57 million was allocated to build three airfields, disguised as civilian airports, on the northern border. After the *New York Times* got hold of the plans and ran a story on the program, it was dropped.

Final resolution of Maine's border didn't come until 1842, when Secretary of State Daniel Webster forged the Webster-Ashburton Treaty. Webster was a canny negotiator and worked with Alexander Baring, Baron Ashburton, a former banker who had come out of retirement to save Britain from what looked like certain war. Ashburton's orders from the British were to preserve the north side of the Saint John Valley, which connected the maritime colonies to Quebec. Webster's job was to convince a half-million Mainers, who refused to give a square foot of territory following the Aroostook War, to let it go.

Webster hired a Portland lawyer to write newspaper articles under a pseudonym, encouraging the citizens of Maine to support negotiation. He then produced two maps. The first, for the British, showed the northern highlands as the clear, agreed-upon border referred to in the Treaty of Paris. The second, used to leverage the

Americans, marked the border more than two hundred miles south along the Kennebec River — nearly cutting the state of Maine in half. The line had been proposed and drawn by Benjamin Franklin himself.

The evidence was enough to convince the two sides to compromise. The treaty drew a line due north from the source of the Saint Croix River to Grand Falls, then west along the Saint John River — giving seven thousand square miles to the United States and five thousand to Great Britain. The treaty also finalized the border between Lake Superior and Lake of the Woods in Minnesota, ended the slave trade on the high seas, and mandated shared use of the Great Lakes.

I motored all morning along the border, past brown sandy beaches and garage-sized boulders poking out of the water. White pines, lodgepoles, and red spruce grew along the shoreline. The border pushed me close to land a few times, and I spotted a black-backed woodpecker and yellow-bellied flycatcher darting through the trees.

It didn't make sense that Americans had lost interest in this. America was born in the wild. Explorers and pioneers shed their European roots as they traveled west and created a new identity. Champlain's expeditions, Lewis and Clark, Thoreau, the emigrant trails, the hunting lodges of northern Maine — all blazed through the wilderness. As the "Frontier Thesis" historian Frederick Jackson Turner wrote, "The American character did not spring full-blown from the Mayflower, but came out of the forests and gained new strength each time it touched a frontier."

Thoreau passed within thirty miles of East Grand Lake on two of his three expeditions to Maine. He published his account of the trip in *Sartain's Union Magazine.* The essays were eventually collected in a posthumously published book titled *The Maine Woods,* which revealed a lifelong fascination with the northland, conservation, and naturalism.

Two of Thoreau's guides were Penobscot Indians — Joseph Attean and Joe Polis. The group traveled by canoe, in French bateaux, and on foot. They slept in blankets by a campfire. The 3.5-million-acre boreal spruce-fir forest between Moosehead Lake and the Canadian border was unmapped at the time. (Much of it still is.) Thoreau drank cedar beer and hemlock tea with homesteaders, ate moose lips, and learned to speak Abenaki. He documented the hard, spartan life of the frontiersman ("We break-fasted on tea, hard bread, and ducks") and the beauty of backwoods rivers and lakes ("a suitably wild-looking sheet of water").

He floated under the stars in a canoe while Joseph lured bull moose with birchbark calls. Northern Maine was still a borderland then. Canadians and Americans alike wandered across the line, looking for timber and game. The endless miles of evergreen changed Thoreau forever: "Thus a man shall lead his life away here on the edge of the wilderness, on Indian Millinocket stream, in a new world, far in the dark of a continent, and have a flute to play at evening here, while his strains echo to the stars, amid the howling of wolves; shall live, as it were, in the primitive age of the world, a primitive man."

Tan stripes marked the high-water line on bluffs across from Blueberry Point. A stand of red and orange maple and oak rose over a small hill and dropped to the lakeshore. A large window at the Fosterville border crossing faced the road. I hugged the American side of the channel under a small bridge between the two border stations. I glanced back from the other side and saw the top of a border agent's head looking the other way.

Cedars swooped over a beach on the

southern shore of North Lake. Water lilies and duckweed turned the water green near the mouth of Monument Brook. A massive, restored farmhouse stood on the eastern end, surrounded by pasture. The water in between was flat calm.

The boundary runs through North Lake into the brook, then to a concrete marker at its head, where it shoots due north to the Saint John River. The marker is called Monument 1 and is the first of more than nine hundred that reach across America to the Pacific. There wasn't a cloud in the sky, not in the sense of the phrase, but literally not a single vapor formation — just striations of light to lighter blue lifting from the horizon. It was the quietest place I'd seen on the border, a no-man's-land at the head of Champlain's Saint Croix.

I heard a single-engine plane but couldn't see it. The only thing watching me right then was a turkey vulture perched on top of a pine tree and a few dozen bullfrogs. I paddled to the mouth of Monument Brook. I wasn't sure how far upstream I would go. The channel twisted left, then right. I made it around the first bend with a breeze at my back. There wasn't enough water around the next turn, and the canoe hit bottom. I stared into the trees for a while and waited for the stream to push the bow around. Then I paddled a few strokes, drifted into America, and followed the current back to the lake.

■ ■ ■ ■ ■

Part II
The Sweet-water
Seas

■ ■ ■ ■

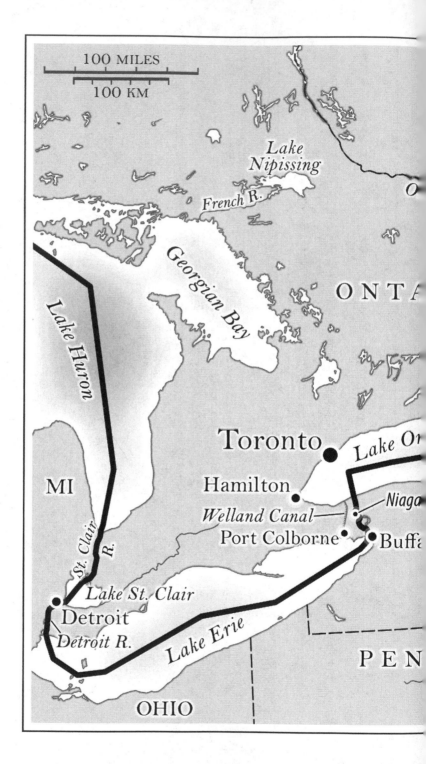

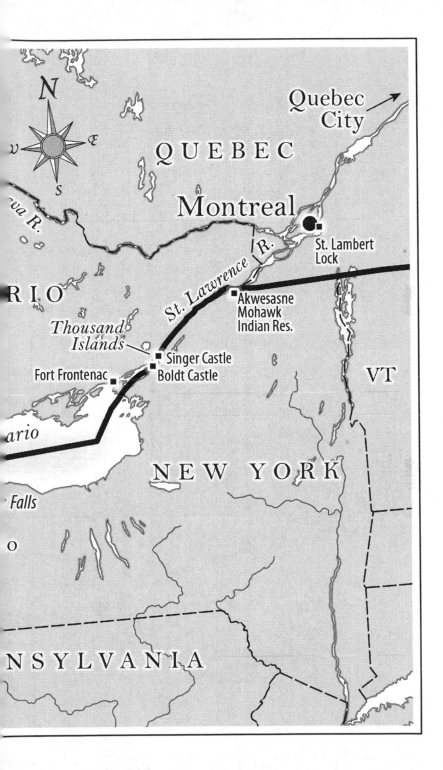

5

The waiting room at Saint Lambert Lock in
Montréal is furnished with two black,
pleather couches, six office chairs, and a
large wooden table pockmarked from what
looks like an all-night knife game. There are
holes in the sheetrock and sand tracked
across the tiled floor. Two windows look out
on a quarter mile of chain-link fence surrounding the building, a parking lot, six
security camera towers, and a guardhouse
where several armed men watch 750 feet of
placid, blue-green water rise and fall twenty-
four hours a day.

It was a warm June day, and a few scattered showers had left puddles in the parking lot. The bluestem growing around the
Saint Lawrence River, where the lock is set,
was brilliant green. The air smelled like
fresh-cut grass. Lachine Rapids, which
Champlain portaged around on several
trips, is a few miles upstream. Sixty miles

beyond that, the US-Canada border enters the Saint Lawrence and continues west, splitting four of the five Great Lakes.

Saint Lambert Lock is part of the oldest and most traveled inland waterway in America — a 2,300-mile corridor that connects the Atlantic Ocean to the Great Lakes and the American Midwest. Since deep-draft navigation opened on the river in 1959, more than two and a half billion tons of cargo, worth about $375 billion, has traversed the Saint Lawrence Seaway. Western coal floats east on the route, along with limestone from Michigan and wheat, sorghum, corn, and soybeans from the upper Midwest. Iron ore, finished steel products, and project cargo are transported west.

I'd been waiting twenty minutes for my ride, a 740-foot freighter called the *Algoma Equinox*. The *Equinox* is owned by a Canadian company, Algoma Central Corporation, that has operated trains, ferries, trucks, and freighters on and around the Great Lakes since 1899. The *Equinox* is the flagship of a new class that Algoma is building. It is the most advanced bulker on the Great Lakes — faster, larger, and 45 percent more fuel efficient than the company's existing fleet. The $40-million ship sails from Quebec across the Great Lakes twice a month, transporting iron ore west and grain back east. Like many freighters around the world, it also occasionally carries passengers. Algoma family and clients, and the occasional journalist, willing to take the slow boat get a private cabin, three meals a day, and shore leave wherever the ship loads, unloads, or stops at a lock.

The *Equinox*'s captain, Ross Armstrong, emailed me the itinerary two weeks before. Pick up at Saint Lambert lock. Follow the border across Lakes Ontario, Erie, Huron, and Superior. Drop off at a grain terminal in Thunder Bay, five hours north of Duluth, Minnesota. It took Champlain three months to make half that journey. We would cover it in six days.

The *Equinox*'s wheelhouse looked like a steel ledge rising above the lock doors when it pulled in. The ship is almost the exact size of the sixty-story Carnegie Hall Tower in New York City, leaned over on its side. The bow is a seventh of a mile away from the stern, and at first it didn't seem possible that the two were connected. The deck floated just a few feet above the water, weighed down by thirty-three thousand tons of iron ore pellets in the holds.

Three crew members lowered a steel gangplank onto the parking-lot curb, and I dragged my ridiculously tiny-looking roller bag onto the ship. All three wore coveralls and hard hats. One, from Newfoundland, introduced himself as Tony. He had a black mustache, pudgy cheeks, and curly, black hair. "You'll be in the owner's cabin," he said. "Better hurry up, supper's almost over."

I carried my bag up five flights of stairs and dropped it in the cabin. The room was surprisingly large. It was generic and time-less in a way that any steel room, like a prison cell, is timeless. The queen-sized bed could have been transplanted from a Comfort Inn. Fluorescent lights gave the room a pale-blue hue. The separate sitting area had a chipboard desk and mini fridge, and there was an en suite bathroom. The walls were covered with white, plastic panels, and the curtains were a kind of textured polyester I had never seen before. Behind them, two oversized portholes looked out on a con-stantly moving scene.

The mess hall was empty when I got there, except for one worker in coveralls, who ate while staring at his plate. He finished his meal, set his dishes in the sink, grabbed a plate of pie, and disappeared upstairs. Great Lakes freighter crews typi-cally work two months on, one month off during the nine-month season. (The seaway freezes over and shuts down in the winter.) Eating is a routine. Sleep is a routine. The man had carried out these routines thousands of times. His job was to repeat: four hours on, eight off, twenty-four hours a day, for ten, twenty, forty years.

The menu that night was chicken curry, steak, spaghetti, meatballs, short ribs, steamed veggies, salad, pie, and a choice of a dozen nonalcoholic drinks. I filled my plate, and the chief cook, Mike Newell, joined me. He has cloudy, blue eyes and gray hair, and he opens his shirt a couple of buttons lower than other crew members. He wanted to tell me about a tragedy. He was the main character. He'd been screwed, shanghaied, taken advantage of every day he was on the water. He'd gotten carpal tunnel syndrome. He'd gotten promoted, then demoted. He'd been punched in the face for no reason. He never wanted to be a cook.

Mike self-flagellated with a dish towel as he spoke. Sweat beaded up on his forehead. He was sixty-two and had worked on ships for forty-one years. He told me about other hardships. "Strange people come here," he said. "Not people you normally see at a job. Mental patients, Hell's Angels, ex-cons. No one else will take them." Mike had seen people die. He'd seen people arrested and others break down in tears. One time, four guys were driving back from a bar in a taxi. One was uncomfortable so he punched Mike in the face. Another time, Mike was walking to the mess hall when a sailor he didn't know pushed him down the stairs. The captain saw the blood and asked Mike if he'd hit his head. Mike told him the story and the captain replied, "Oh," and walked away.

"Killer Kowalski was a chief cook," Mike said. "He was always paranoid about something. Always running around saying, 'What's coming down the lake! What's coming down the lake!' Another guy worked as muscle for the union. His arms were like fire hydrants, and he was mean. He'd been in jail for killing his wife and told people on the ship he was going to kill them too. One day I put pepper on his eggs by accident, and the guy chased me through the kitchen until I locked myself in the pantry."

Back then, Mike said, there were fist fights every day and knife fights once a week. Sailors disappeared overboard in the middle of the night. Mike watched two guys brawl on deck once. One fell a hundred feet into a cargo hold and died. Canadian Mounties investigated the scene for five hours. They left without arresting anyone, and the ship headed down the lake.

Something happens to your mind, your perspective, the way you speak and gesticulate after a few months on a boat. There aren't enough square feet. There is no escape. Mike's hands were all over the place as he told me stories. His tattooed forearms flexed, and a vein in his neck bulged. His silver hair was matted with sweat, and his eyes did not seem to be looking at the same plastic walls, tables, and chairs that I was. Part of him had left the ship a long time ago. "This place is full of lunatics," he said.

Mike missed the days when the crew came to the galley to drink, play cards, and scrap. They gathered around him like boys around a campfire because there was nowhere else to go. Now that ships are computerized, the *Equinox* operates with a crew of sixteen instead of thirty-five. Everyone has a private room, with a television, bathroom, and internet. After their shift and a quick meal, they usually disappear into a cyber world.

I had no idea that life on a freighter was so violent. From the shore, it looked kind of boring. Mike checked on something in the kitchen, and I sneaked away to the deck. It was seven in the evening, and the sun was still above the treetops. The spring air smelled like honeysuckle and musty river water. The ninety-four-hundred-horsepower engine, and a twenty-foot propeller, pushing the *Equinox* through the South Shore Canal toward Lac-Saint-Louis vibrated the deck and every surface I touched. At top speed the propeller turns a hundred times a minute and drives the ship more than twenty miles an hour.

Red and green navigational buoys slipped past either side. A hatch of river flies lifted off the water and hovered above the grasses. Skyscrapers in downtown Montréal looked like vertical shadows. Long, flat clouds slid east. A thunderhead hit with fierce wind and rain. It passed a few minutes later, and the evening sun hammered the deck. You notice things like this moving ten miles an hour: kids playing lacrosse in a dried-up hockey rink; a teenager peeking into his neighbors' windows with a remote-control drone. Acts typically carried out in private are revealed, like a red fox an hour later hunching over and dropping a turd on a perfectly mani-cured lawn.

You also notice the passing of time. In the next six days, Captain Ross said there would be two stops where I could get off the ship. The rest of the time I'd be looking out the window. Or over my shoulder for Killer Kowalski. No alcohol, no drugs, no smoking allowed. A subtle panic washed over me. I was not used to sitting still or watching other people work. From Mike's stories, it sounded like the hardest job on a ship was off-duty time. It made people do crazy things. When Mike hit twenty-five years of service at his last job, he said, the company gave him a clock mounted on a brass helm. Mike told the guy: "You should have given me a fucking congressional Medal of Honor."

The canal opened into Lac-Saint-Louis, then narrowed again at Île Perrot. We were three hundred miles due north of New York City, on the same latitude as Portland, Oregon. Elms and cottonwood bent in the breeze, casting shadowy fingers onto the water. White cedar and ash grew close to the river, where 350,000 cubic feet of water passed by every second. Moraines and drumlins left by glaciers shaped the riverbanks, creating miniature highlands shrouded in red oak and sugar maple. In between, peat bogs lay beneath a lace of fallen trees.

Two bicyclists on the dike pedaled past the ship. It was hard to believe we would be in Thunder Bay in six days. In my mind, it was difficult to connect Montréal and the Midwest by water at all. I was so used to driving and flying that the shape of the continent had become distorted. You get on a plane or a highway in New York and get off in Minneapolis. Or Chicago. Or Los Angeles. Most people don't travel anymore. They arrive. Unless you're riding the slow boat. Then you see every mile.

If the history of the planet took place in a day, humans would appear at 23:59:56, and the Great Lakes would take their current shape across the northland a fraction of a second before midnight. The Great Lakes basin is set in the Canadian Shield, the geological core of North America. The shield floated on a sea of magma around the planet before ending up where it is today. At one point, it straddled the equator on the ancient continent of Laurentia. It was an ocean floor to several prehistoric seas; then it collided with South America and West Africa and created the Appalachian and Adirondack Mountains. Volcanic ash buried it, then glaciers scraped it clean. Geologists predict that in a hundred million years, it will merge with Asia and South America, creating another super-continent they call Amasia.

The Laurentide Ice Sheet gouged the bottom of Lake Superior thirteen hundred feet deep during the last Ice Age. It cut Lake Michigan nine hundred feet down. When the ice retreated fourteen thousand years ago, the basins filled with freshwater. Lake Superior topped out first and spilled into Lakes Michigan and Huron. The Saint Lawrence River was still dammed with ice, so water flowed north through the North Bay Outlet and south down the Mississippi and Hudson Rivers. When the last of the ice melted, water flowed to Lakes Erie and Ontario, plunged over Niagara Falls, and drained through the Saint Lawrence to the Atlantic.

It takes a drop of water about four hundred years to travel from Lake Superior to the Saint Lawrence River, meaning that the water Champlain navigated is still meandering east today. When Champlain first ascended Lachine Rapids, he was in a wooden bateau, headed west to find what he called *la mer douce* — "the sweet-water sea" — and a passageway through the northland to the riches of *La Chine.* It was May 1611. He estimated that China was between eight hundred and a thousand miles away. He had left a young Frenchman with the Algonquin and Huron tribes a year before to learn their language and explore the lakes. In return, he had hosted a Huron Indian named Savignon in France.

Champlain was a week late for the reunion. It had been a difficult crossing and voyage upriver. He described Lachine Rapids as "seven or eight waterfalls" and watched as a Frenchman and Indian died trying to run them. The rendezvous site was empty when he finally arrived. The Huron chiefs had been on time and had left a few days before. Champlain followed them upriver and surveyed the riverbanks for settlement sites. He found a large meadow where the Iroquois had grown maize. His men leveled the ground and built a small structure and a stone wall. He named the site Place Royale, but for the large island across the river, he kept the name that Jacques Cartier had chosen: Montréal.

A few days later, Champlain ran into two hundred Huron warriors onshore. He saluted his friends and summoned Savignon. The three chiefs leading the group were elated to see their friend and brought out the Frenchman, Étienne Brûlé. Brûlé was dressed in a deerskin shirt and traditional leggings. He had flourished during his winter with the Huron, learning both the Huron and Algonquin languages and gathering information about western tribes and waterways. He had unknowingly become the first European to travel up the Ottawa River and explore Huron country. Champlain spoke with him excitedly and, later, questioned the Huron chiefs further about the source of the Saint Lawrence and a possible route to China.

Champlain had been planning for years to train and disperse *truchements* (interpreters) like Brûlé throughout the northland. He recognized the value of Indian knowledge and collaboration and had trained others before Brûlé. But none traveled as far as the young Frenchman did. Very little is known about Brûlé. His story appears sporadically in the journals of Champlain and fellow explorers Gabriel Sagard and Jean de Brébeuf. He was born around 1592 in Champigny-sur-Marne, near Paris, and was likely an attendant on Champlain's ship during the 1608 expedition to Quebec. He would have been sixteen when he arrived in New France. He became interested in Indian culture and languages, and he asked whether Champlain would allow him to winter with them in 1610.

Even less was known about North America at the time. Henry Hudson would not sail into Hudson Bay for two more months.

Jamestown was still struggling three years after being founded. The Pilgrims were ten years away from landing on Plymouth Rock, and the Massachusetts Bay Colony was twenty years away from putting down stakes in the Northeast. Cartier had turned around at Montréal during his 1535 voyage up the Saint Lawrence, as had Champlain in 1603. Beyond that, all Champlain and Brûlé knew about the frontier came from rough sketches that Indians made for them on birchbark or in the sand.

Brûlé spent his first winter with the Algonquin chief Iroquet in the northland near the Ottawa River. The conditions were drastically different from those in Quebec. The Algonquin divided into small groups in the fall and moved upstream to hunt migratory birds, beaver, and large game. After the first snow, they moved into larger camps and lived in longhouses, with multiple clans sleeping in bunk beds. The tribe ate preserved food in the heart of winter and often fasted for days to make supplies last.

Brûlé was likely treated with privilege in the camp. He killed caribou and deer alongside Algonquin and Huron hunters and spent most of his time learning to speak and write their languages. The Huron speak a form of Iroquoian. They were taller than the French and well built, wore beaver skin mantles, and greased their hair and faces. They came from Georgian Bay on Lake Huron and knew western waterways well. Brûlé was so content his first winter with the Huron that he asked Champlain at the rendezvous in 1611 if he could return for another year. Champlain agreed. He didn't see his *truchement* again for years and considered him dead.

On the contrary, Brûlé thrived in the northland. He had been raised in a world of seventeenth-century noblemen and monarchs, where a wrong action or word could land you in a stockade. In the northland, he found freedom and self-determination. He vanished into the woods with natives who prayed to the animals they slayed, honored prisoners of war by torturing them, and lived completely off the land. The Huron Indians were farmers. They moved their villages every twenty years to keep the soil fertile and hunted only when they needed extra food. They preferred female children over males, because females could reproduce. Murderers were tied to their victims and starved to death. Every ten years, the Huron held a Feast of the Dead, during which they reburied corpses in a common pit so that their souls could journey to the "land beyond where the sun sets."

Brûlé spent his second year deep in Huron country exploring the Ottawa and Mattawa Rivers, Lake Nipissing, and the French River. He was the first European to see the broad, blue stretch of Lake Huron and Georgian Bay. He lived hundreds of miles west of the nearest Frenchmen and slogged through swamps, paddled lakes and rivers, and scaled mountain passes in the heart of Iroquois country. While his brothers in France discarded their hose and linen collars in favor of breeches and ruffs, Brûlé dressed in a mix of Huron and pioneer gear: knee-high moose-skin boots, loose-fitting wool tunic, deerskin shirt, wool cap, and a thick fur overcoat.

Champlain was stunned when he saw his *truchement* again in 1615. They were both deep in Huron territory. Champlain was advancing his campaign against the Onondaga Iroquois and was in need of men. He dispatched Brûlé to locate the Susquehanna tribe and ask for their help. Brûlé found the tribe near Binghamton, New York, becoming the first European to explore Lake Ontario, Pennsylvania, and the Upper Chesapeake Bay along the way. He delivered the Susquehanna warriors two days after the battle was lost, though, and found

Champlain wounded and on his way to Huron country to recuperate.

Brûlé disappeared again after the battle. As he trekked, he inadvertently drew the border between New France and New England west across the northland. From Montréal to Ottawa to the site of present-day Toronto and Buffalo, he met tribes and learned their languages, customs, and boundaries. The information he brought back made its way to French fur traders, businessmen, nobles, and the royal court, and trading routes and outposts eventually appeared in his path.

His time in the backcountry had distanced him from the French and their mission, though. He had his own plans and, in his last years, appeared only at trading posts now and then — usually with heaps of pelts to trade. Rumors of his lust for Indian women made their way east. Brûlé had a penchant for double-dealing — with rival tribes and even the English. His knowledge of the interior gave him considerable power in North America. He began his own fur trade and made an excellent profit around Quebec, appearing in the city in 1621 with four hundred beaver pelts. He sailed to France a few times in the 1620s and took a bride there. France's prestigious Company of One Hundred Associates hired him as a consultant, but he was captured by the British on his way back to New France in 1628 — and aided brothers Lewis and Thomas Kirke in their campaign to sack Quebec.

Brûlé did not completely abandon Champlain's orders. In 1621, he set out with another *truchement,* named Grenolle, to fulfill his original mission of discovering the extent of the sweet-water seas. He made his way northwest along the shore of Lake Huron, meeting the Beaver and Oumisagai tribes. He and Grenolle then followed Saint Mary's River upstream to the Sault Ste. Marie rapids, where they encountered the "People of the Falls," ancestors of the present-day Ojibwe tribe. Sagard wrote that Brûlé described the falls and a great body of water beyond them accurately, placing him on the shores of Lake Superior.

The French servant who discovered the Great Lakes died in infamy. Champlain severed ties with him in 1629 after learning of his involvement with the Kirke brothers, and Brûlé vanished into the wilderness again. This time, his lust caught up with him. In June 1633, a Huron chief killed Brûlé over an argument about a woman and, as was custom, ate Brûlé's heart.

What Brûlé left behind was not so much a

legacy as a passageway through the north-land. The first to follow him were more *truchements* commissioned by Champlain — like the great explorer Jean Nicolet, who arrived on the shores of Winnebago country wearing a China damask robe while firing pistols from each hand. (He thought he was in Asia.) Next came Jesuit missionaries who proved to be adept explorers and mapped much of the Great Lakes, establishing missions as far west as Lake Michigan. They were followed by *coureurs des bois,* or "runners of the woods," pioneers of the western fur trade. They all traveled along a line that was slowly trampled through the forests, lakes, and wetlands of the northland, much of which would one day become America's northern border. French soldiers walked it, then regiments of the British army, then American militia, farmers, miners, ship-builders, and finally merchants and captains who sailed schooners and freighters across the sweet-water seas.

6

The room was moving when I woke. The propeller's rotation shook the toilet, chipboard closets, desk, bed, couch, doors. Lakers are less rigid than oceangoing freighters because they don't have to withstand the same conditions. The *Equinox* was built on the Yangtze River in China. Builders welded additional steel supports into it so that the ship wouldn't break in half during the journey back to the Saint Lawrence. The supports have since been removed, Captain Ross said. You can see the hull bend when the *Equinox* hits a big wave.

Living on a moving skyscraper is a strange feeling. I had no idea where we were or what time it was most of the day. The ship's interior is lit with fluorescent light and smells a bit like a hospital. The crew wanders in and out of the mess hall all day and usually eats silently. Some of the men I sat next to I never saw again. Mike was a constant presence in the mess hall. He would come out while I was eating and talk for an hour or more. One day he told me a story about another writer who had ridden on the ship. Mike had spoken with him extensively as well, but the reporter hadn't mentioned him in the piece he later published. "What is that?" he asked me. I said I didn't know. "I'd like to find that guy," he said, swatting the towel. "I'd like to show him a few things." We stared at each other for a moment, then he walked back into the kitchen. He didn't talk to me for two days after that.

The sky looked hazy blue from the wheelhouse, which stands seventy-five feet above the deck. A thick band of clouds blocked the sun. Mustard-yellow exhaust fell from the smokestack and hovered a few feet above the water. The deck was painted rust red, with white handles on cargo covers and bright-yellow safety instructions. Trees glided by at ten miles an hour. The ship crossed the border into Ontario last night, Captain Ross said. We were passing Cornwall Island when I walked into the wheelhouse. The border enters the river there and zigzags two hundred miles to Lake Ontario.

Just upstream, the line cuts the Akwesasne Mohawk Indian reservation in two. Three thousand years ago, the Akwesasne farmed maize on the shores of the Saint Lawrence. They eventually joined the five nations of the Iroquois, and Jacques Cartier documented their villages near Montréal. By the time Champlain reached the area, the Mohawk had wiped out the Akwesasne, abandoned their fields, and taken over their land so that they could trap more furs for the English and Dutch. Now, Akwesasne tribal members have to navigate border authorities on both sides of the Saint Lawrence.

In 2009, the tribe took a page from the Passamaquoddy Indians and surrounded a Canadian border station. Guards were forced to abandon their posts for six weeks. The border station was moved to the Canadian side of the Saint Lawrence, forcing tribal members headed for Cornwall Island to cross a bridge into Canada to check in, then cross back over the same bridge to the island. The three-mile trip can take up to an hour. Akwesasne commuters trying to get to the other side make up 70 percent of the traffic at the crossing. Parents who drop kids off at school on Cornwall Island before checking in have had their cars seized for "aiding and abetting" undocumented travelers. Tribal members have spent an estimated

$300,000 getting their vehicles back.

Green lawns on the Canadian shore west of the island spread from white colonial homes to the water. Every other house had a dock, and most docks had boats tied to them. The residences appeared to be second homes. There were chaise lounges set on riverside patios, swings hanging from trees, campfire rings, teepees, canoes stacked in wooden racks. The American shore was pure wilderness. Scrub brush grows in the lowlands here. Hardwood forests push up against the river.

The helmsman steered while Captain Ross told me stories about shipping on the lakes. He rarely looked away from the windshield when he spoke. If he needed to give a command, he spoke over whoever was talking. If an important announcement sounded on the radio, he tuned everything out and listened. When Tony called from the cruise room to say that the internet was down, Captain Ross hung up on him and gave another order: "Line up the buoys to starboard. Two degrees port. No. Two more."

Captain Ross had spent the last thirty-three years on freighters. He was sixty years old, with receding sandy-brown hair and a graying goatee. He squinted constantly.

Crow's feet reached to his sideburns, and his stocky build easily filled his T-shirt. In Algoma company photos, he dons a navy-blue reefer jacket and a captain's hat. In the wheelhouse, he wore jeans, a polo shirt, and sandals.

Ross was twenty-seven years old when his father, a lifetime Great Lakes captain, called him from Quebec City and asked if he wanted to be a deckhand. It was December 2 and he was working as a data entry clerk for the Hudson's Bay Company — the same company that was formed by a royal charter in 1670 and that now operates a chain of department stores with Lord & Taylor and Saks Fifth Avenue. He was married and had a newborn son. His father said the money was good, so Ross packed his things and moved onto the six-hundred-foot *George M. Carl.*

He watched his father break up a knife fight his first day on the canaller and spent the next two weeks scraping and painting the bridge, cleaning and prepping cargo holds, and tending mooring cables. Captain Ross's father had been at sea for half of his childhood, and Ross had never considered being a sailor. After he got his check for two weeks' work — $700 — he told his wife he was joining the fleet full-time.

It took Ross just four years to work his way up from deckhand to wheelsman to mate to captain. He attended marine school winter sessions, when the seaway is closed, then logged required ship hours during the warm months. In 1986 he captained his first boat, *John A. France,* out of port. "The first time you're out there on your own, you realize there is nobody else to ask what to do," he said. "My second and first mate were sixty and I was thirty, and they were calling me 'Old Man.' "

The first trip went without incident. The next thirty freighters he captained were not as easy. Gangs operated on the ships, and many of the deckhands were ex-cons who couldn't get work elsewhere. The industry needed men so badly that if Captain Ross fired someone one day, he saw him on a competitor's ship the next. Ross watched men get crushed by machines, mooring cables, and cargo hatches. He went looking for mates when they were late for a shift, only to find out that they had thrown themselves off the stern in the middle of the night.

Regulations were looser back then. The crew made swimming pools by spreading tarps between cargo hatches during lake crossings and drank beer poolside all afternoon. They gambled and partied deep into the night and, sometimes, while waiting to get into a lock, they jumped overboard to cool off. "All we had was one TV in the cruise room," he said. "Going past Cleveland we could see an hour of a baseball game until we lost reception. Everyone congregated then; no one stayed in their cabin. We'd have thirty people in the galley playing cribbage, guitar, and cards. It made for a tighter-knit crew."

As for border security, he said, "There was before 9/11 and after." The *Equinox* shadows the border most of the time, especially in lock systems and tight passages between lakes. Cameras watch the boats from shore. Paperwork and communication with authorities is constant. Ships have to notify agents on both sides of the boundary with an exact list of workers, passengers, and cargo. Border agents search boats occasionally, sometimes with underwater drones or radiation detectors to find drugs or bombs.

Heightened security has been a hassle, but it doesn't keep most captains up at night. What worries them, and the entire Great Lakes shipping industry these days, is the health of the lakes themselves. A warmer climate across the northland has made water levels in the lakes fluctuate radically.

Lack of ice in the winter increases evaporation rates, which rain can't always make up for. The Great Lakes saw an unprecedented drop between 1998 and 2013, during which time regional conditions were wetter than average. (Fall gales can evaporate two inches of Great Lakes water per week.)

Freighters are designed to fill canals completely, often running just a few feet above the bottom. A one-inch drop in water levels means a Great Lakes freighter has to shave 270 tons of cargo from its hold so it doesn't run aground. If water levels drop further, as climate scientists predict they will, shipping specialists say that freight companies will have to cut loads — and profitability — by up to 30 percent. When you're talking about hundreds of millions of metric tons of cargo annually, and more than two hundred thousand jobs, low water in the lakes could cripple the business and the region.

A sudden rise in water levels in 2014 — about two feet in Lake Superior and three feet in Lakes Michigan and Huron — brought the lakes to above-average levels. It was one of the most dramatic shifts in recorded history and caught officials on both sides of the border by surprise. Some heralded the rebound as proof that the lakes were immune to climate change. The reality, though, is that a sudden change in either direction costs shipping lines and government agencies millions of dollars. An increase in midwinter rain and extreme spring storms leads to soil erosion and more silt in harbors and canals, requiring wide-scale dredging. Before the 1970s, it took twenty to thirty years for the lakes to see seven feet of change. Now, they can shift that much in eighteen months.

The three-hundred-thousand-square-mile Great Lakes basin spans about a quarter of America's northland. The coastlines of all five lakes combined add up to just under eleven thousand miles, almost half the distance around the world. An average of two hundred thousand cubic feet of precipitation falls somewhere on the lakes every second.

Water and latitude determine what lives or dies in the basin. In the north, the central Canadian Shield forest of fir, spruce, pine, quaking aspen, and paper birch is so dense that you can barely walk through it. Ridges and spires of gneiss and granite rise above the canopy. Move south and east, and sugar maple, yellow birch, white pine, and beech take over the land. All the way south, near the mouth of Lake Ontario, the Great Lakes–Saint Lawrence forest is mostly red maple and oak, with elm, cottonwood, and eastern white cedar at lower elevations.

You think about these things when you have nothing to do but stare for hours at an unimaginable mass of water. You think about the natural border that the lakes and the Saint Lawrence create and how it helped shape political boundaries. You think about the seasons, the intricacy of biospheres, water cycles, heat cycles, the planet's orbit, and its wobbly spin that makes night and day.

Two wood ducks swam away from the bow. The ship missed them by ten feet. Thousands of mayflies swarmed the smokestack. They came from the water as nymphs, rose to the surface, grew wings, and flew. They are ancient insects. Aristotle wrote about their incredibly brief life span. There are other prehistoric creatures around here. The oldest known footprints on the planet were discovered in a Kingston, Ontario, sandstone quarry a hundred miles upstream. Scientists say they were made by foot-long insects called euthycarcinoids five hundred million years ago. They were among the first creatures to migrate from water to land. Before the discovery, the quarry owner used the fossils as lawn ornaments.

Isolation and boredom aren't the only danger on the lakes, Ross said. He pointed to a chart on the wall and showed me locations of a few shipwrecks. Superior and Michigan are the most dangerous because they are the longest — giving storms enough fetch to create two-story waves. Fronts flowing west to east in the fall are particularly rough. The lakes sit in a lowland between the Rocky Mountains and the Appalachians. Cold, dry air flows down from the north and meets warm, moist air coming up from the south. Add prevailing westerlies rolling off the Rockies and you get a vortex of constant and dangerously unstable weather. Winds can blow forty to fifty miles an hour and whip up waves twenty-five feet tall, Captain Ross said.

The Great Lakes Shipwreck Museum in Paradise, Michigan, estimates that six thousand ships and thirty thousand lives have been lost on the lakes. The gale of November 11, 1835, sank eleven ships on Lake Erie alone. The Mataafa Storm of 1905 sank or damaged twenty-nine freighters, killed thirty-six seamen, and caused $3.5 million in damages. Storm losses in 1868 and 1869 led to the first national weather-forecasting system in the US, initially managed by the US Army Signal Corps using telegraphs in Great Lakes port cities. The most famous wreck, the *Edmund Fitzgerald,* which sank in a November gale in 1975 with all twenty-nine crew, went down a couple hundred miles ahead on our route.

A few miles upstream, the river widened to five miles across. We passed Chippewa Bay and entered Thousand Islands, New York — summer home to millionaires for a century and a half. There are 1,864 islands along the fifty-mile stretch. Most have mansions or sleek, modern houses on them. Many were retreats for business moguls and movie stars in the Gilded Age. Back then, a short train ride from New York City to Clayton, New York, left visitors a few steps from a ferry or private launch that would take them to their house or hotel.

I stepped onto the wheelhouse deck to see Singer Castle. Sixty-foot stone walls and terra-cotta roof tiles glowed in the late-afternoon light. The water around Dark Island, which the castle sits on, was deep azure. Frederick Gilbert Bourne of the Singer Sewing Machine Company built the fortress. It is a medieval revival structure with twenty-eight rooms, armored knights guarding a marble fireplace, a walnut-paneled library, and secret passageways from which hosts can spy on their guests. A few miles farther, on Heart Island, was another castle, built by George Boldt, proprietor of New York City's original Waldorf Astoria. Boldt built it for his wife and had hearts inlaid in the masonry. When she died (or ran off with the chauffeur — stories conflict), construction stopped.

Every island has a story. Thousand Island salad dressing was born when actress May Irwin tried it on a fishing trip there. Irwin shared the recipe with Boldt, who added it to the menu at the Waldorf. On a nearby island, a cabin burned down in 1865. In the ashes, a man was found with his throat slit and a knife stuck in his chest. It was allegedly John Payne, a hit man hired by John Wilkes Booth to kill Abraham Lincoln's secretary of state, William H. Seward. When Payne didn't complete the job, and ran off with Booth's money, Booth's associates tracked him down.

A few houses on the north shore looked like French châteaux with steep, peaked roofs and arched windows. Turreted homes and gingerbread-style cabins had replaced a nineteenth-century Methodist camp in Butternut Bay. Cattail marshes and lush reed beds edged the shoreline, and antique boats spanning a century circled the *Equinox:* split-cockpit runabouts, hard-chine sedan commuters, Nathanael Herreshoff steamers, sailboats, and Jet Skis.

The first mate pointed out an old steam-powered dory chugging toward shore as an SOS message was broadcast on the radio. A sailboat had lost power and was floating a few hundred yards dead ahead of the *Equinox.* Luckily, someone was close by to tow it home. I asked the mate how long it would take the *Equinox* to stop if something was in the way. "It doesn't stop," he said. "You should see this place at night. Or in the fog."

Beneath the boathouses and million-dollar yachts, the Canadian Shield runs south across the Saint Lawrence and joins the Adirondacks. Twenty-five feet offshore, the water is two hundred feet deep. Just behind the signal buoys, granite shoals are only two feet deep. Many of the islands here are perched on the edge of the seam. To be counted as part of the archipelago, an island has to have at least one square foot of land above water level year-round and support at least two living trees.

It was interesting to watch people gazing at the ship. I wasn't sure what solace it would give onlookers to know that the three men driving it were wearing Crocs and sweatshirts and laughing hysterically about their in-laws. That is not to say the *Equinox* crew is not highly professional. They are. It's just that enough time on the water makes people a little kooky.

We passed Wolfe Island and broke into a deep-blue sphere. The shores fell away to port and starboard, and the Erie-Ontario lowlands on the southern shore of Lake Ontario appeared as a green streak. Behind us I could see the sweep of Tug Hill Plateau, which divides the Lake Ontario and Hudson River watersheds. Due west was flat calm — liquid silver etched by puffs of wind and three ducks skittering away from the *Equinox*'s wake.

It took ten minutes to walk from the wheelhouse to the bow of the ship. It felt more like a boat up there. Wake peeled away from the bow. The air smelled like pond water. The sun was a bonfire three fingers off the lake. An exact image of the sky stretched across the surface of the water, and the horizon arced with the curvature of the earth.

The first mate throttled up to seventeen miles an hour, and the bow of the *Equinox* plowed forward. The hard part was over. Captain Ross went to bed, and Second

Mate Charles Chouinard took the helm. The only sign of land was a smokestack miles away on the western shore. When Brûlé and Champlain first arrived, they would have seen only water. There is no reason they would have thought the lakes were not an ocean, until they tasted them. There was no reason they would have thought they could cross them either, or that there would be more lakes on the other side.

Some historians believe that Champlain and his *truchement* were not chasing a dream. The elusive Northwest Passage they heard about from Indian tribes might have been a sixth Great Lake. Thousands of years ago, Lake Agassiz contained more water than all the other Great Lakes combined. It reached west and north of Lake Superior. When the ice dams holding it in place melted about eight thousand years ago, a cataclysmic flood raged through the Mississippi Valley, into Lake Superior and up the Mackenzie River to the Arctic Ocean. Scientists theorize that the magnitude of the flood was so great that it might have disrupted ocean currents, cooled the climate, helped spread agriculture west across Europe, and been the source of several flood narratives, like the one in the Bible.

Ancestors of western tribes lived around the shores of Agassiz before it drained, and they passed on stories of the flood through the generations. The Huron may well have drawn the lake on birchbark at Lachine Rapids, leading Champlain to assume it was still there. By the time Brûlé made it to Huron Country, there was nothing left of it. Today, the remains of Agassiz can be seen four hundred miles northwest in Lake Winnipeg.

The man who built the first Great Lakes freighter was never supposed to go to America. René-Robert Cavelier, Sieur de La Salle, was born in Rouen, France, in 1643. His father and uncle were wealthy merchants, and his family was connected to officials in the court of the newly crowned king Louis XIV. As a child, La Salle excelled in math and science. When he was nine, he enrolled in the Jesuit novitiate that his older brother, Jean, attended.

La Salle was brawny for his age. He was an athlete, headstrong, and imaginative. He was attractive and cunning too — all of which made him a terrible fit for the regimented structure of the Jesuit school. He was a dreamer — like Champlain, Cartier, Hudson, Verrazano, and many others in the

Age of Discovery — and it wasn't long before he followed their path across the Atlantic.

La Salle's father died while his sons were at the novitiate. French law disallowed inheritance to be paid to men of the cloth, so the family's wealth was not passed down. La Salle received a small allowance when he left school. He used the money to sail to New France in the spring of 1666, where his brother had taken a post as a priest in Montréal. Before he left, he added the family's estate to his name, "Sieur de La Salle," to make him sound more like a nobleman and gain leverage with officials in America.

Montréal was the most dangerous city on the continent at the time. The outpost was set on the outer fringe of New France and was under constant and bloody siege from Iroquois raiding parties. Gruesome attacks, scalpings, kidnappings, and torture were routine. The town consisted of one street, two rows of houses, a windmill, a hospital, and a stone fort for the governor. The priests of the Sainte-Sulpice church in Montréal owned most of the land and assigned seigniories — feudal tracts — around Montréal's perimeter as a buffer to anyone who would take them. Jean arranged for a large tract opposite Lachine Rapids to be given to his brother, and La Salle moved onto it immediately.

La Salle subdivided some of his land between settlers and built a palisaded village with them. He was energetic to the point of obsession and spent two dangerous years in the wilderness improving the plot. He learned to speak Iroquois and allowed a band of Seneca to winter on his land. They told him about a great river in the west that flowed to the sea. La Salle mistook the Gulf of Mexico for the Pacific and, thinking that he had found a waterway to China, prepared an expedition.

North America was still very much up for grabs then. The British, who preferred to conquer Indians instead of working alongside them, clung to the coasts and had made little progress inland. New France dominated the northland, stretching from Acadia to Lake Superior. Because the British held the Hudson and James Bays, the journey back to Montréal with tons of pelts was arduous and expensive. A route to the Gulf of Mexico or the Pacific could change the colony and the future of the continent.

The following spring, La Salle sold his land back to the priests (at a handsome profit), bought four birchbark canoes, hired fourteen men, and made plans to travel west with little idea of where he was going or what he would do when he got there. His timing was good. The Jesuits were planning an expedition to the Ohio Valley at the same time and wrapped his mission into theirs. They hired the Seneca that La Salle had befriended and a veteran soldier, François Dollier de Casson, to be their guides. To venture west of Montréal in the seventeenth century was wildly dangerous. The terrain was rough, remote, and unmapped. If you got sick, you would probably die. Provisions included bags of dried maize and whatever the guides could hunt and gather. If supplies ran out, expedition members paddled all day without eating. Everyone slept on the ground, no matter their rank, hopefully next to a fire. If it rained, guides constructed rickety tents from overturned canoes, birch-bark, and sticks.

The journey was a moderate success. La Salle paddled the southern shore of Lake Ontario past the mouth of the Niagara River, where he heard the great cataract a few miles away but did not see it. He continued to the western end of the lake, where the town of Hamilton, Ontario, now stands. He faked a fever there so that he could separate from the Jesuits and paddle

Lake Erie and the Ohio River. He explored as far west as the Illinois River, looking for the waterway the Seneca had told him about. It is unclear if he made it to the Mississippi on his first trip west. He would on his next journey. In what became a pattern in his life, his maniacal drive pushed his men to mutiny near the river, and La Salle made his way back to Lachine Rapids alone.

Being an explorer in America in the 1600s meant being a politician as well. You couldn't simply head out and make a claim. Hundreds of charters, borders, territorial lines, and spheres of influence divided the northland. La Salle spent the next five years courting the new governor of New France — Louis de Buade, Comte de Frontenac — and securing a grant from the king to build a trading outpost at Cataraqui, on the eastern shore of Lake Ontario. He built Fort Frontenac with stone ramparts, cannons, officers' quarters, and a forge, mill, and bakery. He constructed a small chapel, watched over by two friars, and cleared a hundred acres of land, where farmers grew crops and raised livestock and fowl. Two military officers, a dozen soldiers, and a surgeon moved in. La Salle created a village for a few French families near the lake and granted them farms. He convinced a band of Iroquois to settle there as well. (His brash and manic way made it hard for Indians to tell whether he was friend or foe.) Four ships anchored on the lake were under his command as well, the largest a square-rigged forty-foot brig.

La Salle's vision of restoring the family name was realized at Frontenac, but he had no intention of settling there. He sailed for France and returned in 1677 with a patent to explore *pays d'en haut* — the "upper country" around the Great Lakes. His plan was to transport supplies for a fifty-foot, two-masted ship above Niagara Falls on Lake Erie. Then he would build the first sailing freighter on the four Upper Great Lakes — and carry furs from the western shores of Lake Superior back to the Niagara River.

That fall, an advance team from Fort Frontenac sailed to the mouth of the Niagara River on Lake Ontario. The crew scrambled up the cliffs around the falls, found a building site on Lake Erie near Cayuga Creek, and contacted the local Seneca tribe. The Seneca lived along the western flank of Iroquoia. The French and Iroquois were enjoying a fragile peace, but the Seneca were not happy about the idea of Frenchmen setting up shop in their backyard. It was December and bitter cold by the time the builders arrived. Carpenters poured boiling water on the ground so they could dig footings for a fortified home and fell old-growth red maple and eastern hemlock for the ship. The snow was knee-deep, and temperatures dipped well below freezing.

The Great Lakes act as heat sinks, cooling the shoreline in the spring and summer and warming it in the fall. Warm fall air blowing off Lake Erie around the Niagara peninsula supports peach trees and grapevines, but when the first frost arrives, humid air becomes lake-effect snow. Lake-effect storms east of the Great Lakes drop more snow than anywhere in America — and left La Salle's men to live and work in a continuous whiteout.

La Salle himself arrived a month later in a second ship, carrying cables, bolts, anchors, cordage, cannons, and other supplies. After landing, the boat dragged anchor in a big blow and was wrecked. La Salle and his crew dredged from a dory in below-zero temperatures, trying to salvage as much cargo as they could. Most of the provisions were lost.

Working in hostile territory in the middle of the winter with primitive tools and no food proved almost impossible. La Salle's foreman, Henri de Tonti — a skilled, one-handed Italian officer — was a taskmaster. Carpenters milled lumber while their Mohegan guides built wigwams and hunted game to keep them from starving. Friar Hennepin, the Récollet explorer who documented the journey, built a chapel and held services for the crew. The men hummed Gregorian chants and celebrated saint's days when they weren't shaping ribs and planking for the ship. Two weeks after they began, the crew managed to lay the keel. In the meantime, La Salle and two men walked 250 miles through three feet of snow — with a single bag of cornmeal to sustain them — to Fort Frontenac to resupply.

Historians have speculated that La Salle's near-demonic energy could have been a symptom of mental illness. His risk-seeking spirit, grandiose visions, and violent mood swings are common signs of manic depression. He did not get along with his men, who thought his erratic behavior endangered their lives. In their journals, they described him as secretive, paranoid, and headstrong.

Tonti made great progress while La Salle was away. When the Seneca saw the massive skeleton of the ship take shape in the stocks, they made plans to sabotage it. The Iroquois traded with the English and Dutch. Even with assurances from Tonti and La Salle, they knew a French shipping route through the Upper Lakes would devastate their business. They made a plan to burn the boat in its stocks, but someone tipped Tonti off and he launched the ship early in May of 1679.

Le Griffon was a forty-five-ton barque with two masts. Nothing like it had ever been seen on the Upper Lakes. It was about fifty feet long and fifteen feet across, with high gunwales and a lofty galley. Beneath the bowsprit, shipwrights had carved an intricate griffon, sign of the Frontenac family. The ship was armed with five cannons, and the crew lit them all off at the launch ceremony. The show terrified and impressed the Seneca, who called the builders *otkon,* or "supernatural beings."

The crew spent the next two months outfitting *Le Griffon,* rigging it with masts, sails, and lines. By the time La Salle returned in July, the ship was ready to push off. Twelve men dragged her to Lake Erie. They dropped anchor in a sheltered cove, far upstream from Niagara Falls, and waited for a following breeze. The wind turned on August 7, and thirty-four men unfurled the sails and headed west on a broad reach.

The crew was sailing uncharted waters that had been crossed only by canoe. A birchbark canoe draws about six inches in the water. *Le Griffon*'s keel likely reached at least five feet beneath the surface. Hundreds of underwater shoals and rocks — now marked by lighthouses, buoys, and charts — were invisible to the pilot. La Salle used a rough map created ten years before by René de Bréhant de Galinée and sounded continuously with a lead line. The pilot passed Long Point, then the grassy shores where Cleveland and Toledo stand today. *Le Griffon* reached the mouth of the Detroit River in three days — a three-hundred-mile journey that would typically take a trader a week or two in a canoe. From there, *Le Griffon* sailed north to Lake Saint Clair and the Saint Clair River, then waited two weeks at the southern end of Lake Huron for the weather to settle.

Not one to take things slowly, La Salle wanted to sail to the edge of Lake Huron on *Le Griffon*'s maiden voyage. The crew set out on the first calm day, but hours later a violent gale blew down the lake. The wind howled from the southeast all day and night. Deckhands lowered the topmasts to keep them from breaking. They lashed sails to booms and let the boat drift for an entire day. At one point the pilot fell to his knees and prayed. The crew followed, promising to build Saint Anthony of Padua, the patron saint of sailors, a chapel if he rescued them from the storm. Saint Anthony came through. The wind blew *Le Griffon* northwesterly through open water, past Presque Isle and Rogers City. When the wind died, the ship was a short sail away from a Jesuit mission on Mackinac Island — seventy miles northeast of Traverse City.

Huron, Ottawa, and a dozen Frenchmen who were camped on Mackinac gawked at the ship as it approached. La Salle put on a show and lit off *Le Griffon*'s cannons as a hundred birchbark canoes paddled out from shore to see the spectacle. It was La Salle's moment. He arrived on land wearing a plumed hat and scarlet cloak trimmed with lace. He attended mass at a small chapel and was welcomed by all, though most seethed at his accomplishment. Jesuits in black robes, *coureurs des bois* in deerskin shirts and moccasins, Récollet priests, and even his own sailors prayed alongside him, while wondering what the madman's next move would be. With one trip, La Salle had changed the fur trade in America and carved a commercial artery deep into the continent. He had also rendered the services

offered by most traders at the camp obsolete.

La Salle departed for Green Bay, Wisconsin, on September 12 to meet an advanced
crew he had sent out months before to
gather furs. He found fifteen of his men with
the Pottawatomi Indians, along with twelve
thousand pounds of pelts. It was a massive
haul to move at one time. And to move it
with such ease, on a defensible floating fort,
was unheard of.

La Salle wanted to continue his mission
to the Mississippi by canoe, and because
Tonti was in Sault Ste. Marie arresting men
who had abandoned the advance group, he
was forced to send his pilot and *Le Griffon*
back to the Niagara River without him. The
ship set out on a calm day, but a violent
storm blew in that night. La Salle's fleet of
canoes was driven up on a rocky inlet for
several days. *Le Griffon* was never seen again.

La Salle speculated that the pilot had
scuttled the ship and taken the furs. Others
guess that competing traders or Indians attacked it to save their business. Father
Hennepin's journal states that the ship was
lost in a storm, but many theories have
circulated since. The wreck of *Le Griffon* has
never been found.

La Salle continued his journey south to

the Illinois and Mississippi Rivers and became the first European to navigate from the Great Lakes to the Gulf of Mexico. Once there, he planted a flag and claimed the region for the king. He called the territory "Louisiana."

Governor Frontenac had been replaced by the time La Salle made it back to Montréal. The explorer did not receive a hero's welcome. His creditors wanted their money back and seized his property. The new governor accused him of threatening the fragile peace with the Iroquois. La Salle's discoveries on the Mississippi were deemed insignificant, but the volatile explorer returned to the river anyway. He traveled to the Gulf of Mexico to set up a French colony in Texas and a string of others reaching all the way back to Montréal. In the end, the man who had claimed a third of America for France died in an ambush carried out by his own men.

It would be fifty years before another ship was built on the lakes. It, too, was constructed by a Frenchman — Louis Denis, Sieur de La Ronde — to move copper from the Keweenaw Point and Isle Royale mines. Thirty years later the ship was replaced by four more. Following the collapse of New France, the British operated sixteen boats on the lakes. By the mid-1800s, the number of freighters had grown to 1,300, and the Great Lakes had become the main corridor of trade and travel in the northland.

7

It looked like night. The sky and land were dark. Flames blazed above tall, cylindrical smokestacks, casting orange light on the ship. The waterfront was barricaded by dunes of iron ore pellets and coal. It was nine in the morning. The water was oily green. I looked through the porthole in my cabin and saw a truck pour molten slag into a ditch. A bright-orange splash flew into the water and incinerated a duck swimming by.

We were north of the border, in Hamilton, Ontario — the same lakeside outpost where La Salle faked his fever and left the Jesuits. The city sits on the western tip of Lake Ontario, thirty miles west of Niagara Falls. The scene outside was the Arcelor-Mittal Dofasco steel mill. The *Equinox* docked there at 5:15 a.m., and the crew began unloading iron pellets from the holds forty-five minutes later.

Hamilton Harbor had been the western

terminus of shipping on Lake Ontario for more than three centuries. Fur passed through first. Then timber, grain, and coal. When iron mines around Lake Superior met Appalachian coal in the 1800s, the Great Lakes became the steel center of North America. Hamilton was a keystone in the evolution of the Great Lakes industrial and agricultural complex that shaped much of the northland that we know today.

Innovators around the lakes fueled the transformation. John Deere developed the steel plow in 1837 in Grand Detour, Illinois — fifty miles from the southern tip of Lake Michigan. Joseph Dart invented the steam-powered grain elevator in 1842 in Buffalo. Chicago's streets hadn't been paved yet when Cyrus McCormick started producing mechanical reapers there in 1847. Patent lawyers were more in demand than investors at the time. McCormick battled Abraham Lincoln and George Harding, both patent lawyers, in court to protect his copyright. Lincoln worked and traveled on freighters on the Mississippi River and the Great Lakes and later filed his own patent for a bellows mechanism to help float ships over shallow shoals.

Industry expanded, and people followed. The first major cities in the northland cropped up in lakeside centers like Buffalo, Cleveland, Toledo, Detroit, Chicago, Traverse City, and Green Bay. Industrial, civilian, and maritime networks connected factories, farms, mines, and cities, creating a singular, multistate economic region now known as the Great Lakes megalopolis. Nearly sixty million people live in the megalopolis today. With a gross regional product of $4.5 trillion annually, it represents the third largest economy in the world.

Third Mate Ian D'Mello was alone in the wheelhouse. He was the youngest officer on the boat. He had a baby face and wide, brown eyes that made him look incredibly excited about every day he spent on the *Equinox.* He graduated from the marine training program at Ontario's Georgian College — along with most other mates sailing the lakes. He grew up in Toronto and sailed on ocean freighters for two and a half years to China, Japan, and South America. "That was more monotonous," he said. "You leave the harbor and go in a straight line for two weeks. On the lakes, most of the time you are in a river or navigating a tight lock. You only get to relax on the long runs."

At eye level from the wheelhouse, two crane operators suspended in glass cabs controlled clamshell loaders over the *Equinox*'s cargo holds. One dropped the claws a hundred feet into a pile of iron ore. It emerged five seconds later with fifteen tons of pellets. Two bucket loaders the size of a two-story garage drove around the bottom of the hold, pushing pellets into piles.

Time is money on a ship, and Ian said the boat would be ready to sail again at midnight. I tried to think of things to do for the next sixteen hours. I hadn't seen anyone in the hallway or mess hall. I'd eaten five meals by myself at that point. The *Equinox* was starting to feel like a ghost ship.

Ian pointed to one of the wheelsmen, Stephen, who was standing on the deck, and said that everyone who wasn't on duty had shore leave until 10:00 p.m. "You can probably share his cab if you get over there in time," he said.

It took me about ninety seconds to grab my jacket and wallet and speed-walk among deckhands, mooring lines, and cargo hold covers to the gangway. (No running on the deck.) Stephen did not look happy to see me. His eyes were bloodshot. He didn't answer when I said hello. He muttered something about crappy cell phone service and gazed at the work lot. One of Stephen's shipmates said that Stephen often told stories on watch that turned unexpectedly gruesome. He started to tell me one while we waited, then the taxi arrived and he jogged down the gangway to meet it.

We loaded in and Stephen asked to be dropped off near Dofasco's gate. Another town car with tinted windows waited for him in a dirt turnout. He grabbed his backpack and jumped out without a word. I continued to Hamilton. The crew described the city as hell on Earth, and so far it fit the description. Something happened when the cab turned onto North James Street, though. We passed a café and a smoothie shop, then a string of art galleries. The cab let me out, and I found a half dozen other galleries, three coffee shops, five restaurants, and two boutique saloons within six blocks. It was a bizarre and unexpected scene. A newspaper article in the window of a gallery explained the renaissance. At some point in the early 2000s, high rents in Toronto, an hour away, had pushed artists west into Hamilton's Jamesville district. A 2006 article in the *Globe and Mail* entitled "Go West, Young Artist!" had galvanized the migration, and by 2015, North James Street looked like a neighborhood in my hometown of Brooklyn.

I browsed hand-cut wood prints and giant

oil paintings at the Hamilton Artists gallery and bought an "Art Is the New Steel" T-shirt at a print and media arts center. I ate lunch on a sunny restaurant patio with fifteen other patrons, who talked about business and art while sipping lattes and microbrews, then got an espresso to go.

Hamilton is the kind of town where you can call the mayor an hour in advance, meet with him, and ask him what the hell is going on there. Mayor Fred Eisenberger was waiting for me fifteen minutes after I phoned his press secretary. He wore a blue button-down and slacks. He was born in Amsterdam — blue eyes, silver hair — and had moved to Hamilton with his family when he was eight. He was in the second year of his second term as mayor, he said from behind a desk stacked with paperwork. One of his campaign promises: clean up the water. "That is an overriding concern," he said. "We've spent hundreds of millions of dollars remediating the aftereffects of industry."

One percent of Great Lakes water arrives as precipitation and eventually exits through a river. The other 99 percent sits right where it is, meaning that pollutants become more concentrated over time. City waste, industrial discharge, agricultural runoff, landfill leaching, and contaminated precipitation are the primary sources. Pesticides, fertilizers, flame retardants, plasticizers, and synthetic fragrances are among the most common chemicals found in the lakes. Recent research shows high levels of pharmaceutical compounds as well. Antibacterials promote resistant bacteria in the lakes. Antidepressants, steroid hormones, and caffeine have been detected in residential wells in lakeside towns. Invasive species are a major issue as well. More than 150 have been introduced to the Great Lakes in the last two hundred years — many via ocean-going freighters that release contaminated water from ballast tanks — and are decimating fragile ecosystems there.

The northland is America's water tower, making water quality — and availability — there a national, not regional, issue. Ninety-five percent of America's surface freshwater sits in the Great Lakes basin. Climate change has already melted spring snowpacks in the north by 20 percent or more. Subsequent lack of spring and summer runoff has lowered water levels in many of the country's largest rivers, most of which originate in the north — the Columbia, Missouri, Mississippi, and Ohio.

In 2014, 90 percent of the US West was in

a state of drought. The Ogallala Aquifer, which waters much of the West, will be 70 percent depleted by 2050. Water shortages in cities like Phoenix, Las Vegas, San Francisco, Los Angeles, Atlanta, New York City, and even Waukesha, just ten miles from Lake Michigan, have inspired plans to tap the Great Lakes, alarming Canadian authorities. Water wars are nothing new in North America. The 1960s North American Water and Power Alliance proposed using nuclear explosions to divert several major rivers into a five-hundred-mile reservoir along the Rocky Mountain Trench. The plan for the Canadian Great Recycling and Northern Development Canal was to dam James Bay and turn it into a massive freshwater reserve. A similar plan in the USSR dried up the Aral Sea, and one that is being built in China will pump the equivalent of three Colorado Rivers from the Yangtze to arid northern cities.

Already, a million miles of water pipelines and aqueducts crisscross the US and Canada. The eight states that regulate Great Lakes water in the US recently loosened rules that control where it can go — allowing more counties to pull water from the lakes. With demand for freshwater in the US expected to grow 50 percent by 2050, former Canadian ambassador to the US, Gary Doer said, water wars in the future will make battles over cross-border oil pipelines like the Keystone XL "look silly."

Four hundred years after Champlain canoed the lakes, fresh fruit and vegetables are still hard to find on freighters. I walked from Eisenberger's office to the Hamilton indoor farmer's market — the oldest in the country, founded in 1837 — and grabbed a dozen apples and pears for my cabin and a few quarts of strawberries for Mike. Then I called a cab and headed back to the steel mill.

Neighborhoods grew progressively darker and poorer, the closer we got to the waterfront. An orange glow hung over the mill five miles away. Giant warehouses and empty lots lined the street. I didn't see a single person or another car. Inside Gate 15, flames flickered above Dofasco's smokestacks, and earth movers roared as they pushed piles of iron. The foundry runs twenty-four hours a day, seven days a week.

Inside the boat, nothing had changed. The forced-air system whirred. The fluorescent lights made everything bright and sterile. A single crewman sat in the mess hall, staring at a plate of spaghetti. Stephen was in the wheelhouse and said that half the crew was still in town. While we were gone, one of the clamshell loaders had punched a hole in the *Equinox*'s hull. The ship has a double hull, so it wasn't sinking. "Until it gets fixed," he said, "we aren't going anywhere."

European schooners, sloops, and brigs hauled most of the freight on the lakes in the eighteenth century. Around the start of the Seven Years' War between Britain and France in 1754, more maneuverable fore-and-aft rigged ships arrived. Hull shapes were designed to carry as much cargo as possible in shallow and variable waters. Early ships were fat with vertical topsides. Flat bottoms allowed vessels to skirt over shoals. A centerboard was added at the turn of the century to improve sailing efficiency. "Canallers" were the workhorses of the mid-1800s and were the model for modern freighters. By 1860, 750 of the 1,300 ships sailing the lakes were canallers.

Most of the steamers in the Great Lakes in the 1850s burned wood. It took an average of 150 cords in four-foot lengths to cross the lakes. One cord cost $1.50. Boats made about thirty trips a season, consuming nearly five thousand cords. Lake Superior had still not been sounded then, and there were no charts. Captains sailed with a compass, a sextant, and a barometer. Look-outs at designated stations warned of coming storms. Sailors Encampment near Nevis Island was a popular stop to heave to and wait for favorable weather.

Steam engines eventually made sails obsolete, and iron ships replaced wooden ones. Boats spoke to each other using "whistle talk," which included everything from what was on a pilot's mind to where he was headed. Each vessel had a distinct whistle — some shrill, some deep. Sailors cut down the masts of old canallers, cleared the decks, turned them into "hookers," and towed them. By 1889, whaleback tows and bulkers, with their flat bottoms and rounded tops, were running the lakes.

After World War II, a few steel ocean freighters sailed up the Saint Lawrence, and the age of the modern laker began. Dimensions were standardized. Boats were built to almost the exact size of the locks. Variations of lakers include longboats, oreboats, straight-deck bulk carriers, and self unloaders. Because the new Soo Locks are larger than any others — 1,200 feet long and 110 feet wide — a handful of thousand-foot lakers operate exclusively on the Upper Lakes.

Until the Welland Canal was built in

Ontario, to circumvent Niagara Falls, there was no connection between the Upper Lakes and the ocean. Canadians built the first Welland in 1824. The canal opened in 1829 with forty locks that lifted boats 325 vertical feet from Lake Ontario to Lake Erie. Large ships needed to be lightened to make it through, and the Ontario Railway was built alongside the canal to carry extra freight. Over the years the canal was widened, deepened, and rerouted four times. The last rebuild was in 1932, and plans are under way to redo it again.

The completion of the canal dropped freight charges dramatically and stimulated economies all around the lakes. The twenty-seven-mile link became so vital that several terrorist schemes targeted it. In 1916, a group of Germans tried to blow up the canal in what became known as the Von Papen Plot. Captain Franz von Papen helped organize a ring of German nationals from his headquarters in New York City, in an effort to stop troops and supplies flowing from North America to the Allies. Dynamite and blueprints for the canal were secured, but the Secret Service foiled the plot after an agent picked up a briefcase full of incriminating documents on New York City's Sixth Avenue El train. Von Papen and the other conspirators were expelled from the US. A grand jury indicted the group, though it had already returned to Germany. Charges were dropped in 1932 when von Papen was appointed chancellor of Germany. (He would later become one of Hitler's greatest supporters and vice chancellor under the Führer.)

The *Equinox* had already passed through the first two locks in the Welland Canal by the time I woke up. It was eight in the morning, and the familiar hum of the engine rattled the mirrors and furniture in the cabin. An Algoma welding team had arrived in the middle of the night and fixed the hole in the hull. Captain Ross made up time after they finally pushed off and was back on schedule by the time he reached the mouth of the Welland.

It would take eight hours and eight locks for the *Equinox* to climb the hill from Lake Ontario to Lake Erie. Captain Ross said I could get off at Lock 3 and return to the ship at Lock 8 if I wanted. One minute late at Lock 8, and I'd be heading home on a bus. I gathered my gear and walked to the deck. The assistant cook, a young woman named Cleo, was getting her seaman's license certified in Saint Catherines and showed me where to wait. When the boat pulled into Lock 3, we climbed a ladder up the lock wall and walked across a bridge spanning the lock doors. Two cabs waited for us on the other side behind a chain-link fence.

The Niagara Escarpment didn't look like much from the cab. The land lifted so gradually that I hardly noticed the incline. Hardwood trees and green lawns bordered the canal. Farther inland was farmland, and a few small roads. The canal itself was so skinny that, from land, the *Equinox* looked like a mini mall sliding through the neighborhood.

My driver left me at the Table Rock Welcome Centre near the Canadian side of Niagara Falls. The border runs through the middle of the Niagara River but not the middle of the falls. The waterfall you see on postcards, Horseshoe Falls, is on the Canadian side. The much smaller American Falls is on the US side. As the limestone riverbed erodes and shifts, the border shifts with it. Erosion has moved the falls seven miles upstream over the last 12,500 years. The current rate of erosion is about a foot a year, meaning that 50,000 years from now the falls will connect to Lake Erie and be replaced by a series of rapids.

A string of midrange hotels, casinos, restaurants, and attractions along the Canadian shoreline is working its way upriver as well. A few blocks north of the welcome center, the sprawling Fallsview Casino Resort stands alongside the Skylon Tower — whose "Yellow Bug" elevators rise 775 feet to a revolving restaurant. I walked northwest up Clifton Hill, past the Guinness World Records Museum, Ripley's Believe It or Not!, the Upside Down House, Brick City (Legoland), Movieland Wax Museum of the Stars, and the Haunted House. A study in the 1990s found that a surge of new construction on the Canadian shore had changed wind patterns over the falls and significantly increased mist from the waterfall there — good news for poncho salesmen on the viewing platform.

Niagara Falls has been a place of business since Étienne Brûlé stumbled across it. Frontiersmen kept an eye out for falling water. Stream-powered gristmills and sawmills were often the first step in settling an area. The first sawmill on the Niagara River was erected in 1725. In 1805, Augustus and Peter Porter bought the entire American Falls from New York State and used cascading water to power their tannery.

In 1891, the International Niagara Commission opened a competition for a commercial generator system that could transmit energy twenty miles to Buffalo, New York. The "Current Wars" were under way in scientific circles then — with Nikola Tesla backing alternating current (AC) and Thomas Edison promoting direct current (DC). Tesla had briefly worked for Edison at Edison Machine Works, but the two soon parted ways. Edison was stuck on the idea of electrifying America with DC, although DC did not transmit well over long distances. Tesla was convinced that his AC motors could do it better, and he was racing the clock to invent one that could transmit power at industrial voltages.

Competition entries were split among AC, DC, and "compressed air," the latter incorporating pistons and water columns that could run machinery and steam engines. Judges did not find a solution among the entries and asked George Westinghouse, who bought Tesla's patents, and General Electric, which had recently merged with Edison Electric, to submit bids. General Electric proposed a DC system to use locally and an AC system to transmit to Buffalo. Westinghouse put its faith in Tesla and designed a plan around his new polyphase AC motor. The commission went with

Westinghouse, helping to decide the Current Wars, and on November 16, 1896, Niagara Falls power lit up the streets of Buffalo.

Plans to dam the entire falls for power generation almost became a reality. Local opposition shut the project down. Frederic Church of the Hudson River school of painters, who painted many of New York's waterfalls, advocated for ending development on the Niagara River. Landscape architect Frederick Olmsted surveyed the falls and recommended that the state buy back the land, which it eventually did. The Niagara Reservation became New York's first state park. Water diversions for hydropower today decrease the flow over the falls so significantly that the US and Canada limit power generation during the day, when most tourists visit.

I was running out of time to make it to Lock 8 and headed to the other end of the canal. Port Colborne sits at the head of the Welland, on Lake Erie. When the canal was complete, concrete plants, nickel refineries, and all of the ancillary businesses that followed the shipping industry across the northland quickly sprang up. As in Hamilton, most of the industry in Port Colborne has dried up, and the town was becoming a chic weekender destination — with gift shops, cafés, and the incredible three-generation Minor Fisheries cafeteria, where your breaded and fried perch comes in daily from the local fishing fleet.

Once I boarded the *Equinox* again at Lock 8, I wouldn't get off until we had crossed Lakes Erie, Huron, and Superior. I took my time looking at shops and cafés along West Street. Sunset comes slowly on Lake Erie. Land on the far side of the lake was a shadowy thumbnail with a few towers and smokestacks poking through. The clouds were soft streaks overhead, weather moving in from the west. An optical illusion takes place on the lakes: when hot air settles over a cool layer, it can bend light. Blinking cell phone towers and skyscrapers a hundred miles away shoot up through the night sky as if they are a short boat ride away.

I found the Alphabet Bookshop close to the lock and spoke with the owner, Richard Shuh. The store is housed in an old, brick Victorian home. The sign out front advertised paperbacks, hard-covers, first editions, and small antiques. Books were stacked on the porch, in the hallway, and all around Richard, who sat in an office chair in the foyer. A photo of Allen Ginsberg and another of Charles Bukowski were thumb-tacked to the wall. I asked whether Richard had known them, and he said he'd met them a few times, in Buffalo and Toronto, back when he sold books there.

Richard had worked on lakers before that. He loaded sacks of grain onto freighters until he hurt his back. The money was good. The work was bad for his body. He did well with his bookstore until 9/11. Half of his business was American, he said. "It's all gone since 9/11. They make you have a passport now. Most Americans don't have one. I guess it's a hundred dollars to get one?" Business had fallen off by 90 percent in the last six years. His best sellers were Victorian-era prints that people hung on the wall. "I guess they have time to read that," he said.

Richard used to live in Thunder Bay. His wife is from there. In the summer they would rent a VW because the clearance was high enough to drive on logging roads. They drove deep into the northland, to a lake in the woods too small to be marked on a map, too big to walk around in a day. They set up camp there and fished, drank, cooked, and disappeared from civilization for a couple of weeks.

"North of that," he said, "you can put

your canoe on a train to James Bay and get an Indian to take you to an island there that is untouched."

"What do you do there?" I asked.

"You explore that world."

Richard spoke quietly about a vintage motorboat he was rebuilding. The only light came from the windows and a single floor lamp. The house smelled like old paper and decaying wood. He had lived in another time, when there were fewer rules, rent was cheap, and it was easier to vanish. That was the northland I grew up in too. My favorite places in Maine weren't even towns. The state still called them "Unorganized Territories."

I bought a few books and met the ship a half hour later at Lock 8. No one said a word when I boarded. I dropped my gear, ate a quick meal, evaded Mike, and went to the wheelhouse. Captain Ross was there. He pointed to another wheelhouse — this one sitting in a ship recycling lot on land. "I used to drive that boat," he said. "I can see myself in the window!" An old steamer used for Captain John's restaurant was tied to the dike. The boat had been built for a Jordanian prince. Captain John found it, brought it back to the lakes, and put a restaurant on it. It was a hit for a while, then started to fall apart. The town eventually shut it down, and now it's in the lot.

Two hundred miles of water extended in front of the *Equinox*. I could see the route that La Salle had sailed ahead: Long Point, Presque Isle, Pelee Island. Haze and fog softened the horizon line. The storm moved south, and the crew chatted and joked, occasionally glancing at the radar. I tried to imagine what it would have been like to sail this stretch in a leaky ship with no idea where you were going. Lake Erie is the shallowest of the Great Lakes, full of shoals and ledges. During the day the crew could use a lead line and take bearings. In the dark, they must have been completely lost.

I couldn't sleep that night, so I walked to the freighter's stern deck. A swinging chair jury-rigged with a chain and shackles hung there. It was the only nonmanufactured object on the deck. I sat in it and watched the electrified glow of Buffalo fade away. Whitewater roiling off the prop glowed beneath stars. The engine room blocked the wind and made the air smell like diesel. I could see running lights on two ships miles behind us. They followed our exact path. Far to the north a single white beam from a lighthouse swept the water.

■ ■ ■ ■

I planned my last days on the *Equinox* carefully — writing, reading, eating — making sure I didn't end up staring at a wall for hours at a time. Captain Ross and the crew were tired of my questions. There wasn't anywhere to get away besides my cabin. The view was either of water or of fog.

I spent most of the day in the wheelhouse. Sometimes I'd say goodbye to the crew on watch, then stay for another hour or two. No one seemed to notice. Sporadic conversations with Captain Ross stretched out over days. He would start a story about how much his wife loved her sailboat in North Carolina, disappear for fourteen hours, and finish it the next day.

The *Equinox* hooked north at the western end of Lake Erie and steamed up the Detroit River. The river was a lighter shade of green than Erie. Waves exploded on docks along the Ontario shoreline, and a few fishermen held on as their boats tipped violently. The shipping channel is two lanes wide at the entrance to the river. A US ship named *American Mariner* ran parallel to the *Equinox* five hundred yards away. I could see its smokestack through the trees on Bois

Blanc Island. The American captain hailed and asked what the *Equinox* planned to do when the lanes merged two miles ahead. Ross replied that he planned to go first. The American said he had entered the channel first — he had — and had right-of-way. Ross replied that he was currently in the lead — he was — so he had right-of-way. The American countered that the *Equinox* was ahead because the American captain had had the sense to power down to avoid a collision. Then he called the Coast Guard and asked for a ruling. The Coast Guard waffled and requested each boat's position. Ross had the throttle pinned, clearly pushing the *Equinox* ahead. Eventually, the radio went silent and the seventy-thousand-ton drag race was decided.

A grain elevator loaded a ship on the Canadian shore. "I don't know why the Americans don't trade in grain," Ross said. American ships also don't travel up the salty Saint Lawrence River, so they last much longer. The *Manistee,* a US ship built in 1943, was still operating a mile upstream. "It's a tough boat," Ross said. "It burns a lot more fuel and takes a much bigger crew, but how do you scrap a boat if it's in perfectly good shape?"

The river angled east, and downtown

Detroit appeared like a house of mirrors. The city was founded in 1701 by Antoine de la Mothe Cadillac as an advance post for the expanding French fur trade. After the British took over the city, Pontiac's Rebellion in 1763 — led by the Ottawa chief Pontiac — destroyed eight British forts around the city and halted British general Jeffery Amherst's plan to invade the American West. Detroit survived, and by 1765 it was the largest city in the northland. It's still the largest city on the border, with 680,000 residents.

A row of smokestacks and billowing steam outlined the southern edge of Motor City. The scene on the shoreline was an apocalyptic rendition of the once-great northland metropolis. Entire blocks were overgrown by trees and weeds. Graffiti covered empty warehouses with broken windows and caved-in roofs. The surrounding land, a short walk from downtown, was layered in rubble.

We steamed past the street where Henry Ford had opened the Detroit Automobile Company in 1898. Ransom E. Olds had started his plant nearby the year before. Ford founded a second business, that would later be renamed the Cadillac Motor Company, before settling on the Ford Motor

Company in 1903 — in a rented shop on Mack Avenue. (His two investors were John and Horace Dodge.) In 1908, General Motors in Flint, Michigan, sixty miles northwest, became the holding company for William Crapo Durant's Buick operation, which suffered greatly from his middle name but profited from his salesmanship. In the next twenty years, 125 auto companies set up shop in the Detroit area.

There were signs of life downtown. A hundred people wearing brightly colored spandex lined up in front of a yoga instructor near the Renaissance Center, a collection of glass-sided skyscrapers. A kayak club paddled along the shoreline. The *Equinox* eased past them, then picked up speed at Belle Isle and steamed up the Saint Clair River to Lake Huron.

At 9:00 p.m. the sun was still out. Fog had set in, and I could barely see the water. I saw my own breath on the wheelhouse catwalk. The dampness and cold penetrated my jacket. There were no buoys, ships, or rocks. You could see them on the radar but not through the windshield. "Lake's too cold," said the wheelsman.

I went to sleep around midnight. At some point after that the boat passed through Soo Locks on Michigan's northern border and entered Lake Superior. I couldn't see land from the wheelhouse the next morning. The water was glassy calm. Captain Ross was at the helm. "We were down-bound on Superior once on a ship that had cracked in half and been repaired," he said. "Forecasters were calling for forty knots. We weren't getting the wind, though. I decided to go through Huron and the Saint Clair. I went for an hour in Erie, steaming south with the north wind behind me. Then the real wind came. The sea was building. Waves coming over the back of the deck. I said, 'Shit, what the hell did I get myself into.' I knew the farther south I went, the bigger the waves would get and the more trouble I was going to get into. But if I tried to turn the ship around and go back to Detroit, I would be beam-on into the sea. One or the other. I slowed down and put the wheel hard to starboard. That was a hell of a turn. All six hundred feet of her was rocking and rolling sideways. The only thing I could see was that repaired crack in the hull. We made it back to Detroit and dropped anchor. I didn't sleep too much that night. You don't get seasick in moments like that; you're just scared. Even the most courageous sailors are praying. You're just a little pimple on the Earth. You're so far from anybody, and looking at your radar screen, there's nobody around."

Captain Ross stared out the windshield for a half hour after telling the story. The helmsman gripped the wheel. Everyone in the wheelhouse seemed deep in thought. "You are like a floating city on a ship," he finally said. "We are our own doctors, lawyers, family, police. You really have to be able to deal with it."

The fog set in again, and the *Equinox* powered into the whiteout. The average depth of Superior is 483 feet. Off Grand Island, the bottom drops to 1,333 feet. Somewhere down there the Midcontinent Rift, a giant scar of hardened magma where North America split in two a billion years ago, runs across the bottom. Deepwater sculpin swim that deep. Native lake trout and lake herring circle above them. Sleek black loons, herring gulls, harlequin ducks, and oldsquaw dive at the fish on the surface, and eagles, falcons, terns, and plovers glide above.

I hung out in the wheelhouse late that night. The claustrophobia was gone. My sense of time and space had adjusted. The isolation and pace of the ship was calming. At home, I realized, I rarely made decisions about what to do next. I simply bounced from one obligation to another, squeezing in sleep and family time in the few hours that remained. The pace on a freighter forces you to think about things, deliberate, and reflect as the landscape creeps by. It was similar to the way Champlain, Brûlé, and La Salle traveled — one step at a time. They wrote in their journals at night, preserved samples of plants and animals they discovered, drew maps, learned native languages. They saw more of America than most modern Americans ever will.

That night I dreamed of a cottony white cloud covering the lake. Above the cloud, the moon seared a crescent into the sky. I saw gray wolves and black bears wandering through stands of paper birch and pine on the two-hundred-foot cliffs bordering Superior. The *Equinox* steamed through the middle of the lake. Just the smokestack poked through, making a long furrow in the mist. It was a clear night above and a white-out below. Lights flickered onshore. Cars zipped along highways. America went on as usual while the giant ship slid through the silver light.

Two massive cliffs passed by my porthole the next morning. They were too close. It looked like we were going to hit. Captain

Ross was at the helm when I got to the wheelhouse. He was wearing a gray T-shirt and had a cup of coffee in his hand. The ship powered down, skirted the cliffs, and made a long, slow turn toward a grain elevator onshore.

"There used to be a lot more of them," he said. "Every year another one shuts down." During the wheat boom in the early 1900s, grain elevators lined Thunder Bay's shoreline. Demand for wheat in Europe hit an all-time high, and wheat coming out of the northland made up a third of the world's supply. (In the 1970s, the US share of world wheat exports hit 50 percent.) The Canadian Pacific Railway double-tracked its Winnipeg–Thunder Bay line to carry grain. The Canadian Northern Railway established facilities there, and the Grand Trunk Pacific Railway opened a route as well.

Ross eased up to the pier, and deckhands tossed ropes and cables at a few workmen onshore. After all the technological advancements the modern world has seen, the shipping process on the lakes is pretty much the same: tie up to shore, load cargo, seal it in the hold, float it somewhere that people need it.

There were fifty silos on the dock, all flat gray and topped by a rusting superstructure.

The crew secured the lines, and I grabbed my bags and said goodbye. Ross asked me to stay in touch. No one else said a word, so I rolled my bag through a web of mooring lines and hatches to the gangway. A few men in hard hats walked up the stairs to start loading. In eighteen hours, the *Equinox* would be on its way again, this time headed east with its holds full of grain.

A taxi waited for me at the end of a long, dirt parking lot. "End of the line?" the driver asked. It was a Tom Petty moment. I told him I was flying home, and he smiled like he'd seen a lot of sailors happy to be getting off a ship.

"Sad what's happened here," the driver said on the way to the airport. A nearby mill had burned down earlier that week. It burned for a day before the fire department came to put it out. Homeless Ojibwe Indians had been trying to keep warm inside with a fire. They fell asleep, and the fire spread. The Ojibwe had it worse than anyone, he said. "They found chromite on Indian land up north. Gold, diamonds, everything. They found it years ago, but no one will help them get it."

My flight from Thunder Bay International Airport was delayed by an hour that afternoon. Passengers sitting at the gate moaned and looked for alternative itineraries on their cell phones. I wondered how sixty minutes was going to change their lives. A skinny, middle-aged woman with an expensive handbag cut the line at the ticket counter and barked at the gate agent: "I have a *dentist* appointment. Can you fly me to a *nearby city*?"

We ended up boarding the plane early and leaving on time. The *Equinox* was still loading when we flew over. The ship looked like a toy. I could make out someone in a blaze-orange suit sweeping the deck. To the west, the forest circled Thunder Bay. I looked for the lumber roads and hidden lakes that Richard Shuh had told me about. The canopy was thick and green. I spotted a single brown line winding northwest. Farther out was a deep blue lake, maybe the one Richard and his wife had found in their VW, canoe on top, Bob Dylan on the radio, counting the miles between them and civilization.

■ ■ ■ ■

PART III
BOUNDARY WATERS

■ ■ ■ ■

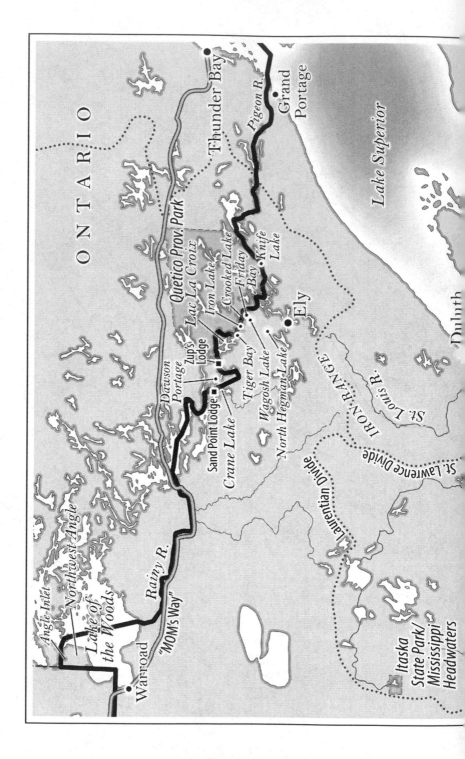

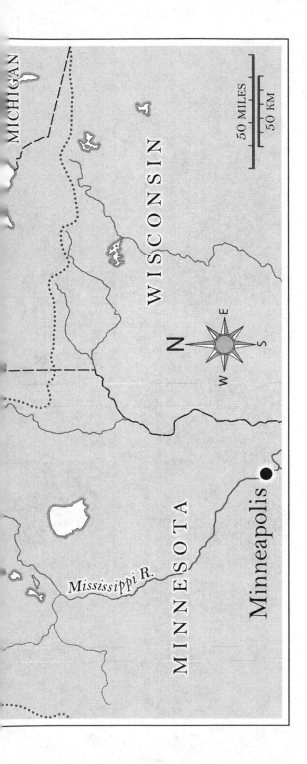

8

There are no roads. No towns or airports. There are no people, gas stations, businesses, cars, airplanes, electricity, phone service. There is water. If you're not on it, you're in the woods. Forests in Minnesota's northland are not as dense as those in the East. There is some light there. Looking down from an airplane, you see a landscape that is marbled blue and green, water and trees.

The Holocene created this wilderness. The Southern Ocean began releasing CO_2 about twenty thousand years ago. The planet warmed and glaciers melted. Bare earth beneath the ice was soggy and barren. It took decades for young spruce and tundra grasslands to crop up. Prickly pear cactus and burr oak spread across the receding glacier's path at a rate of fifty miles per century. White and red pine, spruce, cedar, and hemlock took root. Paper birch and upland maple turned the canopy red and gold October through December. Blueberries appeared in fissures between granite slabs. Thorny raspberry bushes and wild strawberries tangled in clearings. Moose, beaver, bear, deer, bobcats, Canadian lynx, and the largest population of wolves in the continental US live there now. You rarely see them. There is too much backcountry to disappear into.

Minnesota's Boundary Waters is still primitive, carved by nature, and untouched by humans. The watery landscape that flanks the northern border west of the Great Lakes predates Paleo-Indians, Hopewell culture, and the local Ojibwe (Chippewa) tribe. It is unfamiliar to modern man. It wasn't always that way. Commercial logging, fishing, mining, and railroads infiltrated and stripped the northland from east to west in the 1800s. Timber companies built railroads and ice highways deep into Minnesota's backcountry to harvest millions of trees. Miners plowed through the state's Arrowhead region — a triangle of ferrous earth wedged between the Boundary Waters and the northern shore of Lake Superior — searching for iron to feed America's booming steel industry. In 1884 the Minnesota Iron Company completed a railroad between Superior and the Boundary Waters and started loading ore directly onto freighters. Minnesotans in the Iron Range have a saying: half their state is sitting at the bottom of the Pacific Ocean, where armaments from World War II landed.

Relentless resource extraction along the northern border helped spark the nation's first major conservation movement. President Teddy Roosevelt created the 3.9-million-acre Superior National Forest in 1909 to protect the Boundary Waters. US agriculture secretary W. M. Jardine added a 640,000-acre "roadless area" within the national forest in 1926, and in 1941 the Forest Service outlawed cutting along most of the borderline. The region was renamed the Boundary Waters Canoe Area in 1958, and six years later it became the second-largest land parcel protected under the Wilderness Act. The act's definition of wild land: "A wilderness, in contrast with those areas where man and his own works dominate the landscape, is hereby recognized as an area where the earth and its community of life are untrammeled by man, where man himself is a visitor who does not remain."

The million-acre Boundary Waters Canoe Area, which includes a thousand lakes, is now one of the most protected territories in

America. Outboard engines, bicycles, paddleboats, and any other form of mechanized travel is forbidden, except on a few perimeter lakes. All visitors must have a permit. Most homes and businesses operating in the area have been closed and the buildings knocked down. Even the air is protected: airplanes over the region are not allowed to fly below four thousand feet. The effect has been to reverse time, remove humans, and return the Boundary Waters to the days of the Holocene. Today, the only way in is with a canoe.

I didn't arrive by canoe. I traveled by jet to the Minneapolis airport. The pilot told us to observe the crop art on the way in. An artist had planted five acres in the likeness of Van Gogh's *Olive Trees.* The image of twisted branches draped under a swirling sun passed beneath the plane on the approach. The palette was brown and pale green. The image was framed with a grass path where visitors could walk.

The drive north was fast and straight. I passed over the Saint Louis River at seventy-five miles per hour. Three hundred years ago, Indians, explorers, and traders paddled the Saint Louis from the Mississippi to the Great Lakes. During border negotiations in the 1800s, the river almost became the southern boundary of Canada. The Treaty of Paris mandated that the border follow the main trade route through the Boundary Waters. A flawed map and ambiguous language in the agreement led surveyors in the 1820s on a goose chase, searching for fictitious islands and lakes. They drew three possible lines — along the Saint Louis, Pigeon, and Kaministiquia Rivers, from south to north. (The middle boundary, the Pigeon, was eventually chosen.)

A concrete bridge spans the Saint Louis now. A dozen plastic shopping bags hung from the piers. It was mid-September and still hot out. Dry too. Brittle sedges grew along the soft shoulder, and the paled tips of pine trees were nearly white. Three SUVs loaded with kids and canoes cruised in the right lane. The golden hour was coming on: late afternoon, setting sun, lodgepole pines splitting the light. A pink glow spread over a lakeside cabin. A lantern and two Adirondack chairs sat on a dock in front of it. I knew this scene. It could have been Maine. A firefly bobbed through the trees. I heard the *crack!* of a screen door slamming shut. The smell of smoldering charcoal drifted in the car window. The last beams of the day froze the picture: dock, trees, chairs, sun flare, three soggy children wading to shore.

Scandinavian, German, Irish, and Polish families, descended from the first European settlers, still populate Minnesota's northland. Most came to mine the Iron Range or farm the plains. They are soft on their vowels and temper sentences with a slight inflection at the end. They sleep in small clusters of homes huddled on the edge of the Great Plains, throw potlucks, and cook fifty varieties of tater tots. Families still use wooden flails to harvest wild rice; pick serviceberries, chokecherries, and hazelnuts; and make traditional dishes like gravlax, lefse, lutefisk, lingonberries, and sauerkraut. The local name for the Minnesota State Fair is "The Great Minnesota Get-Together." You can see seed art there, butter sculptures, deep-fried candy bars, and two dozen varieties of food served on a stick. In the winter, Minnesotans embrace the cold by skiing, ice fishing, curling, and turning out professional hockey players. They say there are two seasons here: winter and road construction.

Sunlight gilded the highway on the way north. Two hot rods with chrome tailpipes and hood scoops roared past. The Blackberry Barbecue Joint was packed. Nord Lund Auto Repair a few miles down the road was closed. A highway sign said Duluth was a hundred miles east. Fargo, North Dakota, was three hundred west. Ely was twenty-seven miles straight ahead.

Ely ("*ee*-lee") is the unofficial capital of the Boundary Waters. A line of two-story Craftsman homes marked the edge of town. Sea kayaks, canoes, skiffs, inner tubes, water skis, dories, and dinghies sat in driveways and parking lots. A black-and-white photo at a café on north Central Avenue reminded patrons of the town's past. In the picture, two 1960s station wagons wait at a traffic light on East Sheridan Street. One has two sixteen-foot canoes lashed to the roof. The other is carrying a single canoe and two kids. Drivers and passengers wait patiently. They are here for the trip of a lifetime. That's how outfitters describe a journey into the Boundary Waters.

A local outfitter set me up with a canoe guide who had lived in Ely for thirty years and spent much of that time exploring the Boundary Waters. Paul Schurke is best known for an even wilder expedition. On May 1, 1986, Paul, Will Steger, Ann Bancroft, and their team completed the first-ever trek to the North Pole without resupply. They did it with dogsleds and trained around Ely. The feat was documented in a *National Geographic* cover story, a television special, and Paul and Will's best-selling book *North to the Pole.* Paul's wife, Sue, outfitted the one-thousand-mile, two-month journey — which saw temperatures dip to minus seventy-five degrees Fahrenheit — with hand-stitched garments. Her business became the Wintergreen line of outdoor clothing, which she still manufactures in Ely today.

Paul's bio made him sound like a modern-day La Salle. In 1989, he led the joint Soviet-American Bering Bridge Expedition, a dogsled and ski trip that crossed 1,200 miles of Alaska and Siberia in an attempt to melt the "Ice Curtain" between the two nations. In 2014, he retraced Teddy Roosevelt's expedition down Brazil's deadly River of Doubt — a four-hundred-mile stretch of rapids, waterfalls, poisonous snakes, jaguars, and crocodiles. (Only three parties had paddled the entire river since Roosevelt.) Paul is sixty-two years old, returns to the Arctic every year to lead trips, and has crossed Greenland, Arctic Canada, Siberia, Svalbard, and Antarctica's South Georgia Island on dogsleds and skis — the latter to reenact Ernest Shackleton's harrowing 1915 escape from his icebound ship. At six foot two, with broad shoulders, a thick chest, and long, muscular legs, he is ruthless on the trail. His endurance is legendary, and his tolerance for pain and hardship borders on freakish. His friends call him the Iceman.

Sue is often a coleader on trips. She is two years older and about a paddle blade shorter than Paul, with blue eyes and platinum-blond hair cut in a bob. She is sweet, but when something needs to be attended to, she narrows her eyes and whoever is standing in front of her does exactly as she says. Family trips when their son and two daughters were growing up were usually spent with reindeer herders in Greenland, among remote tribes in Africa, or in the hinterlands of Siberia. Every summer, the family also took trips into the Boundary Waters from their house on White Iron Lake.

I met Paul and Sue at their home my first night in Ely. The Schurkes run an outfitting service from their Wintergreen Lodge and had planned a trip for us along the Boundary Waters "Border Route." I thought the trip would be a cakewalk after my first few forays into the northland. Most of the canoeing was on flat water, and there were established campsites throughout the area. When Paul laid out the plan that night, I realized that the Iceman had no intention of taking a lazy weekend paddle.

The Boundary Waters skirts 150 miles of the US-Canada border. (Quetico Provincial Park on the Canadian side of the line extends the wilderness another million acres.) The classic Border Route runs 280 miles from Rainy Lake to Grand Portage on Lake Superior. The trip offers one of the most remote and unique perspectives on the northern border and usually takes fifteen days. We would be doing only part of it over three days, but Paul still planned to paddle a significant chunk. Also, he pointed out, not all the lakes connect. Meaning, we would load our gear into backpacks, carry the canoes on our shoulders, and walk overland on fifteen portages. Some of the portages were a few hundred yards. One was a mile long. All required several trips back and forth to haul gear.

Paul and Sue were barbecuing at a lakeside fire pit when I arrived. Paul didn't stop flipping chicken on the grill as he outlined the route, explained how he and Sue had ended up on White Iron Lake, warned me about what local politics I should be aware of, related a short history of Ely's economy, and pointed out the best places to eat in town. Sue sat beside him in a camping chair, sipping a glass of wine. Paul had been a journalism major and admired the art of storytelling. He spoke like a man from the 1930s, using terms like "hot-dish and hash joint" (diner), "suds" (beer), "laid a rap on" (made a sales pitch to), and "the green screen" (computer).

"My ancestors in the 1800s were from Germany and Norway, and like many Minnesotans who immigrated over here to become wheat farmers, iron rangers, and loggers, I just fit the mold of your typical Minnesota immigrant stock," he said. "Dad was a carpenter. Mom was a schoolteacher. But they had the foresight to know that us kids needed to stretch our wings in places other than downtown Minneapolis. So they bought a piece of forested land in northern Wisconsin when we were kids — which was where we then spent our summers, enjoying Huck Finn adventures rafting down these wild rivers and kinda setting the stage for a life of adventure."

A couple of years after earning a journalism degree, Paul put down stakes in Ely. He and a friend then started an outfitting business for handicapped outdoorsmen. They learned about the Boundary Waters as they went and had some wild adventures, including getting stranded on an island in Lac La Croix with six quadriplegic guests. They hired Sue — a Swedish Californian who, at the time, had camped only once in her life. She managed a handicapped rehabilitation center in Minneapolis and, with Paul, found an Ely musher named Will Steger who was interested in running dogsledding trips for handicapped people.

"We came back in the winter of '79 with a handpicked circle of friends with different disabilities to give this a go," Paul said. "It was another peak life experience. We got the full monty. We got the howling wolves. We got to live in igloos. We got dogsledding on crystal-clear nights at forty below, and it was cool. It was like an epiphany. I saw the light, and the light was good. It's been dogs and our connection with Will ever since."

Eighty huskies howled from a chicken-wire pen the next morning as I packed for the trip. Paul and Sue had been up since 4:30 a.m. Paul's instructions for packing the night before: "Wear pants and a shirt, and pack an insulating layer and a wind-breaker. Dry shoes are nice for the camp."

Paul drove like he was running from the law on the long, straight dirt road connecting Ely with Crane Lake. I white-knuckled the armrest in the back seat. Sue sat shotgun and asked questions about their businesses and who was watching out for what while they were gone. Paul appeared lost in thought, most likely plotting another adventure. Two days into our trip he asked if I would join him and Sue on the first ski traverse of the Antarctic ice shelf.

We pulled into a dirt lot next to the Crane Lake Bar & Grill around eight that morning. A covered ramp led to a dock, a gas pump, and a million acres of raw wilderness. A thick pine forest surrounded Crane Lake. Thin, green marsh fern grew along the rocky shore alongside moonwort, rattlesnake fern, and horsetail. Morning sun reflected off the water, and the only sound was the wind through the trees.

Paul stepped out of the car and pulled a canoe off the roof. In ten minutes he moved most of our gear to the dock, repacked food and supplies in three portage packs, and got the scoop on an approaching cold front from a local guide. He stopped me on the ramp as I ferried a pile of life jackets. "Use the bathroom if you need it," he said. "You're not going to see one for a while."

The Boundary Waters marks the northern edge of the Vermilion Batholith, so most of the lakes are lined with granite. Fault lines run through the Man Chain and Kahshahpiwi Lake, cleaving perfectly straight, granite and greenstone shorelines. Vera Lake is hemmed with jasper. Pink granite batholith circles Ensign Lake, and prehistoric "volcano bombs" — chunks of rock blown off the side of a volcano — lie at the bottom of Kekekabic Lake.

The Laurentian and Saint Lawrence River Divides converge nearby. The intersection is one of four divide junctions in America. Water north of the Laurentian Divide flows into the Arctic Ocean; water to the south runs to the Gulf of Mexico and the Caribbean. The Saint Lawrence River Divide cuts north-south through Minnesota, sending water east into the Great Lakes or west into the Mississippi watershed. "This was the first crossroads of interior America," Paul said as we loaded our gear into an aluminum boat. He had arranged for a water taxi to zip us through the first forty miles of the trip, on perimeter lakes where motors are still allowed. The boat had canoe racks and a semi-enclosed cabin for rough water. After what Paul called a "cultural and historical tour of the Border Route," we would be dropped in Lac La Croix to paddle the rest on our own.

The taxi driver, a tall, goateed man named Ted, pushed off from the dock and headed due north on Crane Lake. A strip of white-gold water painted a line from the bow to the sun. Red pine swooped over the shore-line. Long runs of granite split the forest. Ten-story granite bluffs rose from the depths, and flat swimming rocks the size of tennis courts sat near the edge of the lake.

Paul directed Ted toward a cliff between Crane and Sand Point Lakes. The sheer face was etched with auburn pictographs hundreds of years old. There were handprints and an image of a moose. Ojibwe artists mixed hematite with sturgeon oil to make the paint. It chemically bonds to rock and lasts thousands of years.

The land was barren when Paleo-Indians first walked into Minnesota's northland fourteen thousand years ago. Glaciers were still melting. There was little vegetation, and there were only a few animals to hunt. Lakes were just beginning to see life. Most of the northland was flooded at the time. Giant chunks of ice from retreating glaciers melted in gravel pits. Lake Agassiz covered parts of the region then. While Indians in the south continued traditions they had established centuries before, those who wandered north carved out a new life — learning to forage and hunt in a foreign landscape.

Holdovers from the Pleistocene still roamed North America then: mastodons, saber-toothed cats, five-hundred-pound beavers, speckled bears, and several species of prehistoric horses. Many of the first Indians in Minnesota ended up near what is now Knife Lake in the northern Boundary Waters. Silica-infused mud around the lake hardened into siltstone over millions of years and could be shaped easily. Indians fashioned knives, axes, and spearheads for hunting and butchering animals. Camps were established at the lake to quarry the stone and knap it into razor-sharp implements.

The way a culture hunted, harvested food, fought, and lived determined the size and shape of blades. One way archaeologists distinguish between prehistoric Indian cultures is by the characteristics of their projectile points. The Clovis culture in Minnesota honed siltstone into long, fluted points. The Folsom culture that followed in about 10,800 BC were bison hunters and used smaller heads, fluted along the entire edge. The Archaic period (7000–500 BC) saw upper-midwestern tribes cold-hammering copper tools, while others shaped spearheads and arrowheads with stems to be affixed to a shaft.

Burial mounds, pottery, domesticated dogs, and agriculture appeared in Minnesota around 2500 BC. Tribes there lived on wild rice, fish, squash, beans, corn, bison, and caribou. Ojibwe, Winnebago, and Cree tribes moved into the Arrowhead in the 1500s. The Dakota displaced them, and then the Ojibwe migrated west from Lake Superior and took over the land again. The Ojibwe are originally from the east and speak a form of Algonquin. Origin stories begin near the Atlantic Ocean, where a mystic seashell showed itself over the ocean. One day it sank and never rose again. The shell appeared again on the Saint Lawrence River, and the tribe followed it there and encamped for a while. It disappeared again and rose over Lake Ontario and, eventually, Point Island on Lake Superior — which is the geographic center of the Ojibwe nation today.

The Ojibwe tribe documented its dreams, visions, shamanism, and history in pictographs throughout the Boundary Waters. Ted glanced at Paul as he leaned his long torso over the water to point out how the paintings were placed just above the high-water mark, where an artist could reach from a canoe. He almost fell in, and Ted backed the boat away. "It's America's first art form!" Paul yelled over the engine.

North Hegman Lake has some of the most

interesting pictographs in the area. The style is classic Northern Woodland, a culture that lasted longer in northern Minnesota than anywhere else in America. One of the images on Hegman is of a human with outstretched arms near a four-legged animal, likely a wolf. There is also a bull moose and a series of dashes. Above that are what look like three canoes, two with paddlers. There is a cross at the top, the Ojibwe sign for a star.

Archaeologists speculate that much of the rock art in the northland reflects winter meridian constellations. Theories about the Hegman art suggest that the three canoes refer to the "Winter Maker" constellation of Orion. The paddlers are moving along the Milky Way, which the Ojibwe call the Path of Souls. Placement of the wolf and moose in the piece correspond almost precisely to Ptolemaic constellations set below Orion: Columba, Eridanus, Caelum, and Fornax. A dewclaw drawn on the moose corresponds to a star grouping in the Eridanus constellation. The artist also drew a line beneath the figures that approximates the horizon in the winter months. The horizontal dashes above the shaman's shoulder likely indicate the four moons of winter. (A group within the Ojibwe tribe called the Wabunowin, or

"Dawn Society," kept track of moons.) The three dashes beside it would represent the month of February. In February, Orion hovers just above the horizon, meaning an Ojibwe hunter could calculate his latitude and distance from home by looking at the painting.

We took off again and crossed the border into Canada. Driving through Minnesota's northland at high speed is like traveling through time. You see millions of years of evolution at once. It is an ancient ocean, a dried-up riverbed, an overflowing lake, an old-growth forest. There are no sandy beaches or bays like in the Great Lakes. Even the wide, white slabs of granite surrounding the lakes are gouged from glaciers.

The surrounding woods affect the light, sucking it in and holding it. Onshore, it is shadowy all day. In the middle of the lake it is blindingly bright. When you hike along a portage trail, it is hard to see twenty feet in front of you. When you get to the end, the scene is always different. It is like a slide show: lake after lake, subtle changes in the weather, depth, geology, topography, plants, and sky distinguish each scene.

If you could fly a few thousand feet above the canopy like the Ojibwe's mythic thunderbird, what you would see is Lake Superior 70 miles to the east; Grand Forks, North Dakota, 200 miles west; Lake Winnipeg 250 miles northwest; and Chicago 400 miles southeast. You would see the Iron Range splitting Minnesota's Arrowhead in two, and the Red River Valley running north to the US-Canada border. In the south, hardwood forests dissolve into the corn belt, and west of that, the northern plains roll toward the Rockies.

Ted pulled into a skinny dock on Sand Point Lake. Two Canadian border agents wearing navy-blue uniforms, flat-brimmed campaign hats, and sneakers waited for us behind a makeshift pine podium. Someone had painted a Canadian maple leaf on a wooden pallet in front of the podium. Visitors were supposed to stand on it, hand over documents, and wait to hear if they could enter Canada.

"One at a time," one of the agents said. Ted bowed his head and approached. Things seemed to be getting serious. Paul went next and was uncharacteristically silent. I followed. A white house behind the dock was propped up on cinder blocks. A two-person paddleboat sat on the beach, and I imagined the two guards pedaling together with after-work cocktails.

It was a triumph of field science that there even *was* a boundary in the Boundary Waters. The landscape is so rugged, it took surveyors 150 years to mark the US-Canada border through the region. In some places, crews had to wait for winter to freeze the ground so that they could walk on top of waist-deep wetlands.

Most of the line was left unmarked until 1908, when an American survey team arrived at the mouth of the Pigeon River on Lake Superior, near Grand Portage, Minnesota. It took the group three years, traveling seasonally by canoe and on foot, to reach Gneiss Lake, about forty miles west. Proper surveying at the time required triangulation, meaning that astronomers had to scramble up vertical gorge walls and ferry across dangerous whitewater rapids several times to multiple sites to fix a position. Three additional teams, one Canadian, sped up the process five years later when they started surveying east from the Rainy River toward Lac La Croix.

The Treaty of 1908 and the 1909 Boundary Waters Treaty created a set of rules for surveyors in Minnesota. (Water wars between the US and Canada on the Saint Mary, Milk, Rainy, and Niagara Rivers and on Lake Michigan, where the Chicago diversion had lowered water levels by six inches, inspired the treaties.) American and Canadian boundary commissions were instructed to draw the line along waterways and not bisect land, wherever possible, to avoid claim disputes. Several islands found to be on the wrong side of the line were transferred from one country to the other, though owners were not always informed. George Warren's family on the Canadian side of Lac La Croix mistakenly paid taxes for Warren Island to the US for fifty years.

The east and west survey teams met in Lac La Croix in 1914, and teams were dispatched to install 1,300 permanent markers along the 426-mile line: bronze posts, wrought-iron monuments, and bronze disks. It was a good year for surveyors on America's northern border. A few months before, Canadian and American commissioners informed their superiors that they had finished surveying the Alaska border, the border from the Pacific to the Rockies and a twenty-mile section of the line through Maine's Passamaquoddy Bay.

Our papers appeared to be in order, and Ted drove us to his resort on Sand Point Island. The Sand Point Lodge was just over the line in Canada. Ted's father had started the place in the late 1970s. Ted and his wife visited his father once to help out and never left. "Until now," Ted said. He had just sold the place to a longtime customer.

Ted seemed like a man who had seen a lot of the same thing for a long time. He stroked his gray goatee when he spoke. There were three outboard engines in the resort's front yard and two broken ones mounted on a rail. The lawn was mowed. A basketball net hung above an old snowmobile and two decomposing tractors. A sign in the lodge window read, "Camp Novelties Sold Here. Store Open: 7 AM to 5 PM. Enjoy Yourself."

An elderly guest sitting on the porch did not look like he was enjoying himself. Ted asked if he had heard from his wife.

"No," the man said.

"Still in the emergency room?"

"No way of knowing," he said.

"Let me know when you're ready and I'll take you out of here."

"I'm ready."

It was strange watching guests grow old, Ted told me later. The island stayed the same. The lake was the same. When Ted was young, the guest on the porch was spry and middle-aged. The man escaped to the northland every summer to fish, drink beer, and play horseshoes. He came alone, sat on the lodge deck after dinner, and stared at the sunset until it was gone. In some ways, Sand Point Lake represented his life more than his life at home did. Now his wife was gone, or almost gone, and each trip north could be the last.

He found the man a ride back to Crane Lake, then shuffled behind the lodge to show us some Indian burial grounds. There were two mounds of dirt, fifty feet around and fifteen feet tall. They were made by Paleo-Indians thousands of years ago. When they were first discovered in the 1960s, there was a movement to leave remains in the ground. They have sat undisturbed ever since.

Paul said there were a lot of amateur archaeologists in the area. In the old days, they used to dig up mounds looking for valuable artifacts. Now they pick up whatever washes onshore. "You're not supposed to touch them, but everyone does," he said. "Just about every camp you go to, if you ask nice enough or get the owner drunk, he'll pull out his cigar box. They have spearheads, arrowheads, pottery."

Ted had three cigar boxes. They were filled with spearheads of different sizes and styles, a couple of soapstone pipes that French fur traders had used, a copper spear that Ted says must have come from Michigan. His prized possession had turned up six months before on a path he'd walked a few thousand times: a perfectly carved soapstone fox.

The lodge itself was a northland relic. A bearskin hung from the varnished tongue-and-groove pine paneling. The coffee bar was also home to a VHF radio, 1980s Zenith television, RCA stereo, incoming mail basket, and a faded print of two loons swimming through morning mist. The ceiling was supported by thick beams that looked like they could hold up twenty feet of snow. Sometimes they did. The storms, frost, snow, rain, bugs, and fires in the Boundary Waters are too much for most structures to endure. The lodge reminded me of something a friend had said once: houses in the northland look like they are crouched low to the ground, ready for a fight. He was right about that.

We walked to the dock, and Paul congratulated Ted on selling the place. The lodge had been on the market for several years. Ted didn't seem happy or sad that strangers were moving into his family home. After thirty-eight years cutting the lawn, repairing the roof, toting diesel, fixing outboards, solving guests' problems, cooking, drinking, entertaining, building new cabins, repairing old ones, washing dirty sheets, and telling people where the fish are, he looked tired. He also looked like he wanted to get us on our way and led us back to the dock.

9

The Boundary Waters was the edge of the world in early America. Étienne Brûlé and Jean Nicolet ended their missions across the northland at Lake Superior. La Salle's journey on *Le Griffon* stopped at the border between Lakes Huron and Michigan. West of Thunder Bay, a wall of cliffs, waterfalls, rivers, swamps, and lakes form a natural barricade. There were no reliable maps of the area in the nineteenth century, and no way through. Except the route that *voyageurs* had been paddling for a hundred years.

Voyageurs were the first truckers of inland America. The French Canadian canoe men carried goods to remote trading posts and brought furs back. They followed Brûlé's path and extended it west through the Boundary Waters. They knew more about the American West at the time than anyone except western Indians. The millions of pounds of furs they carried financed British and French colonies. When delegates sat down to draw the US-Canada border at the Treaty of Paris, they charted it right along the voyageurs' route, so that the fur trade in both countries could continue uninterrupted.

In the seventeenth and eighteenth centuries, demand for fur was insatiable. Hats were not accessories back then. They were essential garb, like wearing pants or a shirt today. Hat sales in England in 1688 reached 3.3 million, plus 1.6 million "caps" — or about one hat per person. In 1700, 69,500 beaver hats, made from American furs, were exported from England. In 1760, that number grew to a half million. In all, between 1700 and 1770, England exported 21 million beaver felt hats.

Voyageurs were expected to paddle fourteen to eighteen hours a day. Most came from farms around Montréal and were accustomed to hard work. There were hundreds of portages on the route. One across Wisconsin was forty-five miles long. Voyageurs carried an average of two bales of furs — 180 pounds total. The more bales they carried, the more money they made, so some loaded up four or five. A legendary freed slave named La Bonga carried seven bales for a half mile once. The average life span of a voyageur was thirty-two. The most common cause of death: strangulated hernia.

The voyageurs' uniform was a red wool cap, deerskin moccasins, leggings, and an Indian belt. At night they sang and danced and warded off swarms of mosquitoes and blackflies with smudge fires, until Indians showed them how to make bug repellent from bear grease and skunk urine. There was no time to hunt, so the men carried salt pork and a dried-pea concoction called rubaboo. They ate two meals a day and smoked a pipe every hour. Distance was often measured in pipes.

The Frenchmen paddled halfway across America when most of the continent had yet to see a European footprint. Caravans could be as large as thirty canoes or as small as two. Voyageurs blessed each trip at a monument to Saint Ann, protector of travelers, set on the western tip of Montréal Island. They doffed their red caps when passing wooden crosses placed at rapids where fellow paddlers had died. They paddled the Saint Lawrence, Ottawa, and French Rivers — across Lake Nipissing, all of the Great Lakes, and the Boundary Waters. They chased furs farther west every year — from Rainy Lake to Lake Winnipeg to the Rocky Mountains and the "Oregon River," later christened the Columbia, eventually forging the long-sought Northwest Passage to the Pacific.

Ted drove us along the voyageurs' route across Portage Bay and left us at the western end of Dawson Portage. The portage was an important crossing for settlers and military in the nineteenth century and is still used by the Zupancich family. The "Zups" had been welcoming travelers to the Boundary Waters for eighty years. From the northwestern corner of Lac La Croix, three generations of the family have guided guests on some of the best canoeing and fishing territory in the country.

One of the Zups' guides, Ed, drove us and the canoes over the portage in a 1980s Suburban. Ed said the four-mile drive would take about an hour. His estimate was precise. The Suburban hit four miles an hour and stayed there until we stopped. Ed took us to the Zups' lodge for lunch, after which an Ojibwe man named Jim Eagle dropped us at Tiger Bay. It was almost dark when Jim left us on a rocky islet smack on the border. One of the bronze posts that the surveyors had placed — with "US" embossed on one side and "CANADA" on the other — jutted from a boulder.

Paul showed us a pile of rocks in the middle of the island and said it used to be an Indian lookout. "It's one of the last pre–Civil War ruins left in the Midwest," he said. "The lookout would have put a thatch roof over it. It's in the middle of the trading route, where an Indian scout could see a voyageur coming and signal to prepare the furs."

Paul inspected the stones for a few minutes, and then we paddled into Tiger Bay. It was dead quiet. Water extended for miles in every direction. The horizon was a line of trees, and as the sun fell behind it, I wondered how we were going to find a campsite in the dark.

Paul and Sue paddled with long, steady strokes. Their favorite campsite was taken, so we beached on a wooded island and shuttled gear to a campsite on the point. By the time I got my tent set up, Paul had made a fire and was boiling water in a pot. The site was set on a granite bluff overlooking Tiger Bay. It came with a cast-iron grill that was set over the fire pit and a Dutch oven. It was the most stunning campsite I had ever seen. I asked Paul how many of them there were in the Boundary Waters. "Around two thousand," he said.

Nymphs hatched on the surface of the water as the last light left the treetops. Sue set up their tent, while Paul methodically arranged camp the way he had hundreds of times before: start fire, organize bags, find utensils, cook food. We drank Riesling that night and ate Slovakian pastries that Paul's neighbor had given him. It was fun listening to him tell stories. He pronounced hummus like "*hoo*-mus" and called kebab "*kay*-bob." "Did you know Teddy Roosevelt snuck out of the White House twice a month to sleep in the park and swim naked in the Potomac?" he asked.

Paul had sneaked out of a hotel room once and ended up in one of Teddy Roosevelt's other haunts. It was 2011. Paul had just been honored at New York City's Explorers Club. A man in Ireland found a time capsule that Paul and Will Steger had left at the North Pole, and the National Geographic Society threw a gala to celebrate the recovery. (The magazine had offered $10,000 to anyone who found it.) The time capsule was placed in a display case at the end of the ceremony. After a few drinks, Paul stuffed the capsule into his jacket as a prank and sneaked out. When he saw the thing in his hotel room the next morning, he called the organizer, met her at the club, and returned it.

Sue and the Iceman had the beginnings of a cold, and they both went to bed early. I stayed up and watched the Path of Souls march overhead and disappear into the shadowy canopy on the opposite shore. The fire crackled, and the lake moved through shades of blue and gray. A reflection of a shooting star blazed across the water. A steep rise called Warrior Hill lifted off the opposite shore. Ojibwe warriors had once tested their strength before battle by running up it.

The sky was reconstructed with constellations I'd never noticed: bear, moose, wolf, canoes. Ojibwe shamans interpret and communicate with spirits in heaven and on Earth. Evil spirits live beneath the surface of the water and land. Nanabush is a messenger to humans. He gave the Ojibwe dogs and fire. The Great Mother watches over the Earth. Each of the four winds has a god. Thunderbirds create storms. Windigos walk south during harsh winters, eat people, and transform humans into cannibals. The Great Horned Serpent lives underwater and drags paddlers from their canoes.

The Ojibwe believe that there have been three worlds since the beginning of time. In the first, animals and monsters were masters, and humans existed in a ghostly, transient state. In the second, the monsters died and people inhabited the Earth. The god of the west wind impregnated a mortal woman during this time, and Nanabush was born. Humans and animals spoke to one another, and Nanabush introduced hunting, fishing, and arrowheads. In the final era, in which we live today, humans and animals can no longer communicate. Shamans are the only conduit.

A year after the 1964 Wilderness Act passed, President Lyndon Johnson's daughter turned twenty-one years old. Lynda Bird Johnson was an aspiring journalist and environmentalist. She wanted to disappear into the woods and booked a trip to the Boundary Waters. The area had been a keystone of the Wilderness Act, introduced to the US Senate by Minnesota senator Hubert Humphrey. The legislation did more than preserve land. It changed the shape of America and created a mechanism to conserve millions of acres of backcountry — much of that in the northland.

Lynda paddled and portaged to an island in Tiger Bay — about two hundred yards from where we camped — in August of

1965. Her entourage included eleven canoes, twelve Secret Service agents, a few portable toilets, and a staff of cooks and help. The Forest Service prepared the lakes for her arrival by cleaning and widening portage trails, spraying the island with insecticide, and staging a float plane in the bay to bring in fresh supplies.

Lynda's arrival looks chilly in black-and-white photos of the trip. She is wearing a flannel shirt, a wool zip jacket, and a handkerchief wrapped around her head. Secretary of Agriculture Orville Freeman stands beside her with a camera around his neck. In one photo, Lynda drags her hand playfully through a stream while two men paddle the canoe.

Lynda had banned the press from the outing, but four reporters followed anyway. They canoed to and camped on the same island we were on, Paul said over breakfast the next morning. "They weren't leaving until they got the scoop," he said. "They gabbed with the Secret Service, said they only wanted a few minutes of her time. A couple of days later the reporters floated a bottle of bourbon to the agents. Lynda had also banned alcohol, but the Secret Service took the bribe and convinced her to do the interview. She spent an hour with the reporters. They ran the story on the front page, calling her the Greta Garbo of the North."

Paul told me the story over coffee. It was 7:30 a.m., and he and Sue had already packed their tent and loaded the canoe. Deep, blue water surrounded the point. Sunlight filtered through the trees. We sipped from our mugs and watched the smoldering fire. By the time I finished breakfast, Paul and Sue were ready to go.

We launched at nine o'clock and followed the border south and east to Bottle Lake. It is impossible to see where you are from three feet above water level. Everything looks like shoreline. Paul headed for a tiny slot in the southeast corner of Lac La Croix that looked like a swamp. He lunged gracefully forward, digging his paddle deep into the water and pulling it back with his entire upper body. His pace was close to that of the voyageurs, who were expected to paddle fifty-five strokes a minute. Their day typically began at two in the morning, with a break at eight to eat breakfast. Lunch was typically dried buffalo meat mixed with fat — a concoction called pemmican. The day ended when the sun went down.

It was a relief, for a moment, to get out of the canoe at the first portage. Sue showed me how to load a portage pack, a backpack the size of a large ottoman. She then swung the canoe upside down on top of her shoulders. The motion was like putting on a sweater, except the sweater was a sixteen-foot Kevlar hull.

Pale corydalis and harebell grew near the shore of Iron Lake. Sphagnum, leatherleaf, and Labrador tea spread across the swampy sections of the hike. There was a small gravel beach on one side of the portage, a flat rock for launching canoes on the other. We paddled hard for an hour through Iron Lake, then stopped at Rebecca Falls to have a snack and rest.

Paul and Sue's colds were getting worse, and they took a nap. Then we paddled another forty minutes to Curtain Falls and hiked an epic thirty-minute portage uphill to Crooked Lake. I tried to match Paul's stride and pace. Even with him under the weather, I couldn't keep up. It was hard to imagine how the voyageurs hauled hundreds of pounds of pelts over portages — plus supplies like guns, ammo, flour, and kegs of liquor.

Paul and Sue were lying in the sun when I got to the top of the falls. Flat, silver water gathered at the edge of Crooked Lake and spilled two hundred vertical feet over rocks and cliffs. The water was crystal clear near the shore. It was hot and muggy, and I stripped down to my underwear and swam. Paul had a filter for gathering water, but out in the middle of the lakes, he said, you can just drink it.

That afternoon, we crossed the border into Canada and paddled for hours past granite promontories and tiny islets. The scenery sliding past was like a never-ending film: bluffs, white beaches, beaver dams, eagles, fireweed, hawkweed, bastard toad-flax, and little-leaf pussytoes.

That afternoon we dropped our gear at a campsite, then portaged into Argo Lake to find a cave that Paul had heard about. Someone had told him there was evidence that Paleo-Indians had lived there. We paddled for a couple of hours in a long loop, but all we saw were swooping hawks and an osprey standing watch in her nest. It was almost dark by the time we got back to the site.

I set up my tent and lay down for a few minutes. We had been going for ten hours, and I was exhausted. Paul started a fire, and by the time I sat down beside it he had chili and quesadillas ready. I listened to more adventure stories until the stars came out, then passed out in my sleeping bag.

A thunderstorm hit the lake around midnight with thunder, lightning, hail, and heavy winds. I watched the tent poles bend under the force of the gale. Another storm blew through at dawn with raindrops the size of nickels. I looked outside in the middle of it and saw Paul in his raincoat crouched over a pile of sopping-wet wood. It was 5:00 a.m. Fifteen minutes later he had a fire going and coffee on.

We took off at eight o'clock for what was going to be another long day. The sun was still low in the sky. Everything ahead was a silhouette. We crossed Crooked Lake into Friday Bay, then paddled and portaged among Papoose, Chippewa, Niki, and six other lakes — including a killer mile-long portage from Wagosh Lake to Gun Lake. The canoe was no longer a simple watercraft. It was an amphibious vessel that could go anywhere.

It rained on and off all day. We overturned a canoe on a portage trail and ate lunch under it. An hour later, we ended up on a granite goat path winding along a stream. It was almost dark by the time we made it to Mudro Lake, and it was raining harder. We paddled southwest along the lake and entered an inlet framed by tall reeds. A thick mist settled, and I almost fell out of the canoe when a beaver slammed its tail five feet away.

The wind started up again and slowed us down. We had traveled seventeen miles, and it was almost dark. I spotted a white sand beach ahead but wasn't sure if it was real. I heard a car door slam, and realized it was. It was a strange, unnatural sound. After a few days in the Boundary Waters, everything other than water, stone, and wood seemed unnatural. Paul ferried gear, and we hauled the canoe one last time to the car. The back seat of the Suburban felt incredibly soft, and five minutes down the road, the car was seventy-five degrees. Paul got a cell phone signal at the top of a hill and suggested we order pizza to pick up in Ely. I gave him my order and, just like that, we slipped into the modern world.

10

Water ended the next day 150 miles west of Ely. Dust coated the windshield, my clothes, and houses along the road. The horizon was a shifting channel of light. Minnesota is an anvil split in two: half is in the Great Lakes region, the other half borders the dusty grasslands of the northern plains. Half is Laurentian mixed forest, half tallgrass prairie. Half was once Dakota country, the other half Wisconsin territory. The Mississippi River splits the state in two as well, starting in the north and cutting through Minneapolis to the southeastern border.

I was headed to the Northwest Angle, the northernmost point of the contiguous US. The Angle is a blip on the northern border — an isolated pocket in Minnesota set a hundred miles above the northernmost stretch of the line. It is the northland of the northland — surrounded by Lake of the Woods on three sides and Canada on the other. You have to drive through Manitoba to get to it. It wasn't supposed to be that way. The Angle was another mistake at the Treaty of Paris. The map Benjamin Franklin used indicated that the origin of the Mississippi River was 150 miles north of where it actually is.

Information about the US West was sparse in 1783. Franklin was living in the Hôtel de Valentinois at 62 Rue Raynouard then. He'd been in Paris since the Continental Congress sent him in October 1776 to broker an alliance with France. He stayed throughout the Revolutionary War and led the US negotiating team following the colonists' victory.

America's farewell to the British Empire did not go as smoothly as history books depict. When negotiations began in 1782, George Washington's troops were on the verge of revolt. A majority of leaders in Congress did not want a union — but rather the appearance of a union, followed by the creation of thirteen independent nation-states. The federal government was bankrupt following the war, and appeals to Spain and others for a loan were dismissed. In Paris, Franklin's cohorts, John Jay and John Adams, ran out of money while traveling Europe in search of funding and alliances.

Adams was the taciturn, polar opposite of Franklin and was angry that he had to work with his longtime foe. Franklin was tormented by gout throughout most of the Paris talks and devastated that his son had sided with British Loyalists. Jay's newborn daughter died while he was waiting to hear back from the Spanish court about financial aid. He himself then fell ill in an influenza epidemic.

Somehow the delegates made progress, and in the fall of 1782, all parties were in agreement that America's northern border would extend from the Atlantic to the head of the Mississippi River. The boundary would split four of the Great Lakes, follow the voyageurs' fur-trading route through the Boundary Waters, and continue to the northwest corner of Lake of the Woods. From there it would pass due west to the Mississippi's headwaters.

The map that delegates brought to the negotiating table had been drawn by John Mitchell — a physician-botanist in London who dabbled in mapmaking. Mitchell never traveled to the western US, but rather combined information from known maps of the region into one. His compilation was four and a half by six and a half feet and covered the East Coast to the Dakotas. It was sold in eight sheets and denoted mystical — and often fictional — tribes and places like "Isles Phelipeaux and Pontchartrain" in Lake Superior, "River of the Cherakees," and "Wandering Savage Indians." Descriptions printed on the map suggested that the headwaters of the Mississippi were near the fiftieth degree of latitude, more than a hundred miles north of the actual start of the river. It misplaced other geographic features as well — like the Saint Croix River in Passamaquoddy Bay, and lakes and islands in the Boundary Waters. At the time, the Mitchell map was considered the most comprehensive of the northwestern frontier.

Negotiations continued, and the line was drawn. When the Treaty of Paris was signed on September 3, 1783, US sovereignty was acknowledged by Britain; all British influence was absolved; the Mississippi was to be shared by both countries; British protection of American interests around the world was lifted; American fishermen were given rights to the Grand Banks; confiscated Loyalist property was to be reinstated; and the northern border was set from the northwest corner of Lake of the Woods to nowhere.

■ ■ ■ ■

Cornfields grew between stands of cotton-wood trees, and harvesters cruised down the double-yellow line spewing golden dust on the way north. A series of white signs with red lettering advertised gifts of Minnesota's northland: moccasins, wild rice, Vikings, Twins. The radio played an entire Bruce Springsteen live concert: Rutherford, New Jersey, 1984. I drove past Saint Cloud, Brainerd, and the actual headwaters of the Mississippi in Itasca State Park.

Salt grass and meadow sedge edged the highway in Warroad. Five miles north, I passed by a brand-new, $50-million US border crossing. Drugs and a handful of illegal immigrants had been the only problems along Minnesota's northern border for decades, until 2017, when an American immigration crackdown caused a flood of US immigrants to reverse the flow along the northern border and sneak into Canada. A loophole in Canada's immigration law encouraged more than fifteen thousand to make the journey in 2017.

Many traveled on foot in the middle of winter, a dangerous season in the northland. Two men from Ghana lost all of their fingers on the trek from Minnesota to Emerson, Manitoba, and many others had to be rescued. In May of 2017 a fifty-seven-year-old Ghanaian woman died of exposure trying to cross seventy miles west of Warroad, near Noyes, Minnesota. She was on her way to see her first granddaughter, born five weeks earlier in Toronto.

The agent at the Canadian station a half mile down the road did not smile when I pulled up. He asked where I was going, if I'd been there before, how I'd heard about it. I said I was going to Angle Inlet, and he handed me a piece of paper that read, "Phone Reporting from the Northwest Angle." A map at the top showed the Angle's north–south boundary. Three bubble quotes with telephones on them read "Carlson's," "Jim's Corner," and "Young's Bay." "You'll be reporting from Jim's Corner," the agent said.

I followed Route 12 — "Mom's Way" — through Middlebro, Manitoba, to Sprague. The guard said to take a right at an abandoned gas station there. I did and fishtailed onto a washboard dirt road. Thirty minutes later, the road crossed into US territory, and I spotted four men in their seventies huddled next to a phone booth at an intersection. I parked next to a gray Chevy pickup truck hitched to a bass boat.

"Is this Jim's Corner?" I asked.

The men looked at me, then looked at each other.

"We're wondering the same thing," one of them said.

The men watched as I picked up the phone and pushed a button with an American-flag sticker on it. After a couple of rings a voice answered, "US Customs and Border Patrol." The agent ticked off the usual list of ambiguous and prying questions. "What are you doing? Where are you going? Why are you going there? What kind of fish are you fishing for? Have you ever caught one of those before? What does it taste like?" Then the agent said I was checked in, and I left the old men, still huddled by the booth.

The Northwest Angle is 80 percent water. The other 20 percent is a rectangle of land that juts into Lake of the Woods. Angle Inlet, set on the northern shore, is the only town. The population as of 2010 was 119.

I drove past a few houses in town, a one-room schoolhouse, and a general store that opens daily from 4:30 p.m. to 6:30 p.m. A hundred yards past the gravel greens of a five-hole golf course, a sign pointed to a resort called "Jake's Northwest Angle." Another sign on the office door read: "ring the pager (it works)." I did and Jake's grandson, Paul Colson, drove up in a golf cart. He looked like a backwoods Chevy Chase — handsome, short-cropped brown hair, dimple on his chin, smirk on his face. He wore sweatpants and a baseball hat and flipped a beeper in his hand as we spoke.

I told him I was a writer, and without a hint of sarcasm he asked, "What's your angle?" He seemed relieved when I told him about my trip. Television stations and newspapermen had visited the Angle for the better part of a century to document life in the northernmost point of the contiguous US. "We had a television crew here this morning," Paul said. "They rode with my sons sixty-five miles to Warroad to go to school. The boys do it twice a day. Border patrol stops them in both directions. It's insane what they're doing down there."

Paul's grandfather had pioneered the Angle and built three of the six cabins at the family resort. The old man had also built the road from Sprague and half the town. Paul's boys grew up going to the Angle Inlet School, the last one-room schoolhouse in Minnesota, until the sixth grade. After that they had to commute to Warroad.

Paul had spent the last twenty years fighting US and Canadian authorities who cut off access to hospitals and schools, unfairly taxed Angle residents, and changed fishing and guiding regulations on Lake of the Woods, where most residents earn a living. The town has tried to secede from the US several times. The last effort was in the 1980s. The hassle of living in the Angle has kept families from moving there, and the community was slowly dying. "You gotta think how much longer we can keep doing this," Paul said.

A deep inlet lined with tall reeds connects the resort to Lake of the Woods. A light breeze rustled the grass and cooled what was becoming an extraordinarily hot day for late September. Twenty minutes into our conversation, Paul asked if I wanted a room at the resort. I told him I'd be there for a night, and he tossed me a key and nodded to a cabin behind the office. "The AC works," he said.

After British explorer David Thompson discovered the headwaters of the Mississippi in 1798, well south of Lake of the Woods, British and American officials scrambled to patch the gap in the border. The British suggested that the boundary run straight across the forty-ninth parallel to Lake of the Woods, creating an uninterrupted line. Thomas Jefferson's administration rejected the plan. Britain then offered to purchase the stranded parcel, but that option was also rejected. The Northwest Angle had little value. What was at stake, Jefferson said, was the integrity of the 1783 Treaty of Paris that had given America its independence.

Four decades later, the Webster-Ashburton Treaty extended the line from the northwest terminus of Lake of the Woods due south to the forty-ninth parallel, creating a 120-square-mile chunk of America floating in southwestern Ontario. The US and British Northern Boundary Commission traveled to Minnesota to survey the border in the summer of 1872. British astronomers and a Royal Engineers detachment took a steamship across the Atlantic, a smaller steamer across the Great Lakes, and the Northern Pacific Railroad to one last steamer headed for Fort Pembina in North Dakota. The Americans had arrived by train, two weeks earlier. The commissions started working their way east immediately, dispatching two parties to Angle Inlet and two to the intersection of the forty-ninth parallel and Lake of the Woods. It took three years, working seasonally, to draw the line from Pembina to Lake of the Woods, and from the Northwest Angle south to the forty-ninth. The line wouldn't be marked until 1912, by some of the same surveyors who had worked on the Boundary Waters.

Ojibwe drumming reverberated through the forest in 1917 when Jake Colson moved to the Angle. The Angle was four hundred miles and a boat ride north of Minneapolis. Jake found what he described as a Shangri-la there stocked with fish, game, wild rice, and a wilderness few non-Indians had ever seen. He settled down with a cow, a few chickens, and a garden. The Ojibwe called Jake *Poh-zhash,* meaning "big Indian." He met his wife when his sister arrived for a visit with a friend. The couple lived in a tent until they finished their cabin. They fished, logged, and harvested marsh marigolds to survive. Jake worked as a guide and saved money until 1945, when he built a few guest cabins.

Without a road to his resort — boat access only — business was slow. He added an electric generator and running water. He helped build the first post office and was its first postmaster. He got permission to build a connector road to Route 308. A benefactor tried to offer Jake a college education, but Jake turned it down. When Hubert Humphrey, then mayor of Minneapolis, sent his son to visit the Angle, Jake proclaimed him mayor for the day, and regional newspapers ran the story on the front page. A popular Christian writer named Bernard Palmer rented a cabin and wrote his "Danny Orlis" series about Lake of the Woods — putting Angle Inlet on the map. When fishermen left in the summer, duck hunters arrived. When the hunters left, ice fishermen came.

CB radio was the original form of communication. Jake's black-and-white Zenith television got one channel, from the Canadian Broadcasting Corporation. To deliver a baby or set a broken bone, the family drove 130 miles to Winnipeg. There was often a delay at the border as customs agents tried to figure out which country Angle Inlet was in. Paul's sister, Constance, attended the one-room schoolhouse with Canadians and Ojibwe children. The schoolhouse was built in 1934. Telephone service arrived in 1991.

I spent most of the afternoon at Jake's unpacking and drying out my gear from the Boundary Waters trip. Wind hummed through the trees and rippled water along the inlet. Paul's kids drove an excavator around the grounds after school, and I read a pile of articles and books about homesteading in the Angle.

Transporting settlers and military across Lake of the Woods to the Canadian prairies was big business at one time as Canada tried to keep up with western expansion in America. The first steamer began operating there in 1872. The *Shamrock* had accommodations for twenty-five first-class passengers and fifty in steerage. The three-day trip across Lake of the Woods cost twelve dollars, including room and board. Ferry service expanded in the late 1800s along with mining, lumbering, and fishing. Side-wheelers, stern-wheelers, and propeller boats roamed the waters — ranging from 30-foot lumber freighters to the 150-foot *Kenora* steamer, which had twenty-two state rooms and one hundred passengers.

Fishing was big business too. In 1888, fishermen hauled in 40,000 pounds of of whitefish, walleye, burbot, tullibee, and northern pike. Five years later that number had risen to 1.65 million pounds, plus 124,000 pounds of sturgeon roe. Lake of the Woods was one of the world's largest sources of caviar for a time, producing 1.5 million pounds between 1893 and 1895. By 1900 the fishery was in decline. Less than 60,000 pounds of sturgeon was caught that year, and fifteen years later the number was a fraction of that. Now, sport fishermen chase primarily walleye and muskellunge on the lake.

Paul knocked on my door the next morning to ask if I wanted to go fishing. Lake of the Woods is seventeen hundred square miles, and fishermen pay Paul $500 a day to make it a bit smaller. I grabbed my jacket, and we walked to his boat. Paul's wife, Karen, came along. Paul drove sitting sideways with his legs crossed, one hand on the wheel, the other tucked under his right knee. He was wearing a camo hat and camo sweatshirt and chatted with Karen about their kids' homework. Internet could be spotty in the Angle, and one of the boys had had trouble emailing a paper to his teacher. Karen held her phone over her head trying to get cell service and eventually managed to reach the teacher and get her kid off the hook.

We drove past Fort Saint Charles, a French Canadian fur-trading post built in 1732. A trader named Pierre La Vérendrye had built the fort with his sons, before going on to explore and claim the western half of Canada for New France. The fort had been reconstructed with new logs and asphalt shingles. It sits on the American side of the line now, and someone had hoisted an American flag behind the log palisade.

There were no boundary markers on the lake as Paul crossed into Canada. He drove past long slabs of granite on the shores of Bukete Island and pulled into a bay he made me swear I would not reveal. He handed me a fishing rod, drove a hook through the head of a minnow, and tossed my line overboard. He did the same for Karen and himself, and they cast their lines off opposite sides of the boat. Ten minutes later we had eight fish packed in a cooler.

"Let's find a place where they're biting," Paul said and started the engine. He drove ten minutes northeast. The wind was out of the west, and a light chop was building. There are more than 14,500 islands in Lake of the Woods. Granite and greenstone in the north resisted glaciers, leaving most of the islands there. Glacial deposits on the US side created broad sheets of shallow water, sand dunes, and marshy shorelines.

We dropped our hooks near a granite outcropping and caught eight more walleye in about eight minutes. Paul added them to the cooler, looked at his watch, and said we had to get back to meet the school bus. He said he wasn't sure how long his family would last in the Angle, as the boat skipped over the chop. His sister wasn't interested in running the resort. Border security and tense relations with Canadian game wardens were hurting his business. The Angle school had closed when his youngest boys graduated, and it didn't look like there were many more kids on the way.

Karen hopped off the boat at the dock and headed home to meet the kids. I followed Paul to a fish-cleaning station, where he emptied the cooler onto a stainless steel counter. He filleted each fish with one sweep using a long, thin knife, then tossed the head, tail, and spine into a bucket. "We put up this building to keep the flies down," he said. "You wouldn't believe it in the summer."

Paul asked whether I wanted to join the family for fish tacos. I declined and packed my things for the trip home. He was already dropping fillets on the grill when I passed by on my way out. I drove west past road signs riddled with bullet holes and a few commuters headed home from Warroad. A wall of hardwood lined each side of the dirt road that Jake Colson had cut.

The road had been graded recently and ran straight and smooth for fifteen miles. I couldn't imagine the old man and his neighbors chopping their way through the forest. It must have taken thousands of man-hours, hauling brush and removing stumps. Jake would probably be proud that his grandkids drove the road twice a day, following the dusty finger through Canada back to the US.

■ ■ ■ ■

PART IV
SEVEN FIRES

■ ■ ■ ■

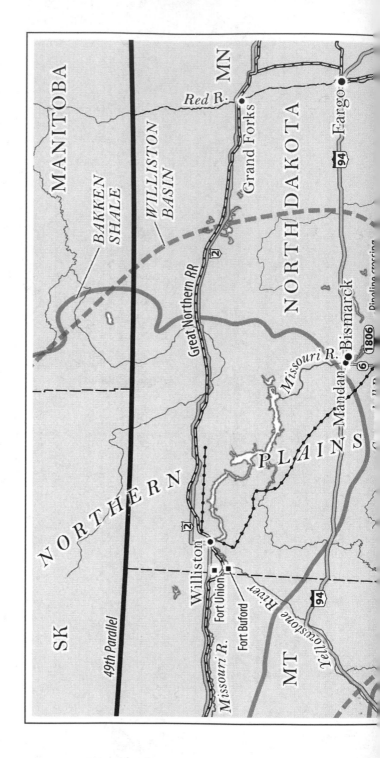

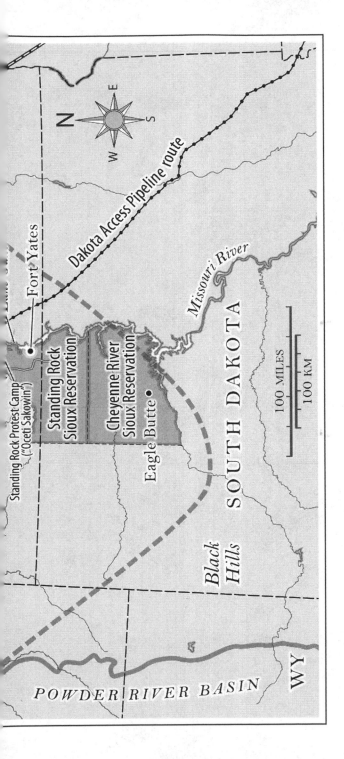

11

Route 1806 was closed. Then Highway 6 closed, and 1806 reopened. An hour into my drive from Fargo, North Dakota, to the Standing Rock Sioux Reservation three hundred miles west, police outfitted with body armor, assault rifles, and concussion grenades blocked both roads. Military-grade vehicles, National Guardsmen, cops from ten different states, and a private security company were stationed farther down the highway. Some officers held tear gas launchers; others had shotguns loaded with rock salt.

The imminent threat thirty miles south was two unarmed Lakota Sioux protestors. They had secured their arms around construction equipment with plaster a few miles north of the reservation. One, named Happi, wore a red bandanna and a gray, button-down shirt. In photos, he looks bored, and a bit pleased at the spectacle he helped create. The excavators around the pair had been installing a pipeline that would cross the Missouri River a half mile north of Standing Rock. Tribal members had set up a protest camp to fight the pipeline the previous spring, saying that construction crews were destroying cultural sites and ancestral land and that a spill would be devastating to the reservation. The camp had since made headlines around the world and swelled to more than fifteen hundred people. A federal judge had ordered the company building the pipeline to stop a few days before, while the judge figured out whether it was destroying centuries-old Sioux burial sites and sacred rock formations.

The tribe's legal team said that the company responded by bulldozing the sites in question. In the months leading up to the completion of the 1,172-mile, $3.8-billion Dakota Access Pipeline (DAPL) — which runs through North Dakota's northland, then dips through South Dakota and Iowa to refineries in Illinois — Texas-based Energy Transfer Partners (ETP) had proved that it was not afraid of protestors or the law. It was fined for not reporting Indian artifacts in the pipeline's path and for rerouting the line without permission. The

Environmental Protection Agency, the Department of the Interior, and the Advisory Council on Historic Preservation all noted that the environmental impact study that the company had submitted — and paid for — was insufficient, and they recommended that the US Army Corps of Engineers revisit the study before issuing permits. In Iowa, lawyers for some of the two hundred affected farming families — many of whom had been on their land for more than a century — claimed that ETP had improperly used eminent-domain laws to take their property.

The Army Corps regulates crossings on navigable waterways in America and is required to consult with tribal governments before processing permits that might affect their land. The Corps appeared to fast-track the project, though, regardless of risks that a spill would pose to Standing Rock residents and millions of others downstream. It accepted ETP's incomplete environmental study and failed to communicate with local tribes through proper channels. The Corps's final assessment: "The anticipated environmental, economic, cultural and social effects [of the project are] not injurious to the public interest."

The Corps had come to a different conclusion months earlier when the original pipe-line route crossed the Missouri upstream of Bismarck. Given the history of pipeline spills in the United States — an average of one a day in 2016 — the threat of polluting the state capital's water supply was too great. Sixty-one thousand people live in the city; 92 percent of them are white. So, engineers moved the crossing thirty miles south, directly upstream of Standing Rock's primary source of drinking water.

It was ninety-six degrees the day I drove across North Dakota's northland. The state cuts across the northern plains — the boreal tip of the 1.5-million-square-mile Great Plains that has existed in the rain shadow of the Rocky Mountains for sixty million years. The landscape was a one-dimensional, silver-green stratum. Golden sunlight spilled through the windshield. Telephone poles lined up like birthday candles for miles. Rows of cottonwood wandered along streambeds. Strands of barbed wire and dusty farm roads were the only visible boundaries.

The forty-ninth parallel caps the state for three hundred miles. Stretching from Minnesota to the Pacific, the forty-ninth is the longest straight border in the world. It was marked by wooden stakes and wandering waterways until 1873, when the same Canadian and American surveyors who had marked the Northwest Angle turned around and drew the line nine hundred miles west to the Continental Divide.

The Northern Boundary Commission fought off clouds of mosquitoes, extreme heat, thunderstorms, and prairie fires while painstakingly making their way across the plains. The border ran straight through Sioux territory, and commissioners were wary of marching 270 white men onto the Indians' land. British and Canadian surveyors, who had never had any problems with the Sioux nation, were particularly concerned — realizing that raiding parties would not be able to distinguish them from their American colleagues. Major Marcus Reno, with two companies of the US Seventh Cavalry — the same that would fight at the Battle of the Little Bighorn three years later — escorted the American commission. The British and Canadian surveyors hired thirty multiracial Métis guides and Chippewa Indians, dubbed the "49th Rangers," to ride ahead and suss out trouble.

Sioux scouts were uninterested in the bearded and bespectacled foreigners dressed in Hudson's Bay Company hooded greatcoats, moccasins, and sealskin pants. Astronomers and their assistants took sixty readings from Ursa Minor, Cepheus, and Polaris, at dozens of stations along the line to ensure accuracy. Surveyors dragged sixty-foot Gunter's chains, made of eight-inch steel wire links, to measure the border: a quarter chain was a rod, ten chains a furlong, eighty chains a statute mile. The team also used theodolite survey telescopes, air levels, sextants, fifty compasses, and eighteen synchronized chronometers — top-of-the-line equipment for mid-Victorian field science.

It took two seasons — the commission took the winter off — to reach the divide. Despite their efforts, none of the monuments along the forty-ninth parallel actually touch the line. Instead each segment veers an average of three arcseconds (295 feet) north or south. In two cases, the line deviates 575 feet north or 784 feet south, placing properties, roads, and half a town in Washington on the wrong side of the border.

In the half-light of late summer, the cropland between Fargo and Bismarck was dull green. I'd never seen the northern plains before. Silvery flecks of cottonwood bark and broad, galvanized-steel barn roofs reflected the dim light. Thunderheads cut shadows into the fields. Light falling from the underbelly of the clouds touched one-story ranch homes and domed silos. There were no mountains or valleys to deflect wind and rain. Everything was flat.

A hundred miles north of Bismarck, in Rugby, North Dakota, is the geographic center of North America. Montana is three hundred miles west. Saskatchewan and Manitoba are another hundred to the north. The distance to the North Pole and the equator are exactly the same — creating an impact zone between two hemispheres of weather. The confluence makes North Dakota the most extreme weather zone in the world, with hurricane-force winds and temperature swings of 180 degrees between seasons — from minus 60 degrees Fahrenheit to 121. Studies of lake beds across the state reveal similar fluctuations for thousands of years. Extreme droughts and floods have lasted as long as a century. The Dirty Thirties blew soil from millions of acres away in "black roller" dust storms. In 1997, floodwaters in Grand Forks reached more than three miles inland and caused $3.5 billion in damages.

I could have ridden a bike along this stretch. I could have hiked or saddled a horse. But that's not how they do it here. People drive across the northern plains. They load up minivans, pickup trucks, and sedans, tune in a talk show, and eat up the miles. The road is the link. It is a conduit for families, public services, and business. When your neighbor lives ten miles away and fresh milk and eggs are forty, you depend on it. North Dakota is one of the only states in the country that casts its highways in concrete so they never fall apart.

I drove west over the ancient beaches of Lake Agassiz to the Drift Prairie, the Missouri Escarpment, and the Missouri Plateau. The plateau tops out at thirty-five hundred feet in Slope County before crumbling into the Badlands on the Montana border. There, the Missouri — America's longest river — cuts the state in half along the Missouri Trench.

Eastern North Dakota marks the northern edge of America's Central Lowland — a trough of shale and limestone that once sat twenty-five hundred feet below the Western Interior Seaway. The seaway was six hundred miles wide sixty-five million years ago and divided North America in two. Another shale formation in the Northwest, the Bakken Formation, is the epicenter of

North Dakota's oil boom. Oil companies tried to tap it for half a century without any luck. Hydrofracking and horizontal drilling technology in the early 2000s achieved what had until then eluded them. Overnight, North Dakota became the second-largest oil producer in America, after Texas.

Between 2002 and 2008, oil production doubled North Dakota's GDP. Williston Basin oil fields, which the Bakken is set in, pumped a half-million barrels of oil a day in 2010. Between 2010 and 2014, the boom created two thousand new millionaires in the state every year. Speculators renamed it Saudi Dakota. The massive yield put America on a path to energy independence and helped make the US the number one oil and gas producer in the world. Ten percent of domestic oil in 2015 came from the Williston Basin.

Existing pipelines, trucks, and trains couldn't handle the surge, and moving the oil became a problem. In 2014, ETP announced a solution. ETP, Phillips 66, Sunoco Logistics, Enbridge, Marathon Oil, and seventeen of the largest banks in the world — spearheaded by Citibank — financed the Dakota Access Pipeline. The thirty-inch pipe would carry a half-million barrels of oil a day from the northland to refineries and other pipelines in Illinois.

Thousands of farmers, Indians, ranchers, and residents living along the proposed route protested, saying that a spill would be catastrophic. A few years before, a pipeline 150 miles north of Standing Rock had ruptured and spilled 840,000 gallons of Bakken shale oil into a farmer's field. It was one of the largest onshore oil spills in US history. Cleanup crews began working around the clock on the seven-acre site, digging fifty feet down to remove contaminated soil. The pipeline management company Tesoro Logistics estimated it would take two years to clean up the mess. Three years later, still working twenty-four hours a day, they had completed a third of the job and had no timeline for finishing.

In September of 2016, ETP announced that despite the protests, its pipeline was almost complete and DAPL would be operational by the end of 2016. The final section would tunnel under a dammed section of the Missouri called Lake Oahe, near Standing Rock. Things there did not look good. The Sioux Nation had a long history of standing up to corporations and the US government. They were the only Indian nation to have defeated the US Army in a war — and to have received everything they asked for in peace negotiations. The government had been taking from them ever since. It sold off millions of acres of their land and violated multiple treaties. Mining corporations had recently started digging for uranium and dumping radioactive waste on Sioux land. In September of 2016, the protest camp, set on the Cannonball River, prepared for what many saw as a last stand against a century and a half of oppression.

I took a chance on route 6 and found it open. The road runs perfectly straight through the northland, past thirty miles of ranchland and sunflower farms. I passed Saint Anthony and Breien and pulled into the Cannon Ball Pit Stop, a few miles from the protest site. The Lakota woman working the cash register appeared genuinely frightened by the number of strangers walking through the door. Fifteen hundred "water protectors," the name protestors gave themselves, from all over the world occupied the camp. (More than eight thousand others would show up in the coming months.) Hundreds arrived every week, from tribes as far away as Florida, Maine, and Japan. Many came to protest how the pipeline would dampen America's climate change initiatives. Susan Sarandon, Leonardo Di-

Caprio, Willie Nelson, and other celebrities spoke out in support of the camp, and nearly every major news outlet in the world had covered it.

I bought two boxes of mac and cheese, and a few cans of black beans, then asked the woman if she had seen the camp.

"I try to keep a low profile," she said.

"How many people are down there?"

"If people need things, they come here," she said. "We will be here tonight. Food stamps for this month are activated at midnight. We stay open late for that."

I followed 1806 around a long bend and saw dozens of large, white teepees spread across a field near the Cannonball River. In between were horse trailers, eighteen-wheelers, pickup trucks, tents, camper trailers, RVs, and rental cars. Pale-green cotton-woods growing along the river circled the hundred-acre camp. Army tents, shelters made from plastic tarps, geodesic domes, and upside-down American flags flapping from makeshift poles huddled against the waterway. The Missouri was a blue streak in the background. Twenty paint horses walked in circles around portable steel corrals, and people wandered muddy, rutted roads past bright-green portable bathrooms. The council tent, where leaders met, stretched eighty feet across the middle of the field. Hundreds of Indian-nation flags, erected by tribes that had joined the protest, flew from white flagpoles alongside the dirt driveway.

Organizers called the camp *Oceti Sakowin,* the actual name of the Sioux tribe. It means "Seven Council Fires" and refers to the seven tribes that make up the Great Sioux Nation. Two young Lakota men guarded the entrance. They asked an elderly white lady in front of me whether she was carrying any weapons, alcohol, or drugs. She said no. One of the guards searched her Buick and pulled a four-foot, double-bladed axe from the trunk. "I'm going to keep this here for now," he said.

I told the guard I was a writer, and he grabbed a thick media packet and told me to follow him. He led me to a faded-blue pavilion tent that he said was the media center. North Dakota's legendary wind had blown down one of the tarp walls. Rocks held down stacks of calendars, information packets, and registration forms. Carol Two Bears introduced herself as a media liaison. She was my height, with square shoulders and long, black hair. She told me that there were some rules I had to abide by. I was not allowed to take photographs of ceremonies, drum circles, the council lodge, or certain

275

religious events. "Rule of thumb," she said, "ask before you shoot." I asked her where different tribes were camping and if there was an area for visitors. "Five days ago I could've told you where everybody was," she said. "Now I have no idea."

The camp was well managed, with a chain of command and various services for protestors. There were full-time medics, a legal team, security, a radio station, an elementary school, and a sprawling kitchen staffed by volunteers. A water truck supplied drinking water. A disaster response trailer and an ambulance stood ready. Most people coming through the entrance brought donations of food and clothing that lay in heaps behind the kitchen. By the end of September, the camp was one of the largest towns in North Dakota.

Carol suggested I find a place to pitch my tent, then meet back at the central fire circle for the evening's presentation. The security guard at the gate was supposed to stay with me at all times, but he had wandered off. A veil of dust and woodsmoke hung in the air. I set up my tent near a temporary horse corral and went back to the fire circle, where another northland tribe, Washington's Lummi Nation, was blessing a twenty-two-foot western-red-cedar totem pole on its way to Winnipeg. Since 2001, Jewell Praying Wolf James had been carving poles with the House of Tears Carvers on Lummi Island, near Bellingham, and delivering them to causes around the country.

Sioux tribes weren't the only Indians fighting environmental injustices. The Lummi Nation had been taking the US government and fossil fuel industry to court for fifty years, mostly to protect their fishing rights. Four other northwestern tribes were protesting an oil terminal in Vancouver, Washington. The Western Shoshone Indian Nation was trying to stop contractors from burying nuclear waste on Nevada's Yucca Mountain. A confederation of tribes in Texas was combating another ETP pipeline, the Trans-Pecos, which would transport fracked natural gas through the Big Bend region to Mexico. Jewell's last four totem pole journeys were to oil pipelines, coal trains, and tar sands regions. As environmentalist Bill McKibben said, the indigenous environmental campaign had become "the vanguard of the movement."

"We are spiritual beings here to have a human experience," Jewell said through a scratchy PA system. He was dressed in black and looked like a sixty-year-old Johnny Cash. A line of pavilion tents and blue tarps tied to teepee poles framed the circle. On the left, the kitchen was crammed with folding tables, water dispensers, and aluminum trays. The last meal the cooks had prepared: an entire moose donated by Donald Soctomah and the Passamaquoddy tribe.

Fifty protestors, guests, tourists, facilitators, cooks, security, Lakota in full dress, and others who looked like they had simply stopped by to see what was up listened around the fire. Lakota women sat in camping chairs bundled in wool blankets, most holding children. "This is starting to feel like a real Indian visit," Jewell said. "Arrive in October and don't leave until March."

He spoke about the 1950s, when fellow tribesmen went to prison for singing traditional songs or possessing eagle feathers and peyote — when Indian children were forced to go to boarding schools, dress like white children, and speak English. "Our elders had to practice their rituals in the woods," he said. "They had to wait until the reservation agent was asleep or gone." He spoke about broken treaties that took thousands of square miles from his tribe, and thousands more from the Sioux — some of which was now being excavated by ETP pipeline crews.

Jewell and many other tribes learned long

ago that the only way to fight the US government is in court. Jewell got his law degree when he was in his early twenties. He is sixty now and has been fighting for tribal rights ever since. He'd walked with US senators and sat with presidents. He'd recently helped a coalition of northwestern tribes defeat the largest coal export facility ever proposed in America. An advantage that tribes had over fossil fuel companies, he said, was a history of treaty law. The US Constitution recognizes treaties as the "supreme law of the land," and Indian treaties that have not been abrogated by Congress still have significant power. In an ironic twist, the agreements that the US government pushed on tribes in the 1800s, in exchange for their land, were coming back to haunt it.

"Our white brothers and sisters are lost," Jewell said. "They are starting to remember they have a duty to the Earth. We're fighting multibillion-dollar corporations with peanuts. We have to turn it around or your children will have nothing. We have always been the Earth's protectors, and now we must help our brothers and sisters."

Silhouettes of gulls glided a half mile above the fire circle. It was six in the evening, and the sun fell slowly over a low ridgeline behind the camp. Jewell gave the stage to his brother, "Uncle Doug," who hunched over the microphone and sang a Lummi song. His voice was high-pitched and oscillated between octaves. Brown blades of prairie grass looked like gold tinsel sprinkled across the field. Eight teenage Lakota boys with long, black hair rode bareback down the road. They wore red and blue bandannas, and their bony frames jostled as the horses trotted. They gazed straight ahead, unaware of or uninterested in the crowd of two hundred watching them. Two raised their fists when they heard Uncle Doug's song.

There was a feeling in the air that the protest had morphed into something larger. Things were not good on American reservations. Of the 4.5 million people from 565 federally recognized tribes in the US, 30 percent lived in poverty. Alcoholism and mortality rates were 500 percent higher than for the rest of America. (One in ten American Indians dies of an alcohol-related death.) Suicide rates were double the national average, with 40 percent of the victims between the ages of fifteen and twenty-four. Only half of Indian youth graduate from high school, and 40 percent of on-reservation housing is considered inadequate. At Standing Rock, per capita income was $13,474 in 2016. Unemployment was over 80 percent.

Youth at Standing Rock were discovering a connection with their tribe and their ancestry. For many, it was the first time they had seen various tribes working together. The Sioux and Crow Nations, enemies for centuries, signed their first peace treaty at the camp. It was also the first time that the seven bands of the Lakota tribe had stood together since the Battle of the Little Bighorn, in 1876. The last Indian protest this large was the armed standoff at Wounded Knee in 1973, when two hundred Sioux protestors took over the South Dakota town — to bring attention to neglected Indian treaties — and fought federal agents for two months.

Doug's voice reverberated around the field, and a college-aged white kid with a bushy beard threw more logs on the fire. The boys rode away. The wind died, and mosquitoes floated through the air. The temperature dropped from ninety degrees to fifty in an hour. Lights flickered in teepees, campers, and tents. A few elders placed their hands on the totem. There was an eagle with a twelve-foot wingspan on top, a wolf, a bear, and a white buffalo —

symbols of leadership, cunning, and courage. The scent of woodsmoke and bug repellent spread through the camp. Doug finished his song and handed the microphone back to his brother. Jewell gave a Lakota representative a check for $10,000 to support the cause and $500 in cash to buy food. "This is the awakening we've been waiting for," he said.

12

The Sioux tribes were relative newcomers to the northland in the 1500s. Lakota "winter counts" — pictorial histories that the tribe records every winter — set the tribe's spiritual and ancestral home in South Dakota's Black Hills. Archaeologists say that their ancestors originally moved from the Southeast, near the Gulf of Mexico. Either way, they passed through northern Minnesota around the time the Ojibwe arrived. The two did not get along. The Ojibwe named their new enemy *Nadowessi,* or "little snake." Early French traders who made first contact with the nation added *"oux"* to make it plural. The names merged into *Sioux* — a word that has no meaning in any language and, for two hundred years, referred to the most powerful nation in the northern plains.

Borders in the northland were more fluid then. They followed environmental and demographic shifts. Hunters in the northern plains in the 1500s followed herds of bison, while sedentary, agrarian communities, like the Mandan and Hidatsa on the Missouri River, stayed put. When Spanish horses arrived from the south, and French and English guns from the north, Plains tribes and their territory changed drastically. Sioux braves were natural horsemen and marksmen and became an efficient war machine in the 1700s. While epidemics annihilated stationary villages, bands of hunters roaming the plains avoided the worst of them. Many of the Sioux Nation's enemies were wiped out without the Sioux raising a hand, allowing them to further expand their borders.

By the time the first white settlers arrived in the northern plains, Sioux tribes controlled 740,000 square miles — from Colorado through Nebraska, Minnesota, and Utah to the Canadian border. It was the largest territory ever amassed by a North American tribe. One day it would represent one-fifth of the United States. Traders, explorers, US Army expeditions, and a few frontiersmen who wandered into the northern plains came to respect and fear the Great Sioux Nation. They weren't like other tribes that white men had met. They didn't make art or ceramics. They didn't keep wampum. They made war instead.

Sioux tribes considered battle the best means by which a brave could prove his courage, and courage was the measure of life. Children were given bows and arrows as young as three years old and told to compete in target practice and games like King of the Hill. The games were often violent, and the winner was allowed to keep the other kids' weapons. Adult warriors rode dare rides, alone and often armed with only a war club, a few hundred feet in front of enemy lines. Crazy Horse, an Oglala Lakota, got his name after charging a band of Arapaho solo. He returned wounded and carrying two scalps. Years later, at Wyoming's Fort Phil Kearny, he lured US war hero Captain William Fetterman and eighty-one of Fetterman's cavalry into one of the greatest defeats the US Army sustained in the Indian Wars — by dismounting his horse within rifle range, lifting his breechclout, and mooning the soldiers as shots whizzed by. Red Cloud, a legendary Oglala Lakota chief, also dismounted his horse in front of a US Army skirmish line. He then sat down, lit his pipe, and smoked while lead shot from Springfield rifles and Colt .45's hit the dirt around him.

Like the Ojibwe, the Sioux consider the Road of the Spirits — their name for the Path of Souls — a portal to the afterlife. The seven stars of the Big Dipper lift souls onto the road, making 7 a sacred number. The number 4 is also sacred, and the two numbers form the tribes' numerical systems. Political and cultural divisions are made in sevens. The Sioux nation is divided into seven tribes. Each tribe is divided into seven bands. Bands changed their names so often in the 1700s that explorers ten years apart documented what they thought were completely different groups. The number 4 is associated with nature, people, and place. There are four divisions of time: day, night, moon phase, and year. There are four kinds of animals on land: creatures that crawl, fly, walk on four legs, and walk on two. There are four celestial entities: sun, moon, sky, and stars.

When settlers began showing up in the northland in the 1840s, the tribe looked on with indifference. Prairie schooners had been carrying white settlers south along the Santa Fe Trail for twenty years by then. Subsequent emigrant trails — like the California, Mormon, Oregon, and Bozeman — each angled a bit farther north. The last two, the Oregon and Bozeman, passed directly through Sioux territory for a thousand miles. Fort Laramie, Fort Phil Kearny, and Virginia City — a gold mine boomtown in the 1860s — were all located on the Bozeman Trail and set deep in Sioux country.

The tribe was impressed by the whites' mystical inventions but thought little of the people themselves. They found whites smelly and were disgusted by their hairy bodies and balding heads. They considered them inferior simpletons. Sioux society is matriarchal, where a man moves into a woman's home after marriage, and the woman is considered the head of the household. They were shocked at the way white men scolded and hit their women and children. Early explorers often wrote about how undisciplined Sioux children were, how they were allowed to stay up all night and were rarely punished. When a trickle of whites began to show up on Sioux land, tribes figured there were no more than a few thousand of the silly beings in the East — and that they would soon be gone.

The June 1850 US census calculated twenty-three million residents in America, a 36 percent increase from ten years before. Ninety percent of the population lived east of the Mississippi. When James Wilson Marshall, a New Jersey carpenter, discovered a flake of gold at John Sutter's California sawmill in 1848 — exactly nine days before Mexico signed the Treaty of Guadalupe Hidalgo, ceding the entire Southwest and California to the US — a flood of white immigrants spilled over the Appalachians.

Ferries dropped homesteaders on the banks of the Missouri, where they could purchase and outfit a Conestoga wagon for about $400. It took three to six months to make it from the "Big Muddy" across an overland trail. Relocation was the norm among early-American families. Some settlers were escaping religious persecution or poverty, some were looking to get rich. In the late 1700s, four out of ten households moved every ten years. Most settlers had moved across state lines previously, and 30 percent had moved at least twice. Many had adopted a nomadic lifestyle, searching for opportunity on the frontier. In 1850 alone, fifty-five thousand Mormons, forty-niners, and homesteaders took to the trails. Between 1843 and 1869, five hundred thousand emigrants followed the Oregon, Mormon, and California Trails.

The shores of the Missouri, where buffalo had once scratched themselves on thick cottonwood bark, became crowded with stern-wheel steamboats, ports, farms, and small frontier towns. A stream of settlers marched along the Oregon Trail as thousands of Mormon handcart pioneers — hauling their possessions in hickory carts with steel wheels — filed along the Platte River to Salt Lake City. Mass migration along the trails transformed them into apocalyptic highways, littered with dead livestock and human corpses. Whites brought cholera, smallpox, and other European diseases that devastated western tribes. Hunters used .50-caliber Sharps buffalo rifles to fell up to a thousand buffalo a week. In sixty years, the population of buffalo in the West plunged from thirty million to less than a thousand. Statistically, it was the greatest slaughter of warm-blooded animals in human history, including the whaling years.

Settlers crossed Indian land in the northland, most illegally, and Sioux braves made sport of stealing their horses, guns, steel tools, and knives. If they caught a family of whites on their land, they treated them as they would any interlopers. Women were often beaten while braves gang-raped them. After the victim was dead, her private parts were cut off and laid in the grass. Couples were disemboweled, then tied together with their entrails and roasted over a fire.

The violent ways of Sioux warriors were not abnormal on the plains. Many tribes — and US soldiers — did the same. In 1864, volunteers in the Third Colorado Cavalry killed 163 Cheyenne and Arapaho, two-thirds of them women and children, in the Sand Creek massacre. Soldiers raped dead women in relays, used toddlers for target practice, and sliced off breasts, vaginas, and testicles, then displayed the body parts at Denver's Apollo Theater and saloons in the city.

Starvation, weather, raids, and ignorance killed five thousand settlers on the trail in 1850. In the following years, one in eleven emigrants left this world between Saint Louis and Salt Lake City. The statistic did not go over well in Washington, DC. American politicians had learned from the British that to control the land, you had to occupy it. They also knew that the English were moving west and south quickly in British Canada, and that the first nation to settle the West would likely control it.

The War of 1812 and deteriorating relations with the South left Congress with little money and no confidence that they could defeat western tribes in battle. They had learned from several embarrassing losses that Plains Indians were more formidable warriors than others they had encountered. It would take too much time and money to beat them on the battlefield, so Congress resorted to an approach that had proved fail-safe in the past. They offered them gifts and money and convinced them to sign lengthy treaties that would eventually rob them of their land.

US Indian agent Thomas Fitzpatrick was tasked with gathering Plains tribes to sign their first major treaty in 1851 — the same that Standing Rock lawyers would reference 165 years later. He rode from the Arkansas River into the northland, asking headmen along the way to parlay at Fort Laramie and find a solution to the white emigrant problem. The invitees — Sioux, Cheyenne, Arapaho, Shoshone, Crow, Assiniboine, Mandan, Hidatsa, and Arikara — had fought one another for centuries. They had never convened as a group and had no intention of calling a truce. But they were intrigued by the trinkets, cash, firearms, alcohol, and gifts that Fitzpatrick promised. The former fur trader had been allocated a budget of $100,000 to give to tribes that attended the rendezvous.

Red Cloud, a thirty-year-old Oglala Lakota and the tribe's head warrior, led his
band in formation to a field outside of Fort
Laramie in late summer. Red Cloud was six
feet tall and towered over other braves. He
had a wide forehead and hooked nose and
adorned himself with eagle feathers and ribbons. At important meetings, he slicked his
hair back with bear grease and braided in
the wing bone of an eagle. Red Cloud was
the son of a drunk and a fierce warrior who
had fought his way to power. He did not
drink and did not accept gifts from whites.
Legendary acts of bravery and cunning had
made him a supernatural figure to many.
He was a shaman who practiced the sun
dance — a four-day purification ceremony
in which dozens of pieces of flesh are ripped
from a warrior's body. His followers said he
could talk to animals, fly, and be in two
places at once. They said he was also capable
of casting spells and interpreting omens.

Red Cloud rode into the 1851 rendezvous
on a paint with a few hundred of his three
thousand warriors. Chiefs marching with
him wore buffalo split-horned headdresses,
feather trailers, painted buckskin capes, leggings, and war paint. Twenty-year-old Sitting Bull, a Hunkpapa Lakota, marched in
the ranks, as did an eleven-year-old boy

nicknamed "Curly," who would one day be called Crazy Horse.

The Sioux contingent camped alongside their Arapaho and Cheyenne allies and sang death songs when the Shoshone, who had killed many of their kin, marched into camp. Fitzpatrick and US Army officials watched nervously as the gathering swelled to ten thousand. The next day, they moved it to a pasture on Horse Creek, where army engineers had built an amphitheater out of wood and canvas. Cavalry dragoons prepared to intervene when Sioux headmen surprised the Shoshone with a feast of boiled dog, then watched in awe as the two tribes danced and sang until dawn. In the morning, Fitzpatrick, who had lived among the Indians for years and earned their respect, paid homage to the Great Spirit and shared a three-foot peace pipe with the elders.

The rendezvous continued for two weeks, with brief negotiations interrupting celebrations, horse races, feasts, and dances. Government officials selected heads of each tribe to sign the treaty — though most had no authority or any idea what was in it. The headmen did not write, so they tapped the fountain pen the secretary held instead, and he signed for them. Their primary concession was to allow settlers to pass on the overland trails unmolested and for forts to be maintained on their territory. The other terms of the treaty forbade intertribal raids and defined the territory that each tribe controlled. It also recognized that the US did not claim any of that land, and it bound the US government to protect tribes "against the commission of all depredations by the people of the said United States." Finally, it promised gifts equaling $50,000 a year for fifty years.

After the tribes disbanded, most went back to living the way they had before, rich with coffee, beads, blankets, tobacco, sheets of brass, US Army dress uniforms, and medals featuring President Millard Fillmore. For years after, tribes showed up at Fort Laramie in the spring to meet the annuity train and gather their gifts. Shipments continued sporadically through the Indian Wars and beyond, as the US government bought off whoever was willing to come to the table and lay down their arms. Government-approved brokers extended Indians additional credit, often settling debts by taking land for pennies on the dollar. For any tribe willing to stop fighting altogether, Congress drafted more treaties — defining smaller and smaller reservations that Indians could live on, while signing the rest of their territory over to the federal government.

From 1853 to 1856, western Indians ceded 174 million acres of land to the US in fifty-two treaties. The US government ratified 370 more treaties over the next fifty years. They offered hunting grounds, autonomy, citizenship, friendship, goods, and money to tribes. On a map, territory that Congress guaranteed the Sioux Nation at the 1851 Fort Laramie Treaty looks like an inkblot covering nearly half of Nebraska, Wyoming, Montana, and North and South Dakota. Once the Indians were safely registered on reservations, administered by a US Indian agent and a detachment of soldiers, Congress amended, canceled, or ignored every Indian treaty it ever signed.

I wanted to see the former Sioux territory for myself and drove through it for two days. Freight trains crisscrossed the northland east–west. The highway rolled north–south. Silos broke through the plains like fingers. Underground, a third of America's intercontinental nuclear missiles sat in temperature-controlled shafts, many in the Bakken oil fields. I put the car on cruise control and sat cross-legged for an hour. Silver oil tankers rushed in the opposite direction. Silver guardrails edged the road. The only points of reference were billboards and gas stations.

Americans didn't want this swath of the northland at first. Long trains of prairie schooners passed the northern plains on their way west. Emigrants wanted gold, silver, farms, furs, water, timber, or a route to the ocean. The hardened, windswept plains over their right shoulder didn't interest them. The soil there was alkaline and hard as cement. Lewis and Clark called it "astonishingly dry," and Thomas Jefferson estimated that it would take a thousand generations to settle. It rarely rained in the "Great American Desert," as the territory was labeled in an 1822 atlas.

The one-hundredth meridian marks the border between life and death on the northern plains. Twenty or more inches of annual rain falls to the east, less than fifteen in the west. Tall prairie grass grows in the east, short grass in the west. Settlers west of the line, who had little wood to build with, burrowed dugout homes into the ground to withstand brutal plains' winds. For almost a century, banks wouldn't give a loan to anyone farming west of the line.

Hardy, land-seeking Scandinavians from Iowa and Minnesota were the first immigrants to move to North Dakota. The Homestead Act of 1862 allowed them — and any American, including freed slaves and "intended citizens" — to settle up to 160 acres of federal land for free. They put down stakes near stands of cottonwood along the Red River so as to have logs to build with. The ground around Fargo appeared so infertile that gardens were for family use only. Frustration with farming the northern plains ran so hot then that a man was killed in the 1870s near Fargo for claiming that he could grow crops in the Red River Valley.

Yale Law School graduate Oliver Dalrymple changed that. He took on more than seventy thousand acres of farmland in the Red River Valley in 1875 and employed six hundred men, two hundred plows, two hundred self-binding reapers, thirty steampowered threshers, and four hundred teams of horses to irrigate and reap thirty bushels of wheat a day on one of America's first commercial farms. By 1881 he was threshing enough wheat on his "bonanza" farm to fill three trainloads a day. The US government publicized his profits. Word spread quickly, and a wave of Norwegians from Minnesota and Iowa settled in Cass and Traill Counties. Canadians followed in

Walsh and Pembina Counties. By 1885, North Dakota's population was 150,000. A half-million acres of land had been plowed under in the Great American Desert, and twelve million bushels of wheat was being harvested annually.

Flare stacks spewed fire above wheat fields and ranchland as I approached Williston, the nexus of North Dakota's oil boom, set in the northwest corner of the state. The town was once in the heart of Sioux country — less than a mile from the Missouri and twenty-five miles northeast of Fort Buford, where Sitting Bull surrendered in 1881. It was ten in the evening, and the sky over town glowed dull orange. Light from the flames turned grazing cattle into silhouettes. Oil derricks appeared every quarter mile. Some were pumping; many were frozen in place. Four iron walls surrounded a blazing vent twenty feet off the shoulder. Tall prairie grass grew around silos, tractors, and plows. A white picket fence circled a red barn and ended at another stack launching fire into the air.

Eighty thousand people flocked to North Dakota at the height of Williston's boom. Roughnecks in the field made $100,000 a year, and farmers took in $50,000–$200,000 a month leasing their land. Some

Indian tribes profited too. The Mandan, Hidatsa, and Arikara nations on the Fort Berthold Reservation received $91 million for drilling rights there. In 2014, the Standing Rock Reservation tribal government leased nearly two hundred thousand acres of their land for oil and gas exploration. (The Department of the Interior estimates that more than 20 percent of America's fossil fuel reserves sit on Indian land: 5.35 billion barrels of oil, 37.7 trillion cubic feet of natural gas, and 53 billion tons of coal.)

An influx of oil from the Williston Basin, which includes the Bakken shale play, was a factor in the collapse of oil prices in 2014. The effect in Williston was devastating. After years of surpluses, North Dakota was $6 billion in debt in 2017. Oil companies that had been fighting for land leases left the state without a trace. United Airlines ended direct flights from Houston to Williston, and the little town once known for the bushels of durum wheat it turned out was left to clean up the mess.

The next morning I had breakfast with a Williston hotel manager. He had a graying beard and bags under his eyes. A few guests holding Styrofoam coffee cups sat at tables around us. The manager had been working at a hotel in Georgia when he was called up to run a new hotel in Williston. Housing was so tight during the boom that he and his wife slept in a pop-up camper for six months. There were no homes for sale, nothing to rent. "Man camps" sheltered thousands on the outskirts of town in cramped, temporary structures. The grocery store ran out of bread by 10:00 in the morning; produce was gone by 9:30. The staff at the Home Depot stopped stocking shelves and made piles of flat-screen TVs and barbecue grills in the middle of the floor instead. "You had to survive," the hotel manager said.

He and his wife eventually found a house to buy, an hour and a half away. He commuted every day and spent as little time as possible in Williston. "There were drugs," he said. "You could get a hooker if you wanted. It was like a city; you could get anything. People also got paid well, but the rents were higher than in Manhattan." The number of federal prosecutors in western North Dakota tripled to 336 in 2010. A year before, two members of the international Sinaloa Cartel were apprehended nearby, one of several foreign and domestic gangs that infiltrated the region. Meth and heroin were smuggled through Indian reservations, where tribal officers are not allowed to arrest non-Indians. Two hours away in Ward County, meth seizures increased sixfold. One member of a Williston drug gang arrested in the spring of 2014 had nine rifles, six pistols, four shotguns, and three revolvers hidden in his apartment.

The Williston Brewing Company was empty when I drove through town, and R Rooster BBQ looked like it was closed. The apartments and storefronts at the $15 million Renaissance on Main complex were empty. Developers built ten thousand apartments in town between 2009 and 2016. Vacancy in 2017 was 40 percent. An old department store on the west side of the road displayed poofy red and white prom dresses. Someone had planted flowers at a few intersections to spruce them up. Five blocks outside of town, a row of heavy-equipment rental agencies, which had been sold out for years, were full of excavators, bulldozers, pump equipment, and portable urinals.

I passed a Halliburton truck and more wells on my way south that afternoon. Dust swirled behind a UPS van driving down a dirt road. Steel check valves broke through the soil. Wheels and gauges on the pipes were painted the same bright yellow as late-summer blossoms in nearby sunflower fields. Utility trucks that service the oil fields were yellow as well, adorned with cranes, welders, lockboxes, toolboxes, extra fuel tanks, and compressors. A man stood beside a Suburban with a flat tire and gazed at the scene. His tire hadn't popped. The entire structure of the wheel was gone, leaving the axle sitting on the ground.

A few miles down the road I pulled into another reminder of northland profiteering. Fort Buford and nearby Fort Union boomed during the fur trade. Fort Union was the largest trading post on the plains in the 1800s and sold British muskets, Sheffield knives, Cologne pipes, falcon bells from Leipzig, and "rattlesnake whiskey," made from a gallon of water, a cup of whiskey, a splash of strychnine, and a pinch of gunpowder. Set at the confluence of the Missouri and Yellowstone Rivers, Fort Buford was a vital military post and supply depot. When Sitting Bull surrendered there in July of 1881, he handed his rifle to his son, Crow, and instructed him to give it to the fort's commander, Major David H. Brotherton. Sitting Bull's only request was that he be known as the last Plains Indian to give up his weapon.

I was alone at the fort. There were no staff members or other visitors. I walked around a re-creation of the regimental headquarters where Sitting Bull had turned himself in. It is gray clapboard with brown trim. Five brick chimneys emerge from the cedar-shingled roof. The bay window in the northeast corner was the first ever installed in a western post. The yellowed curtains were drawn, and the sills were layered with dead houseflies. Workers at the Fort Buford State Historic Site had rebuilt several of its original structures, including a barracks and a stockade. Soldiers' accounts of living at the fort in the 1800s recall sporadic attacks from surrounding tribes, baseball games in the yard, and eating boiled buffalo boss ribs with yeast powder biscuits.

The wind blew so hard off the river that it sounded like a voice in my ear. Fence posts hummed. Barbed wire whistled. Interpretive signs near the buildings rattled, and shingles on the fort looked like they were about to blow off. I stood for a while looking at the buildings, then across the field at the swirling Yellowstone and Missouri. Meriwether Lewis, coleader of the Corps of Discovery with William Clark, had camped at the confluence with his men in 1805. He was so exhilarated by the sight of the merging rivers that he handed out drams of whiskey that night to the corps. Later, someone picked up a fiddle, and the group sang and danced around the campfire into the early hours of the morning.

Joye Braun was more worried about security guards and broken treaties than Williston's boom-and-bust cycle. I found her at Oceti Sakowin under the "legal tent" near the kitchen. Protestors sat around the sacred fire circle, sipping coffee and smoking cigarettes. Car-camping gear was abundant: roll-up tables, folding sinks, rocking camping chairs, cooking kits, solar flashlights, campfire spits. The cooks had set out stainless-steel bowls of sliced watermelon and boxes of pears donated by Washington's Yakama Nation. An older white man poured coffee from a five-gallon Gatorade water cooler. Two men stood around the dispensers talking about how to replace the generator at the camp, which burned diesel twenty-four hours a day.

"Solar panels are on the way," one of them said.

"Sustainability," said the other, nodding.

Joye is a forty-seven-year-old Cheyenne River Lakota activist. She works for the Indigenous Environmental Network and erected one of the first teepees at the Standing Rock protest. She had camped near

Bridger, South Dakota, the previous year, fighting the Keystone XL Pipeline. Bridger was on the front lines of that battle from early on. TransCanada had planned to run the XL pipeline directly across the Cheyenne River Reservation just south of Standing Rock at first. When the tribe blocked that plan, the company shipped megaloads of tar sands mining equipment through Bridger. Lakota actions to block them helped bring the XL campaign into the public eye and get President Obama's attention. After the president shut down the XL project in 2015, Joye drove north to block another "black snake" planned for Standing Rock. "Next thing I know," she said, "April 1, we saddled up and had a big ride from Fort Yates to Cannon Ball and I put my teepee up in the snow."

Joye has soft, brown eyes, a motherly demeanor, and a wild, percussive laugh with which she punctuates her most salient points. Over the course of the hour that we spoke, six different people walked up to her, hugged her, and walked away without saying a word. She told me how a stroke in 2010 had confined her to a wheelchair. Her husband had brought her back to Eagle Butte, on the Cheyenne River Reservation, where she grew up, and she went to ceremony for the first time in years. One day while recovering, she saw a man on TV lie down on Highway 34 to stop a TransCanada megaload. The trucks are three-quarters of a football field long and two stories high. Joye was so inspired that she wheeled her chair in front of a megaload the next day. "We made a law forbidding oil production equipment from crossing the Cheyenne River Reservation," she said. "I stopped the truck, and it turned around. The next night, three megaloads came through Bridger and tried to run people off the road. We caught up to them, and they stopped. The National Guard was activated that night."

It was approaching noon, and the wind was picking up. A yellow ETP helicopter flew overhead. The FAA had imposed a no-fly zone over the camp to stop protestors from recording ETP's activity with drones. ETP's private security company continued flying over anyway. Joye flipped off the chopper and lit a cigarette. In a few days, a judge would decide on the injunction that could stop pipeline construction. Two weeks before, North Dakota governor Jack Dalrymple — great-grandson of wheat farmer Oliver Dalrymple — had declared a state of emergency at the camp, stating that it was a public safety hazard. Police departments from neighboring states, using a "good neighbor" rule that Bill Clinton had passed to help natural-disaster response, converged on Standing Rock. The officers had no connection to the area or knowledge of the Sioux reservation and used military-grade sound cannons, concussion grenades, water cannons, Tasers, and tear gas on protestors over the next three months. Much of the gear had been gleaned from the controversial "1033" military-police exchange program that the Defense Department enacted in 1997, and the subsequent tactical-arms cottage industry that Homeland Security now finances.

No weapons were allowed at the Standing Rock Reservation — including the axe that the old lady in front of me had inadvertently tried to smuggle in on my first day. Leaders of the movement relied on the courtroom instead. Joye and her fellow water protectors could recite the dates of broken treaties from memory. Lawyers from Earthjustice, the National Lawyers Guild, and the tribe's own legal team were arguing multiple lawsuits in North Dakota and Washington, DC. Many briefs led with the 1851 and 1868 Fort Laramie Treaties. "There is something poetic about these documents coming back after all these years," Jan Hasselman, lead counsel for the Standing Rock tribal government, told me. "In the past, a lot of people on the reservations thought, *What was the point?* Now, for the first time, people are actually listening to them."

School let out, and children scattered into the camp. One by one, parents sat in the grass to listen to Joye. There were protests planned in Bismarck that night, and a few more on the construction site over the next few days. No one knew the details; they just happened. Ten thousand people were expected at the forty-seventh annual United Tribes International Powwow in Bismarck that weekend, a few miles from the Morton County courthouse, where David Archambault II, chairman of the Standing Rock Sioux tribe, was arguing to release protesters from jail. "Someone's delivering two hundred pounds of buffalo meat here on Saturday," Joye said. "This place is going to be nuts."

Joye agreed with Jewell Praying Wolf James that something larger was taking shape. "There are prophesies that talk about how the First Nations people will rise up and become so enlightened they will enlighten the world," she said. "This is indigenous rising. We have been the most oppressed, suppressed, people in the world. Indigenous populations, specifically here in America. We were so decimated, but we have been growing and educating ourselves. The common goal is water. Water is sacred. Without water there is nothing. There is an alternative for everything oil makes. There is no alternative for water. And yet they want to commodify it and poison it." I asked if she thought the camp would be able to outlast a standoff with a multibillion-dollar oil company. "If there's one thing we know how to do, it's camp," she said.

Oceti Sakowin was quiet the next morning. In the early days of the protest, women had gathered by the riverbank every morning to offer handfuls of tobacco to the water. There were nearly two thousand people living at the camp now, and the daily schedule was more spontaneous. Orange light washed over the teepees in the field. Their smoke flaps looked like preacher's collars, and the lacing pins like jacket buttons. In Lakota culture, the circular floor inside represents the earth. The walls are the sky, and tent poles connect the two spheres.

Wind whipped a streamer dangling from a smoke flap and pulled at the flags along the dirt driveway. An older man with an image of Chief Sitting Bull stitched into his denim jacket wandered past. Three young boys from the Lake Traverse Indian Reservation in Veblen, South Dakota, chopped wood nearby. Helena La Batte of the Sisseton Wahpeton Oyate — a branch of the Santee Dakota — organized their trip to Standing Rock. She was standing by the van they'd driven, watching the boys, when I walked up. She said she was not as interested in oil as she was in the dairy business in Veblen. Three farms that keep thousands of cows within a mile of the reservation had contaminated the water supply there. The stench of the methane cloud in homes near the farms was overwhelming. Flies buzzed constantly, and children had been infected with a strain of bovine bacteria.

Helena researched the issue and found that seven aquifers beneath the reservation had been contaminated by hormones and bacteria from manure runoff. She had never been an environmentalist or activist. She was simply tired of watching her town waste away. She worked for the tribal council at the time and brought the issue to their attention. She said the council dismissed her, and she now runs a riding camp at her house. She doesn't charge children to attend. She invites them to her home to learn to ride. She has to be stern with some of the bad actors, she said. One girl walks eighteen miles, once a week, to go to the camp. "She does it to get away from the meth at home," Helena said.

One of the kids' favorite activities is swimming with the horses. Helena had brought their favorite horse to Standing Rock, a dappled gray named Silver. She called him "dirty white boy." At home, the kids hang on to his mane as he walks into the ruddy water of Lake Traverse. Then he swims in wide circles with the children dragging behind. When his front hooves touch the beach again, he lurches forward, and the kids scream and cling to his neck as he drags them out of the water.

I left the camp at noon to continue my journey across the northland. I followed Route 1806 past the pipeline access road that protestors had been blocking. It was barricaded and papered with Lakota banners, ribbons, and feathers. A quarter mile farther, plywood signs read, "No More Stolen Sisters" and "Law: 1851." Just beyond that, over a small hill, a herd of fifty buffalo grazed in a rolling green pasture.

There were no excavators, no houses or people in sight. Just buffalo grass bending in the wind, the pale-blue Missouri sliding around an oxbow, and the furry, brown beasts wandering in circles. It was a perfect system, all of the parts moving in synchronicity. In two hundred years, a scheme that took millions of years to evolve was methodically being taken apart.

I pulled over and watched for a moment. A white sedan that had been following me parked a hundred yards back. When I drove away ten minutes later, the sedan made a U-turn and drove toward the encampment. I passed a police barricade near Bismarck. Lights flashed on an SUV, and a deputy directed traffic between several beige and white tents. A state trooper with a flat-brimmed campaign hat inspected cars and passengers as they drove by. The troopers wore bulletproof vests and holstered their pistols where a belt buckle would normally be.

I passed piles of pipe meant for the Dakota Access line stacked along Interstate 94. Two trucks driving the opposite direction had Frac Shack logos painted on their sides. Ten miles later I was in the plains of southwestern North Dakota. The land buckled into small hills and ravines until Sully Springs, where the red-and-white-striped Badlands filled the horizon.

Route 47 veered to the south, drawing a

clean line through a sea of cornfields. The nine-hole Fort Custer Golf Course was bright green with weeping willows dividing the fairways. Giant hay bales leaned against a silo next door to a KOA campground. Hawarden, Montana, was straight ahead; Sheridan, Wyoming, to the south. Light broke through a rain shower thirty miles away and painted the Little Bighorn River silver.

The entrance to Little Bighorn Battlefield National Monument is marked by a concrete gatepost. The road runs southwest through a coulee to a cluster of brown National Park Service buildings. Rows of white tombstones welcome retirees driving massive RVs, families crammed into minivans, motorcyclists, and tourists to the park. The graves continue from the parking lot over the hills to the southwest. Most of the headstones are blank. Several dozen lay on the ground, surrounded by orange construction barricades. Veterans and their spouses are allowed to request a grave site at Little Bighorn. The soldiers buried here fought in the Indian Wars, Spanish-American War, World Wars I and II, Korean War, Vietnam War, and Gulf Wars.

Concrete pathways lead away from the visitor center to various battle sites. A conference room with panoramic windows hosts interpretive talks three times a day. An attached stone courtyard looks out on battle sites like Greasy Grass Ridge, Medicine Tail Coulee, and the site of Custer's last stand. At the bottom of the hill a run of cottonwood trees hides the river and much of the terrain where an Indian encampment had been set before Lieutenant Colonel George Armstrong Custer attacked it on June 25, 1876.

Eight thousand Lakota, Cheyenne, Arapaho, and others had gathered there. They came together to discuss how to survive in an increasingly white world. It was a stroke of luck that Custer and General Alfred Terry found them at all. The US Army had a miserable record of locating Indian camps. Custer's orders had been to flank the group from the east with 475 men of the Seventh Regiment of the US Cavalry. Terry would march from the north with 400 soldiers to stop anyone trying to escape. After Custer's movements were detected on Wolf Mountain, twelve miles from the camp, he decided to continue anyway.

The first to die in the Seventh Cavalry's charge were two Lakota women and a young girl. A sentry had warned the tribes a few minutes before the attack, and warriors quickly returned fire. Major Marcus Reno, the same man who had escorted the Northern Boundary Commission, retreated into the woods, then back over the river. Lakota fighters inflicted heavy casualties as Reno's company sought cover up a line of steep bluffs, then fell back into a stand of trees. In the distance, Reno saw gun smoke and chaos around the site of Custer's charge. Exactly what happened is still a mystery, but most accounts suggest that Custer rode north and descended the Medicine Tail Coulee leading to the encampment. Custer's men then retreated to Calhoun Hill and Battle Ridge, where they were surrounded.

Only 50 of the original 210 men with Custer made it to the site of the last stand. Hundreds of whooping Lakota and Cheyenne warriors surrounded them, picking them off one by one with old British muskets, arrows, spears, and a few modern Spencer rifles. Several soldiers tried to break through Indian lines. All were pulled from their horses and killed. By the time the sun set on June 25, all five companies under Custer, plus the colonel himself, were dead.

Braves hacked apart the soldiers' bodies and collected their weapons. They did not scalp Custer. They stripped and washed his body instead. Historians postulate that they did this out of respect. Since Custer usually wore buckskins for battle and not a uniform, they more likely mistook him for a civilian.

I followed one of the paths up the hill toward a concrete memorial for those who had stood with the colonel. Tombstones on the western face of the hillock are set wherever a soldier's remains were found. The battlefield is a rolling tan carpet with a few trees and squares of soy and cornfields beyond the river. There is a small cluster of graves on each hilltop. The first officers to visit the battle site after the slaughter were not sure what they were looking at. They found Custer's Indian scouts in tears and didn't believe them when they described the bloodbath. Most of the bodies were so mutilated that it was impossible to identify them.

The air was hot and humid. A stiff wind preceded a line of thunderheads in the west. Two gray-haired couples gazed at a placard near the last stand. A young family marched dutifully up the hill toward Reno's entrenchment, and a sparrow hawk flitted through the breeze and landed on a tombstone. A guide in the visitor center announced over a PA system that the Battle of the Little Bighorn video was about to start. There were no gravestones for Indians. A single monument to them had been installed 120 years after the battle.

13

A few days after I left Standing Rock, the federal judge hearing the pipeline case denied an injunction, allowing construction to continue. On the same day, the Justice Department, the Department of the Army, and the Interior Department asked ETP to voluntarily pause while they reevaluated permits that the Army Corps had issued. ETP did not stop and announced that the pipeline would be online in early 2017.

Over the next three months, encounters with security and police grew increasingly violent. The media reported that a private security firm working for ETP, with experience in Iraq and Afghanistan, unleashed attack dogs on unarmed men, women, and children from Oceti Sakowin. According to press reports, the firm filed briefs with ETP for dealing with "jihadist-like uprisings" and infiltrated the protest camp to gather intelligence. Cell phone signals at the camp were jammed to inhibit communication and stop photos and video from getting out, and surveillance flights continued. The police reportedly worked in conjunction with the firm and ETP, fired tear gas canisters and rubber bullets at protestors, and arrested hundreds. On a twenty-degree November evening, water protectors were beaten back from Highway 1806 with water cannons, concussion grenades, and tear gas. More than three hundred were injured, including twenty-one-year-old Sophia Wilansky, who nearly lost her arm when, she said, a concussion grenade hit her and exploded.

The first snow fell, and temperatures dropped to minus twenty. The Standing Rock Sioux Indians are a northland tribe that knows how to survive in the cold. They built new lodges and installed wood and pellet stoves. Locals in Cannon Ball and the reservation's casino made rooms available on especially cold nights. Days after reportedly promising to protect the tribe's First Amendment rights, Army Corps colonel John Henderson signed over jurisdiction of the camp to the state. Governor Dalrymple followed by ordering everyone off the site. Protestors didn't leave. Two thousand US veterans arrived December 4 to back up the water protectors, and the following day, on the brink of another clash with authorities, the unthinkable happened. The Army Corps rejected ETP's final permit to tunnel under the Missouri River. Overnight, the project was stopped.

Protestors danced and chanted to workers and security guards: "Don't ever come back!" They sang and made proclamations about freedom, history, and the rights of a sovereign nation. It was the biggest and most publicized American Indian victory in modern history. The awakening they spoke of reverberated across the country. There were other pipelines, other issues on Indian land that they could stand up against: the Diamond Pipeline between Oklahoma and Tennessee; the Rover in Ohio; the Sabal Trail between Alabama and Florida; the Trans-Pecos in Texas; the Atlantic Sunrise in Pennsylvania and Virginia; the Pilgrim in New York and New Jersey; the Bayou Bridge in Louisiana; the Downeast pipeline in Passamaquoddy Bay, Maine.

Tribal leaders reminded everyone that the fight wasn't over. They were right. ETP reportedly continued its work without the permit. The chairman of the Cheyenne River Reservation, Harold Frazier, asked the government who was monitoring the construction site. He was told that ETP's private security team was acting as observers. On January 20, a new administration moved into the White House, and a familiar scenario played out. A memorandum from the Oval Office ordered the secretary of the army to expedite approval of the Dakota Access Pipeline.

Familiar names surfaced. Former ETP board member Rick Perry was sworn in as secretary of energy. Former Exxon CEO Rex Tillerson was named secretary of state. Big Oil champion Scott Pruitt took control of the EPA and immediately began to disassemble the agency. The Corps had little choice but to comply. Two months later, the embattled Keystone XL Pipeline was revived as well.

In February, ETP announced that the Dakota Access Pipeline was complete, and in mid-May it was filled with Bakken sweet crude. The line suffered several leaks in the first few months, spilling more than a hundred gallons of oil. The same month that the pipeline started flowing, ETP spilled two million gallons of drilling fluid into an Ohio wetlands area while installing the Rover Pipeline. ETP's response, according to the Ohio EPA director, was "dismissive" and unlike anything he had seen in the twenty-seven years he'd worked there.

■ ■ ■ ■

I headed back to North Dakota's northland in the spring of 2017 to see what had become of the movement. There were no roadblocks or police on Highway 1806. To anyone driving through, it looked like it always had. The Missouri ran wide and fast past Fort Abraham Lincoln State Park. The grass was bright green, and delicate spring leaves were just unfurling from elms on the riverbank.

Traces of the protest were hard to find. I spotted a fluttering shred of banner material on a barbed wire fence a few miles north of the camp and a duct-taped wooden pole that had once held a sign. Roads that construction crews had made across the prairie were covered with new grass. Gates to neighboring ranches had been replaced with new red ones. I almost drove past the Oceti Sakowin site a few miles later. There was nothing there. Less than nothing. All of the structures were gone. The horse corrals, council tents, fire circles, and teepees had all vanished. The field looked like every other field along 1806.

Barbed wire and a sign that read "No Trespassing: Government Property" blocked the entrance. I stepped over the wire and walked into the field. Dozens of hand-warmer packets stuck out of the mud. A pair of black winter gloves was half buried, and a gray wool scarf fluttered on the driveway. It must have been cold in the final days, unbelievably cold. I found the remnants of a woodpile and a few smashed Pepsi cans. The sacred fire circle where I had listened to Jewell James was the only patch of earth the grass had not overtaken. It was as if too much had happened there for nature to reclaim it just yet.

I wondered whether there were security cameras or motion detectors on the property, some kind of defense that ETP had installed. But there was nothing left to defend. ETP got what it wanted, covered its tracks, and moved on. Cell phone signals were no longer being jammed. The summer before, I couldn't send a text message; now, I had three bars of high-speed service. I saw the Missouri from a hilltop near the road, a green-brown strip of spring floodwater rushing downhill. The sky was like it always is in North Dakota's northland: six layers of varying clouds, capped by a misty blue circle around the sun.

I drove south and found four teepees and a few tents at a roadside camp. A familiar sign hung from the entrance: "Media Must Check In." I parked next to four stretched buffalo skins drying in the wind. A kid with tattoos on his face and scruff on his chin approached. He held a small drum he had just made. "He's in the teepee," he said. "By the white truck." I followed his gaze to a plywood enclosure attached to a teepee and knocked on the door.

Leon Red Dog moved a Styrofoam plate holding his dinner so that I could sit in a chair. "Been here since February," he said. "A church gave me the pellet stove." Leon was sixty-seven and a member of the Itazipco band of the Cheyenne River Sioux tribe. He had kids on the Cheyenne River Reservation and "enough grandkids for a basketball team." He looked like he hadn't showered in a while: brown long-sleeve T-shirt, gray sweatpants tucked into cowboy boots. There was some gray in his hair, and the way he moved made it seem like his joints could use a night in a real bed. Leon fiddled with his hands as he spoke: "I first came to Oceti Sakowin with some veterans last August. The headmen asked me to join their meetings. We met every morning, mostly deciding where to send the young people. Young people never do what you tell them."

After the camp was cleared in February, Cheyenne River chairman Harold Frazier asked Leon to set up a surrogate site nearby. Frazier, who was instrumental in the protest and was one of the last to leave, wanted to keep the Oceti Sakowin spirit alive and teach young Sioux activists how to camp and pray. He got a lease for twenty-five acres and helped Leon set up the first few teepees. Then Leon and some volunteers built a kitchen, made a fire circle, and got down to the business of surviving a northland winter. "We mostly clean the camp and keep the kitchen running," Leon said. "We had eighteen people here for a while."

Leon's camp didn't have a website or a fund-raising scheme. Most guests were water protectors on their way to court to fight federal charges relating to the protests. Nearly eight hundred had been arrested over the course of six months. Some faced mandatory sentences of ten to fourteen years if convicted. "They come for healing," Leon said. "They come and pray and go to Oceti Sakowin. A lot of them cry when they go there."

I drove to Joye Braun's hometown the next day. She was away at a speaking engagement, so I spoke with Harold Frazier instead. He is fifty-one years old and barrel-chested, with short-cropped black hair. Like Joye, he laughs after he makes a good point. Harold sat behind a cluttered boardroom table in the center of the tribal office. Secretaries and officials working in cubicles sat in orbit around him. A young man with a tight ponytail and a three-piece suit fried fresh walleye fillets on an electric grill at the other end of the table while we spoke.

Harold had been busy helping water protectors who were facing jail time. "We were told our First Amendment right to protest would be protected, and these guys are going to jail," he said. "North Dakota spent $15 million fighting unarmed protestors at the Standing Rock camps. They asked Congress to pay them back. That money will come from taxpayers. So we're paying them guys to hurt us? It's a vicious cycle."

The Cheyenne River tribe gets its water from the Missouri as well, and Harold had discussed the pipeline at a private roundtable meeting with President Barack Obama the previous fall — along with Barbra Streisand and "a few rich guys from California." Harold has a way of saying exactly what's on his mind, and he told the group about the recent violence that police had brought to Oceti Sakowin. "The president said he would send federal observers to keep an eye on things," Harold said. "They never came. They wanted that pipeline. That's the only answer."

The man with the ponytail said the fish was finished, and Harold sent me on my way with a golden fillet. I drove along the Missouri for the rest of the day, past sprawling ranches, hay fields, and tiny compounds surrounded by rusting machinery. Chain-link fences wrapped around gas terminals, and high-tension power lines swooped across the prairie.

The dark shadow that is Lake Oahe appeared near Snake Creek. In the 1960s, the Army Corps built a series of dams along the Missouri to prevent flooding in downstream cities like Saint Louis and New Orleans. They built the dam that formed Lake Oahe without properly consulting the tribe — and submerged more than two hundred thousand acres of land on the Standing Rock and Cheyenne River Reservations. There is no shoreline around the lake. Water eases into grasslands like a giant puddle in the spring and contracts in the fall. The final resting place of Sitting Bull in Fort Yates a few miles north overlooks a forest of dead trees, still standing fifty years after Lake Oahe flooded it.

It's no wonder that so many young Sioux tribal members on the reservations turn to drugs, alcohol, and even suicide, a bartender told me that night. He was a Lakota Sioux himself. "We're invisible," he said. "Half the country doesn't even know we're here." The bar was set in a small blue shack, situated in the middle of a pasture a few miles south of Oceti Sakowin. Three cattle skulls hung on the wall, and sawdust covered the floor.

No alcohol or drugs were allowed at Oceti Sakowin, and some protestors had visited the bar to get a drink. "I like everything that they stood for," the bartender said. "It seemed like the right thing. But if you ask me, they never should have crossed that river. It's not our land. Everything that pipeline company was doing was fucked up. Everything the cops did was fucked up. I think what we stood for was honorable, but I just don't like how we did it."

The bartender handed me a Coors Light and told me about life on the reservation. He was missing a tooth and wore steel-rimmed glasses. His forearms were thick and muscled. He didn't want me to use his name; he didn't need the trouble, he said. He told me that Lakota men got fired in Williston's oil fields because of the protest.

Others had been chased or intimidated by the police or kicked out of stores by whites in Bismarck. "I've traveled all over the country, and Bismarck is the most racist place I know," he said. "The payback is coming now. They're boycotting our casino. They want to take away funding for the tribe. You wait and see what they do and what the state does. Every other protestor went home when the camp was cleared. We have to live here."

Williston oil production had picked up again. By spring, drilling operations had grown by 80 percent, and production broke a million barrels a day. Half of that now ran through the pipeline.

Two boys and a girl in their twenties walked into the bar and bought a twelve-pack of Budweiser. They came up short, and the bartender told them to bring the rest when they could. He and his boss had plans for the bar, he said. They'd known each other since they were seven. "We're gonna expand in the corner," he said. "We've got another building we're gonna drag over and attach. Pool table, darts, new sound system."

I left him a twenty and wished him good luck. I was no different from the other visitors: my time here was coming to a close, and I was headed home. Outside, the sky was blood red. Clouds in the west hugged the prairie, that's where the rain comes from. There isn't much left after the Rockies wring them out. Storm fronts recharge over the Great Lakes and pour down on forests and cities in the Midwest and on the East Coast. That's the cycle the Sioux tribes pray to, and the one the oilmen were messing with.

The fate of the pipeline and the Sioux reservations continued to flip-flop. A federal judge handed the tribe a victory in June of 2017, stating that the required environmental impact study filed by ETP was indeed insufficient. He ordered another review to be conducted, but allowed the pipeline to continue operating in the meantime.

I opened the car door and heard a *Whoop!* and the sound of hooves behind me. A dozen paints raced by a hundred yards away. A man wearing a cowboy hat swung a lasso over his head and herded the horses in a wide arc. It was a scene from a different time, another postcard from the northland: cowboys and Indians, oil patches and water wars, boom and bust, flood and drought.

"That's my boss," the bartender said, stepping into the lot. We watched as the herd disappeared over a hill. There was a house on a ridgeline behind it, a pickup truck stacked high with hay parked in the drive-way. A long shadow slid over the hills, and a few lights flicked on upstairs. I said goodbye again and got into the car. The bartender gazed at the field for a few seconds. Then he walked back inside to wait for another customer.

■ ■ ■ ■

PART V
THE MEDICINE LINE

■ ■ ■ ■

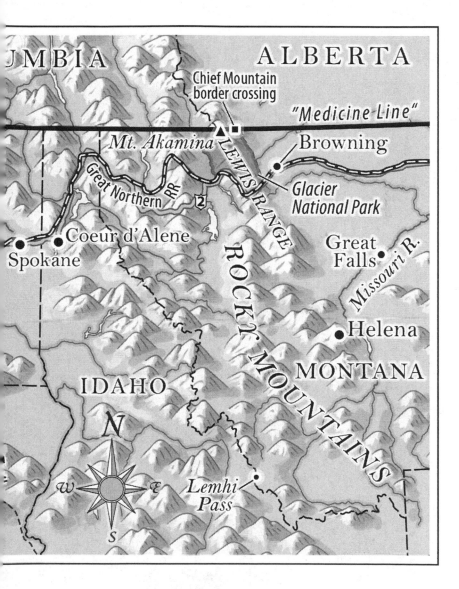

JMBIA

ALBERTA

Chief Mountain
border crossing

"Medicine Line"

Mt. Akamina

Browning

Great Northern RR

2

LEWIS RANGE

Coeur d'Alene

Glacier
National Park

Spokane

Great
Falls

Missouri R.

ROCKY MOUNTAINS

Helena

IDAHO

MONTANA

N

W   E

Lemhi
Pass

S

14

Power lines glided over the road. Ribbons of asphalt, steel, water, soil, and trees ran parallel with the highway, cutting the northland off from the rest of the country. I was on US Route 2, somewhere in eastern Montana. The two-lane "Hi-Line" shadows the northern border twenty-five hundred miles from Maine to Washington, with a break over the Great Lakes.

There were curves at the western end of the northland: river bends, winding train tracks, Swainson's hawks banking low, wide arcs over the road. The earth slanted to the east. Sage flats skirted the road. There were sacred formations south of the highway: the Black Hills, the Bighorn Mountains, the headwaters of the Missouri.

"Montana" is a Spanish name, though Spanish explorers never made it that far. Francisco Vázquez de Coronado crossed the Rockies in 1540 near present-day Santa Fe, but he chose to trek east to Kansas instead of north. Montana license plates call their home Big Sky Country. It was easy to see why. The state is larger than Japan. You can see a good chunk of it from almost any vantage point. Humidity averages in the low sixties. The whipsaw crest of the Rocky Mountains is visible from a hundred miles away. Big Sky Country averages seven people, one pronghorn antelope, one elk, and three deer per square mile. Eighty percent of the counties are still classified as "frontier," meaning they are occupied by six or fewer people per square mile. There are more elk, grizzly bears, loons, and trumpeter swans in the state than anywhere else in the continental US.

The air was so clear that I could see the legs of an antelope five miles away. A stand of whitebark pine three miles beyond that swayed in the breeze. A teenage boy cruised past in a beige 1970s Lincoln Continental. Square head, square shoulders, pale blue eyes. Looking in the mirror, he parted his hair with his left hand while dangling his right hand on top of the vinyl steering wheel. He didn't have to steer; the car steered for him. He didn't look like he was driving at all. It was like something was pulling the road out from under him. Time stopped moving in eastern Montana some-time around 1973.

Montana and "Oregon Country" were some of the last unexplored and unmapped regions on the planet in the early 1800s, along with interior Africa, Australia, and both poles. Oregon Country stretched 250,000 square miles from the Pacific coast to the Continental Divide in western Montana. Thomas Jefferson considered it the last piece of America, that would someday complete an "Empire of Liberty" from sea to sea. It was a pipe dream. America was having a hard time managing the territory it already had. And the Northwest was already claimed by Russia, England, France, Spain, and dozens of Indian nations.

The Northwest was the final stretch of the northland for me as well. I was twenty-five hundred miles from home, fifteen hundred from the Pacific. It was fall again and getting cold. The last miles were not going to be easy. Montana, Idaho, and Washington are home to some of the tallest peaks on the continent, scattered across remote wildernesses, rain forests, alluvial plains, and a matrix of lake and river systems. I would be driving and camping the whole way. The weather forecast predicted a hard frost by the end of the week. I needed to make it to the coast before the first snow.

Low-angle autumn light glanced off buttes alongside Route 2. Barn swallows flitted over hay fields. Dirt driveways in Culbertson and Blair were dry and dusty. Covered porches had been closed up for winter and storm windows installed. The Continental floated ahead of me. The car was an apparition. Wheat and flax fields moved by like they were on a studio set. The land wasn't flat like in North Dakota. Combines ran up and over knolls and ravines, harvesting wheat. Bright-red fire hydrants had been installed every quarter mile in one field, thirty-foot-tall iron sculptures of birds in another.

Sitting Bull made his last stand near here. Shortly after the Battle of the Little Bighorn, he had led what was left of his tribe through Montana's northland. They camped and hunted across the northern plains, outwitting Colonel Nelson Miles and six companies of the US Fifth Infantry Regiment. America wanted blood after Custer's defeat, and Generals Sherman and Sheridan initiated a policy of killing every Indian their troops could find. Mainly they found women and children headed to a reservation to turn themselves in, most of whom were shot or hung.

The winter of 1876 was severe, with fierce wind and temperatures dipping to minus thirty. Miles outfitted his men with buffalo robes, mittens, and face masks cut from wool blankets. Sitting Bull went largely undetected, but freezing temperatures and a lack of game weakened the tribe. They retreated farther north and, the same month that Crazy Horse and nine hundred Sioux tribal members surrendered at Camp Robinson, Sitting Bull crossed into Saskatchewan over what Indians had begun to call the "Medicine Line."

The "strong medicine" of the forty-ninth parallel stopped US forces in their tracks, allowing Indians a measure of peace to the north. American officers wouldn't have thought twice about pursuing an enemy across the US-Canada border twenty years earlier. But cross-border bootlegging skirmishes in the 1860s had alerted Canadians to the porous and dangerous state of their southern boundary. After Britain granted Canada dominion status in 1867, and the line along the forty-ninth was marked in 1873, Canadians and their North-West Mounted Police let it be known that the border was real.

Montana's "Medicine Line" was not the first in America. The Iroquois used the same sobriquet for the French-British boundary in the Seven Years' War. They documented the border on their wampum as a white line between two black ones. Great Lakes tribes used the term as well for the line between British Ontario and the American colonies.

Wallace Stegner wrote about Medicine Line country. He grew up thirty miles north of the Montana border in a small Saskatchewan town called Eastend. Like many northland settlers, Stegner's father was a roamer. The author spent time in an orphanage when he was four, then lived in an abandoned dining car near the Canadian Pacific Railroad in Saskatchewan. The family moved to a shack on the border in the summer, where they farmed wheat. In a memoir of his childhood, *Wolf Willow,* Stegner wrote about the evolution of small towns in the region: "The first settlement in the Cypress Hills country was a village of métis winterers, the second was a short-lived Hudson's Bay Company post on Chimney Coulee, the third was the Mounted Police headquarters at Fort Walsh, the fourth was a Mountie outpost erected on the site of the burned Hudson's Bay Company buildings to keep an eye on Sitting Bull and other Indians who congregated in that country in alarming numbers after the big troubles of the 1870's."

I drove Route 2 past draws, moraines, hollows, arroyos, rift valleys, and mesas in the east near Frazer and Nashua. This is the language of Big Sky Country: laccolith, dike, shonkinite, marine shale. The state is split in two along the Rocky Mountain Front. East is prairie; west is the Northern Rockies. The front is a fifty-million-year-old thrust-and-fold jumble of wetlands, forests, and vertical subranges. The wall of rock is so formidable that it shapes weather across America. Western-flowing air from the Gulf of Mexico hits the front and reflects it back onto the plains, helping to create a vortex of wind and storms across the Great Plains known as Tornado Alley.

The single-engine plane sticking out of the roof of the Hangar Bar in Glasgow, Montana, looked like it had seen some weather. Another plane, a US Air Force T-33 trainer, sat in the front yard of the Valley County Pioneer Museum. There were six casinos, one rodeo arena, one Taco Shack, three car-parts stores, and the Busted Knuckle Brewery downtown. Afternoon light dropped out of the sky on my way through, touching the tips of Sudan grass growing along the soft shoulder.

The sun became a spotlight just before it set, shining through an opening in the clouds and splintering on my bug-splattered windshield. I'd been following the Continental for hours. A barbed wire fence bordered the road most of the way. Rifts and mesas lifted, fell, vanished, then reappeared. The bluffs on the horizon looked bigger than anything I'd seen in a while. I drove past a steak house, a bowling alley, a hundred wide-screen TVs shining through double-paned windows. A pharmacy at the edge of one town was closed, but a string of Christmas lights had been left on.

I passed a grain elevator, and the sky darkened like an eyelid closing. A sliver of sun held out just above the horizon. A silver moon shone through the clouds before the sun went down. It was simultaneously night and day for about seven minutes. A freight train rushed past, and the rumble shook the car windows. The train was a mile long and stacked double high with forty-foot containers. A string of black, cylindrical oil cars took up the rear. The train blasted east, and the eye closed. Then everything was gone: traffic, tracks, Continental, casinos, town. It was thirty-five degrees. Snow tomorrow in the high peaks, the radio announcer said. The last of the light leaked out of the clouds, leaving me at the dark edge of the Rocky Mountains.

It was a Canadian who first traversed the Northwest in 1793. Alexander Mackenzie was a young Scotsman who grew up in New York City and Montréal. He was a fur trader with the North West Company and was working in central Canada. He had been searching for new trapping ground and a Northwest Passage and, after a few false starts, decided that the Peace River, two hundred miles northwest of present-day Edmonton, Alberta, was likely it.

Mackenzie set out from Fort Fork in May in a twenty-five-foot birchbark canoe. A crew of voyageurs and several others joined him. The canoe held three thousand pounds of supplies, gear, and gifts for Indians. Emptied of its cargo, Mackenzie wrote, "two men could carry her on a good road three or four miles without resting." The crew didn't rest much paddling and portaging upstream on the Peace, then up the Parsnip River and overland to the Fraser River. They eventually met a band of Carrier Indians, who saved them from rough water and a dead end, advising Mackenzie to follow West Road River. Mackenzie took their advice and followed a network of Indian trails to six-thousand-foot Mackenzie Pass and the Bella Coola River. Two days downriver from there, he happened upon an Indian village built on stilts. From that vantage point, he said, "I could perceive the termination of the river, and its discharge into a narrow arm of the sea."

The fact that a Canadian logged the first traverse of North America, north of Mexico, infuriated Thomas Jefferson. He immediately accelerated plans to explore and win the Northwest. The exact location of the northwest coast had been discovered only a year before. On May 11, 1792, captain Robert Gray, the first American to circumnavigate the world, sailed into the Columbia River and calculated a longitude of 124 degrees — making Jefferson's "Empire of Liberty" just under three thousand miles wide.

Jefferson's campaign to extend America's northern border to the Pacific got an unexpected boost in January of 1803. That month he sent James Monroe to Paris to meet Robert R. Livingston, US minister to France. (Monroe had to sell his family's silver flatware, porcelain plates, and a china tea set to afford the trip.) Their orders were to purchase the port of New Orleans, where a quarter of America's produce floated south, avoiding taxes and encouraging a separatist movement. Napoleon countered with a stunning offer. He wanted the US to buy all of Louisiana, the same territory La Salle had named.

The French emperor had had visions of restarting New France at one point, but a rebellion against a French colony on Haiti soured his enthusiasm for colonial ventures. That, plus dwindling finances and a desire to check the growing British Empire in North America, pushed him to sell. Monroe and Livingston agreed to buy 828,000 square miles for $15 million, doubling the size of the US.

Seven months before, Jefferson had put in another bid. This one was to Congress for a secret mission to explore the northland through Louisiana and Oregon Country. He wanted a "Corps of Discovery" to see how far west the seemingly endless Missouri River went, find a Northwest Passage, and document the remote northwestern corner of the continent. He entrusted the journey to his secretary, Meriwether Lewis. The two had been neighbors when Lewis was a boy, and they lived like bachelors in the recently finished White House. Jefferson was a widower. Lewis slept next to his boss's extra files, clothes, and furniture in the unfinished

East Room — where Abigail Adams had dried her husband's underwear during the previous term.

Lewis was unqualified for the job but had military experience and the leadership skills needed to guide a group of three dozen men on a seven-thousand-mile journey. Lewis's partner would be William Clark, a veteran of the Northwest Indian War and younger brother of commander George Clark, the highest-ranking American military officer on the northwestern frontier during the American Revolutionary War.

Not knowing where they were going or what they would find made preparation difficult. The northland west of North Dakota was rumored to be another El Dorado. Bits of information gleaned from voyageurs, Indians, and explorers suggested that the territory held endless forests, croplands, gold and silver veins, active volcanoes, prehistoric animals, a mile-long mountain of salt, and a wide plateau from which all the rivers of the West flowed. Some thought that Indians living along the Missouri River descended from the twelve lost tribes of Israel. Others thought the Mandan people in the Northwest were a roaming band of Welshmen.

Lewis's shopping list was eclectic: two

hundred pounds of "portable" (dried) soup, fishhooks, guns, black powder, chronometer, dried tobacco, shirts, lead canisters, ink powder, crayons, pencils, flannel, mosquito netting, oilskin bags, salt, needles, flint, and a collapsible iron boat that he designed. Jefferson gave Lewis a starter course with a sextant on the White House lawn, then sent him to Lancaster to continue studying with the preeminent astronomer in America, Andrew Ellicott. Lewis continued his studies in Philadelphia with Dr. Benjamin Rush, the leading physician in the nation — and signer of the Declaration of Independence — where he learned how to preserve and document specimens.

The expedition left Wood River, north of Saint Louis, at four in the afternoon on May 14, 1804. Most of the journey would be on the Missouri, upstream against a five-mile-per-hour current. It took twenty men, rowing full tilt, to make headway against the flow. Several lightweight pirogues rowed alongside, sounding and scouting. The Missouri runs through present-day Omaha, Nebraska, the Dakotas, and western Montana. By late fall the group had made it to a site just north of present-day Bismarck, North Dakota, where they built Fort Mandan to winter in. They met the Shoshone woman Sacajawea there, through her husband, the French Canadian trader Toussaint Charbonneau. Both were hired as interpreters, and they guided the corps over the Continental Divide at Lemhi Pass the next spring. From there the group paddled the Clearwater, Snake, and Columbia Rivers. Using Mount Hood as a landmark, they reached the Pacific in November of 1805. After a cold and hungry winter on the north shore of the Columbia, they returned to the Missouri, arriving in Saint Louis again on September 3, 1806.

The expedition lost just one man in the two and a half years it was in the field. Lewis made 140 maps of the region and documented over two hundred unrecorded plant and animal species. It would be another fifty years before someone created a comprehensive map of Oregon Country, during which time the British occupied it. In 1818, British and American authorities came up with a plan to coexist in the region. It lasted until 1846, when Jefferson's dream came true. America's northern border was drawn along the forty-ninth parallel from the Rocky Mountains to the Pacific.

Meltwater flooded a nearby stream. The air smelled like sagebrush, horse manure, and pine. It was fifty degrees, and last night's snow in the peaks was already disappearing. This was the West that you saw in movies: log cabins, buck and rail fences, wooden sidewalks, deep-blue rivers, and intersecting mountain ranges. Cumulonimbus clouds hung in the high-pressure desert air. Wind was out of the south at five miles an hour.

Lewis and Clark came through here. Three Forks, Montana, is a few miles from the Missouri headwaters that Jefferson sent them to find. Lewis spent several days exploring the region, remarking that it was an "essential" point of geography on the continent: "The country opens suddonly to extensive and beatifull plains and meadows which appear to be surrounded in every direction with distant and lofty mountains."

I wanted to cross the Rockies like Lewis and Clark had, but not here. I wanted to see where the forty-ninth passed over the mountains a few hours north in Glacier National Park. I followed the Missouri out of Three Forks, past buckwheat fields and side-roll sprinklers to Helena. Sheds, barns, and garages clad with vertical pine planking were stained auburn by sap and the sun. Elk and deer antlers hung over doorways. A few thousand feet higher, auburn scree tumbled toward the road from rocky summits.

Birch leaves were dry and pale. Woolly buckthorn and red mulberry bushes were still green, but the sunlight was weak. Fields lifted into foothills, which folded into the ten-thousand-foot peaks of the Lewis Range. Central-pivot irrigation systems made bull's-eyes in every other field. The temperature had been ninety-six degrees in Bozeman the day before. At two in the afternoon, when I drove through Choteau, it was forty-five. A few miles north, in Browning, Montana, a world-record temperature drop had occurred in January 1916: the thermometer fell from forty-four degrees to minus fifty-six in twenty-four hours.

I followed Highway 89 through Browning and the Blackfeet Indian Reservation. It looked like the tribe was stocking up for winter at the Exxon station. A dozen tribal members stood around the pizza display. Another dozen chatted by the gas pumps. The Blackfeet have lived in the northland for more than ten thousand years. Four bands of the tribe — North and South Piegan, Blood, and Siksika — were hunting in the northern plains when Europeans arrived. Isolation protected them then. Now, it cuts off nine thousand Blackfeet on the reservation from basic social services.

Browning has served as the eastern gateway to Glacier National Park since 1910. The town stands in stark contrast to the surrounding wilderness that two million, mostly white, people visit every year. A family driving a brand-new SUV stacked with bikes, tents, and canoes cruised past a destitute neighborhood while I was pulled over at a convenience store. Two children in the back seat watched iPads as they drove by two Blackfeet children on the sidewalk who were pushing a baby in a stroller. The Blackfeet were invisible to the white children. Psychologists describe the phenomenon as an extreme form of color blindness. The "invisibleness" of Indians to most Americans comes from the fact that most social representations of Indians today are historical ones. To the average American, Indians are a thing of the past.

It was getting late, and the forty-ninth was another forty miles north. I stopped at the Saint Mary Ranger Station to find a campsite, but the ranger there told me that all three thousand sites in the park were full. I did a U-turn and headed to the Chewing Blackbones campground on the reservation instead. The man who met me at the front desk said the campground was named for a famous Blackfeet warrior, and that his family line descends from one of the original Blackfeet chiefs who settled on the reservation. He asked where I'd driven from, and I told him Standing Rock. "I worked for Keystone," he said. "I interviewed tribes between the Canadian border and Nebraska and mapped sacred sites. Then I advised them where to build the pipeline . . . I couldn't tell people what I did."

I asked him how he felt about the protests at Standing Rock, and he said he wished the Sioux tribes well. "But you got to understand that some people need some things and other people need other things," he added. "Everybody's fighting for what they think is right, but whatever you think is right usually turns out being wrong, and whatever you think is wrong somehow ends up getting through anyway. You can't fight the people in Washington. You can't fight the money."

I asked him how things on the reservation were. "Terrible," he said. "The schools are terrible. They've got meth, and I know they've got pills. The doctors give out pills to anyone. Kids are dying in car wrecks. Doctors give pills to the survivors. They don't understand, we are addictive people.

There's eighty percent unemployment here. A hundred miles away it's at three percent. But you can't tell people to stop doing something they don't want to stop doing. Every now and then you'll get someone who stands up and does the right thing. There were a couple people in our family who did that. We were lucky. Our family got out. You see someone straighten out and things start to work out for them, and you think maybe I might do that. The next thing you know it passes around. We're almost all out of it now. I haven't had a drink or done anything in twenty-five years."

Saint Mary's Lake, where the campground is situated, is mentioned in a Blackfeet creation story. The man at the front desk told me he still "holds ceremony" there twice a year. "I'll be doing one this fall," he said. I paid him seventeen dollars for a bundle of firewood and a campsite and drove to the lake to set up my tent. Seven teepees in a wide meadow bordered the water. A few families camped nearby. A group of college-aged kids had set up by the teepees and were barbecuing off the trunk of their car.

The sky was clear, and the blocky summits of the Lewis Range were reflected in the lake. The 160-mile-long range forms the northernmost leg of America's Continental Divide. Ten summits crest ten thousand feet. Triple Divide Peak sits in the middle and is one of two "hydrological apexes" of North America, marking the intersection of the Continental and Laurentian Divides. Water on southwestern slopes makes its way to the Columbia River and the Pacific Ocean. Drops hitting the southeastern side just inches away flow to the Gulf of Mexico, and those to the north end up in Hudson Bay.

The ten-million-acre "Crown of the Continent ecosystem" surrounds the mountains. The region has gone virtually untouched since Lewis and Clark first documented it on their return trip to Saint Louis. It is the largest intact wilderness in America, with more than a thousand native plants and threatened species, like the Canadian lynx, cougar, grizzly bear, and gray wolf. It also holds some of the last glaciers in the northland, though many are now melting out.

There are 25 glaciers in the park. There used to be 150. The number of glaciers shrank by more than a third between 1966 and 2015. One of the country's oldest climate change research facilities is based in the park. Glaciologists there forecast that the glaciers will be gone by the end of the century.

The temperature dropped quickly that night. A three-quarter moon lit the sage and crushed mullein stalks in the field. The Blackfeet still weave the red osiers growing around the lake into baskets. I could see my breath through my headlamp's light. There wasn't another sound. I thought that old Chewing Blackbones would have liked a moment like this — a peaceful night with loons calling on the lake and winter still a few weeks off.

The *Spirit of the West* announcer told stories on the radio the next morning about how Wilf Carter was a ranch hand before he became "Montana Slim" and how the death of Kit Carson's father had shaped the young western hero. The weather report at 7:00 a.m.: "The snow line dropped last night to six thousand feet in the Golden Triangle. Chance of rain today: one hundred percent."

The hills behind Saint Mary's Lake were white. The peaks were shrouded in fog. The park was gone, completely socked in. A family camping next to me huddled around a fire. Three of the college kids were passed out in their car. Winter comes in the middle of September in northwestern Montana.

I packed up the tent before the real rain started and drove north to find the border. Black and brown cattle led their calves down the middle of Route 17. The valleys around Chief Mountain were mostly hardwood, and the leaves were starting to turn. It looked like Vermont for a moment, with perfectly straight, hundred-foot lodgepole pines every few yards.

The highway dropped down to the Chief Mountain border crossing. The 1939 station was built in National Park Service rustic style — stone chimneys, cedar shingles, stone foundation, aluminum lap siding. A shingled porte cochere reached out over the road where two officers checked in a line of cars. Orange barricades and traffic cones blocked the highway. I pulled into a small parking lot near the head of the Belly River Trail, put on a rain jacket, and followed a path into the woods.

I was hoping the trail would parallel the border, so that I could get a look at it. There were no signs indicating whether you were allowed to wander off the trail. There were a half dozen that reminded hikers how likely it was they would be eaten by one of the three hundred grizzly bears living in the park. If you saw a bear, the signs said to stand tall, act casual, and not run — kind of like when you see a friend in a crowd. If the bear charged, you should hold your ground, as it was likely a bluff. A bear charges at about forty miles per hour, which means that at two hundred feet, you have two and a half seconds to decide whether the bear is faking. If a bear ever sneaks up behind you, the signs said, you are to assume it is a man-killer. At that point you should run faster than the bear and fight it with whatever weapons you have, "including fingernails and teeth."

I felt like a bear was following me the rest of the hike to the Belly River. The Crown of the Continent ecosystem bloomed alongside the trail. Pines were spaced almost exactly fifteen feet from each other, as if they had been planted. Stunted mountain ash and maple grew beneath the conifer canopy. Three of North America's largest river systems start in the crown: the Saskatchewan, Missouri and Columbia. There were natural borders here as well. Four floristic regions — the Cordilleran, Boreal, Arctic-Alpine, and Great Plains — meet at the crown, and many of the thirteen hundred plant species in the area exist at the edge of their latitudinal range.

Four hikers approached and told me it was extremely muddy a mile ahead. They carried massive packs and had muck caked up to their knees. They'd been on the trail for a week. I asked if they'd seen a bear. They laughed and said no. Then I asked if it was possible to bushwhack from the trail to the border.

"Why?" one of them asked.

"I want to see it," I said.

They glanced at each other, paused, then walked away. I kept hiking and a mile later hit the mud. It was indeed deep, nearly impassable. The GPS on my phone said I was nowhere near the border, so I turned around and decided to use the traditional route instead.

A middle-aged woman wearing a US customs officer uniform greeted me an hour later at the Chief Mountain Border Crossing. The border patrol agent standing next to her had a brownish coif and blue eyes. He kept his hand on the butt of his gun the entire time we spoke. His uniform was army green, and he seemed anxious. Whenever I said something, he opened his eyes wide and leaned toward me as if he was hard of hearing — or was not used to civilians walking up to his station and asking a bunch of questions about the border.

"Can I walk to the border?" I asked.

"What?" the agent asked, leaning in.

"The cut," the woman said. "He wants to see the cut."

The agent shrugged, and the customs officer said I could go if I showed her my passport when I came back. I walked down the road past a sign that said "Welcome to the United States" and continued toward the Canadian border station three hundred yards away. Halfway there, the forest opened up, and a twenty-foot clear-cut running along the forty-ninth parallel met the road.

It was a massive slash, the first visible representation of the US-Canada boundary I'd seen on the whole trip. It was perfectly straight and dropped down the flanks of Chief Mountain to the Belly River. The US-Canadian International Boundary Commission is tasked with keeping the cut clear and walks the line every five to ten years. Crews of ten pack up chainsaws, camping gear, and surveying tools and walk 1,349 forested miles of the northern border, including Alaska, trimming trees and shrubs and repairing monuments.

It was bizarre to see a boundary on a map transposed into a real line on the earth. It looked ornamental, like an environmental art piece. Juniper and cottonwood saplings growing on the floor of the cut colored it light green. Western hemlock and red cedar trunks along the edges were dark brown. The line launched up the opposite side of the valley, then disappeared into a scree field on eight-thousand-foot Mount Boswell, the final obstacle that the Northern Boundary Commission had to navigate in 1874 before reaching the Continental Divide.

The US commissioner, Archibald Campbell, gathered his American survey crew at Fort Buford in June of 1874 to prepare to mark the final section of the forty-ninth parallel. They had made it more than halfway to the divide the previous fall, after marking the Northwest Angle, and had about four hundred miles to go. The Americans spent a week riding an overloaded steamer — crammed with the commission's 140 horses and mules, 38 wagons, and 270 tons of supplies — four hundred miles up the Missouri from Bismarck. Marcus Reno and his troops met them at Fort Buford, and the assemblage marched north to meet the British and Canadians on the line later that month.

Both groups divided into smaller parties to reconnoiter, measure, and mark the border with iron monuments and earthen mounds. They moved quickly across the northern plains and arrived at the thick forests of the Lewis Range in September. Crews dumped the last of their supplies at a depot set at the foot of the mountains and began the arduous job of cutting the boundary across the first few ripples of the Rocky Mountain Front. The forty-ninth passes six miles north of Chief Mountain. It took axe men ten days to cut a slash down to the Belly River and back up Mount Boswell. On the other side of Boswell, the commission continued to Waterton Lake, then cut the last stretch to Mount Akamina and a pyramid of limestone rocks that the North*west* Boundary Commission — the commission that marked the line from the Pacific to the Divide — had left in 1862. The limestone cairn was the terminal monument connecting the longest straight border in the world.

The customs officer was waiting for me when I returned to the station. The bright lights, yellow pilings, and security cameras at the crossing were a stark contrast to the old post-and-beam structure next to it. The building was a reminder of a different time, when the world's friendliest border was just that: a line of monuments and cuts through the woods that no one paid any mind.

I handed my passport to the officer and

asked if it was possible to hike along the line.

"No one does that," she said.

"Is it illegal?"

"You're gonna want to tell the patrol before you do something like that," she said.

15

I drove south toward Highway 2 that afternoon. The storm was getting worse, and I could barely see the road. I hooked a right in Browning and headed into the park. Heavy wind knocked the car around, and freezing rain iced the windshield. Snow had already closed the park's famous Going-to-the-Sun Road — a fifty-mile scenic highway that crests the Continental Divide at 6,646-foot Logan Pass — and roadside signs warned of icy conditions ahead.

I pulled into the Glacier Park Lodge ten minutes later. Fifty-foot cedar timbers framed the entryway. Two 1930s White Motor Company buses waited for guests. James Hill's Great Northern Railway opened the hotel in 1913, across the street from its East Glacier Park station. The Great Northern was the last of the transcontinental railroads built in the 1800s. It started in Minneapolis and zigzagged along the northern border over eight thousand miles of track, ending with a spur in Seattle and one in Portland. It was the northernmost route in the US and delivered millions of emigrants to the Great American Desert, shaping nearly every northland county between Minnesota and the Pacific.

The Glacier Park Lodge lobby hadn't changed much since it was originally built. A stack of four-foot logs blazed in the fireplace. Forty-foot Douglas firs, forty inches around with the bark still on, held up rafters above. Log banisters and railings wrapped around the second and third floor. I asked a young woman at the registration desk if it was all right to take pictures. She looked at my drenched raincoat and said, "There's a special on rooms tonight." A half hour later, I hauled my soggy gear into a hundred-year-old corner room and draped my tent over an upholstered chair to dry.

The man who settled the last stretch of the northland didn't grow up in the white-gloved world of J. P. Morgan, Pierre Samuel du Pont, or John Jacob Astor III. James Hill was raised in a log cabin in Upper Canada's Eramosa Township. His father was a journeyman farmer who died when Hill was fourteen. Hill attended middle school and was tutored in math and English by a local reverend. The reverend noticed that his student was an avid reader and excelled in algebra and geometry. Hill was ambitious and independent from a young age and took on extra reading and schoolwork. When he was seventeen, he set out to travel the world. His first destination: the Orient. He got as far as Saint Paul, Minnesota.

Saint Paul was the northern terminus for more than a thousand steamboats a year coming up the Mississippi in the 1850s. From there, settlers typically headed to northland outposts in Minnesota or Dakota Territory. Hill took a job as a bookkeeper for a steamboat company shortly after he arrived in 1856, then worked for a wholesale grocer. He learned how freight moved, how to cut corners, and how to profit in the transit business. When the railroad came to Saint Paul, he built a warehouse and ferry pier to make transitioning goods between the two easier. The business did well, and he invested profits in the coal trade. When he was thirty-two years old, he started his own steamboat line with a partner — delivering settlers to Winnipeg country and bringing wheat back.

When the Saint Paul and Pacific Railroad went into receivership following the Panic of 1873, Hill bought it with a partner and extended the line to the US-Canada border — where it met the Canadian Winnipeg train. In 1879, the renamed Saint Paul, Minneapolis, and Manitoba Railway Company was valued at $728,000. Five years later, with Hill at the helm, it was worth $25 million.

In his memoir, *Highways of Progress,* Hill writes: "Nations, like men, are travellers. Each one of them moves, through history, toward what we call progress and a new life or toward decay and death." Hill was not one to understate. He was a towering, thickset man with a bushy white beard. On a reconnaissance trip for his steamboat company, he rode a dogsled to the Red River and set his guide's dislocated shoulder on the way home. He scouted potential train routes on horseback, inspecting the terrain and grade. If a locomotive was stuck in the snow, he got out of his private car and shoveled. After service began on a line, he would buy a ticket and ride the train undercover in a fifteen-dollar suit to inspect his employees and equipment.

The transcontinental-railroad boom was long over when Hill decided to build the Great Northern. The Panic of 1873, caused mainly by overbuilding of railroads, had bankrupted more than a hundred US rail lines, including the Northern Pacific. Hill had made a hobby of flipping bankrupt businesses throughout his career, and he had a reputation for making money where others could not. He founded the Great Northern Railway in 1889 and completed the line to Seattle four years later. The railroad was the only transcontinental built without government subsidies.

The first passengers boarded the train in June 1893. Selling tickets and hauling cargo was only half of the railroad business. Transcontinental lines in the West built entire civilizations around their tracks to keep the railroad profitable. If a section of the route was unpopulated, they bought a company and relocated its plants alongside the tracks. If workers or homesteaders needed a center from which to conduct their businesses, they built a town, sent out marketing literature, and hired agents to populate it.

Railroad companies found millions of willing settlers in Europe, Scandinavia, and Russia. They offered credit to buyers, free passage across the Atlantic, and land for two to eight dollars an acre. "Buyer expeditions" left American port cities for elaborate reception houses on the plains. Railroads maintained agencies in London, Liverpool, Germany, Holland, and Scandinavia. The Northern Pacific created its own Bureau of Immigration. Buyers could land on the East Coast, transfer directly to a train that would take them to their homestead, and be processed as US citizens along the way.

Much of the marketing literature was fiction. Holland immigrants in 1892 were told that the climate around a new colony in Alamosa, Colorado, was "Mediterranean." During their first arctic winter, many died of diphtheria and scarlet fever in dilapidated barracks. The Northern Pacific, on the verge of bankruptcy, told customers: "Every disease in the U.S. West has been cured." The Union Pacific described the parched Platte Valley as a "flowery meadow of great fertility clothed in nutritious grasses and watered by numerous streams." Brochures pointed to the financial success of farmers like Oliver Dalrymple in North Dakota, claiming that all it took was a plow and some hard work to get going.

Twenty years after the last spike was pounded in the Great Northern line, the land around it represented some of the last open territory in the West. Hill needed farmers to populate it, but he needed them to grow agricultural commodities — things he could then transport to metropolitan markets. Companies like the Dutch house Prins & Zwanenburg executed his vision, creating entire towns across the northland. The towns Friesland and Groningen, north of Minneapolis, offered prebuilt farmsteads, including a house, barn, and stable on forty acres of land. German investors from the Ruhr Valley bought in, and developers built grain elevators and hotels along the tracks, then sold off parcels around them.

Hill's agents curried favor with newspaper editors in Sweden, Norway, and the Netherlands by buying full-page ads promoting homesteads. They donated money to churches across Europe and kept close ties with the clergy, who put in a good word for them regarding the integrity and goodwill of the Great Northern Railway. Great Northern brochures stated that "chinook winds" made winters temperate in Montana, that "heat prostrations" were unknown. They claimed that Montana farmers were so prosperous that they all carried checkbooks.

The US government, which was heavily invested in the railroads, doubled the size of homestead grants to 320 acres in 1909. Homestead entries in Montana grew from five million in 1909 to thirty-five million in

1919. The Great Northern hauled a thousand emigrant cars west in the first three months of 1910. In one month, the railroad's land office in Havre, Montana, recorded sixteen hundred entries taking possession of half a million acres of land. After the new owners arrived at the station, a locator would find them and take them to their plot. Some turned around and caught the first train east. Others broke down in tears.

Much of the farmland that Hill was trying to sell along his tracks was located west of the one-hundredth meridian, in the heart of the Great American Desert. Global weather patterns were no match for his vision. He built a laboratory in Saint Paul to examine soil along the railroad and study ways to make it more fertile. He dispatched special "seed improvement" trains to inform farmers about new technology, and he embraced the dry-farming movement of the early 1900s. The sometimes dubious science behind the campaign claimed that techniques like subsoil packing and deep plowing allowed seeds to grow anywhere, without water. The Great Northern, the Northern Pacific, and the Montana State Board of Agriculture, as well as anyone with a stake in western real estate, got on board. The

Dry Farming Congress pulled huge crowds throughout the West — and even larger grants for "scientific research." Promoters, scientists, and US Geological Survey officials added another lucrative theory: "Rain follows the plow." The concept: steam engines, plowing, and human activity induced precipitation. The Santa Fe railroad advertised its own rain line, a fictitious meridian that progressed west at eighteen miles a year, just in front of new construction.

Hill proselytized on irrigation, summer fallowing, strip farming, and the virtues of homesteading from the caboose of his train as he rolled through northland settlements like Saint Cloud, Fargo, Grand Forks, Billings, Helena, Portland, and Seattle. He awarded prizes to the most productive farms in the region and set up display cases of golden northland-grown wheat. He hired an agricultural expert to manage forty-five experimental farms along the line — and figure out a way to make something sprout. His sermons caught on, and the northland grew behind him, earning Hill a new nickname: the Empire Builder.

A guided tour leaves the Glacier Park Lodge lobby every day at 5:00 p.m. I joined a group of elderly tourists and listened to a young guide dressed in railroad overalls. He told us that James Hill's son Louis W. Hill designed the lodge — and a chain of interconnected alpine hotels in the park. Louis Hill built the lodges between 1910 and 1915 to compete with "healing chalets" in the Alps and marketed them to wealthy easterners. Guests could hike or take a car between each lodge, spending weeks touring the grand peaks of the Northern Rockies.

The tour shuffled around the ground floor as the guide told stories about the Hills, the Blackfeet, and the many antiques in the lodge. James Hill wanted buffalo skulls to hang in the lobby. Because there were no more buffalo in the West, he hired archaeologists to recover skulls from the site of a Blackfeet buffalo jump. Plaster replicas were illuminated from behind at night. Louis added Japanese lanterns as well — a bid to attract the growing Japanese travel class.

The tour group itself was a thing of antiquity. I was the only one under the age of eighty. The comb-over on the man beside me was a work of art. It looked like eagle feathers were woven into it. A man on the opposite side of the crowd had his eyes closed for 90 percent of the tour. Most of the trivia that the guide shared was met with blank stares. Hill had hired Blackfeet families to pitch teepees in the hotel's front yard and wear traditional dress. The Blackfeet wanted ninety dollars an acre for the land when Hill first approached them. Hill refused. He then had Congress pressure the tribe into selling their land for thirty dollars an acre. The price was so good that Hill bought an extra thousand acres for a golf course.

The guide announced that he had a special treat for the end of the tour. We followed him into a side room where luggage was stored. "You can't usually get in here," he said, pushing a few bags to the side. Six large-format, black-and-white photographs, shot by Roland Reed in the late 1800s, hung from the walls. They were stunning pictures of the Blackfeet and the mountains they once lived in. Reed had staged most of his photographs, the guide said, but these were realistic scenes. Behind the riders, massive white glaciers clung to the mountains. There were no roads, buildings, or red buses. Before whites arrived, Blackfeet Indians harvested lodgepole pines, furs, and berries from the Lewis Range in the summer, before heading back to the plains to hunt buffalo.

"If I could have anything in this lodge," the guide said, "I would take this one photograph." The image was of two Blackfeet riders on a grassy knoll. Behind them were a forest and a few high peaks. Their hair was braided. The one in the front wore deerskins; the one behind wore blankets. Mist covered a valley at the foot of the mountains. There was no sun — just a dark line between earth and sky.

Amid the cedars, buffalo skulls, and antique china, the photo was indeed the only object in the lodge of extraordinary value. It was a split second in time from a lost world. "I like showing people this last," the guide said. "I like them to know that we weren't the first people to live here."

The storm let up the next morning. I followed the Great Northern tracks west out of the mountains and across the Idaho border. A black wall of clouds hung over the peaks behind me. The front broke apart twenty miles down the road, and I saw the sun for the first time in three days. Striations of cloud, precipitation, and wind swirled in the foothills. There were clouds within clouds — puffy cumulonimbus up high, lenticulars capping the high peaks — and rain streaking to the prairie.

Hill's train, now called the Empire Builder, steamed east on the opposite side of the valley as I turned south toward Coeur d'Alene. Idaho's northland sits like a bookmark between Washington and Montana. It is a no-man's-land between the West and the Pacific Northwest. Many northlanders there stand alone as well. I followed the Kootenay River past Ruby Ridge — where white supremacist Randy Weaver was shot by US Marshals and the FBI in 1992. In Coeur d'Alene, a man dressed like Uncle Sam waved a flag at an intersection that read: "Do you know your constitution?" Twenty miles south, in Benewah County, separatists had recently advertised a "fortress" housing community called the Citadel. Requirements for members included keeping an AR-15 rifle and a thousand rounds of ammo nearby at all times, maintaining provisions for at least a year, and being able to shoot targets at twenty yards with a handgun.

I met a leader of one of Idaho's many militia groups in Coeur d'Alene. Jeff Stankiewicz cofounded the Idaho Light Foot Militia in 2009. Light Foot battalions — there are eight across the state — call themselves a "constitutional militia." They recognize their right to exist under the

Second Amendment, which reads: "A well regulated Militia, being necessary to the security of a free State, the right of the people to keep and bear Arms, shall not be infringed."

The line has been interpreted in many ways. To Jeff it represents an obligation to gather regularly in a field, wear a camouflage uniform, carry various "tactical" items, set up communication and medical tents, and shoot thousands of bullets at paper targets. "We are not a political organization, and we are not a private organization," he said. "We exist mainly because the state legislature isn't doing what they are supposed to be doing. The legislature is supposed to be arming, equipping, and disciplining the militia, and they don't. The only part of the militia that they do is the National Guard. And they're all in Iraq or Afghanistan."

Jeff waited for me outside the fabrication company he manages. He is not the kind of muscled militia leader you see in the movies or on the internet. He is average height and a bit portly, with dark-brown hair swept back from his forehead and a thick mustache. He wore a red button-down shirt and blue jeans with an elastic waist the day we met. He gave me the kind of cheery welcome you'd expect from a car salesman, then led me to his office.

Jeff grew up in Connecticut and moved to Idaho in the 1990s. He migrated to the northland for the same reasons many did — freedom, space, nature, isolation. "I wanted to get away, to be more independent," he said. "I wanted to rely more on myself for things." He was walking the aisles of a gun show in Boise when a man sitting at a booth handed him a pocket copy of the Constitution. The booth was run by the John Birch Society, a far-right, anticommunist advocacy group formed in the 1950s. Jeff bought a copy of *New American* magazine that the man was selling and over the next few months changed his worldview.

"Look at the ten planks of the communist manifesto and then look at our government," he said. "The Constitution? We don't follow that at all. The confines on their power are not there. Almost everything was supposed to be left to the states. Start reading the Federalist Papers and Anti-Federalist Papers, then start to figure out where the founders came from and why they wanted the government this way."

Most militia in Idaho's northland are "secret squirrel groups," Jeff said, that meet in basements and spend their time collecting and firing guns. "They typically start with one person who declares himself a general, then tells others that they will be his men," Jeff said. "In Montana, some groups use a cell structure, where only one person in each cell knows the contact information of another."

Six jars of preserved cucumbers and carrots sat on a shelf behind Jeff's desk. He keeps a pump bottle of hand sanitizer next to his keyboard and a three-by-four-foot target of a mustachioed man holding a revolver on the back of his office door. There were ten bullet holes between the man's navel and forehead. "I did that reaction-shooting at the range," he said. "Where you don't aim, you just go."

Jeff's cheeks get red when he gets excited, and he gets excited when he talks about training. He is not a prepper, because part of being in the militia means you have to leave home during an emergency. He does stock up on canned food at the grocery store when it's on sale and stores fifty-five-gallon barrels of wheat that he buys from a Bonners Ferry farmer. He keeps an AK-47, several pistols, and an 8-millimeter Mauser rifle with plenty of ammo on hand. In training sessions, his battalion practices map reading, land navigation, first aid, battle tactics, discerning fields of fire, hand signals, field marches, noise and light discipline, patrolling, directing traffic, and "halts." At a recent training event, members learned how to suture using pig's feet and how to insert an IV by sticking each other with expired IVs donated by a local EMS unit. A few months before, the Light Foots had been called up in Sandpoint. They wore blaze-orange vests over their camo and managed traffic for a five-kilometer run. "Someone calls the Sheriff every now and then and says there are thirty guys marching down the road in camo," he said. "It's funny because our rally point if comms go down is the sheriff's office."

Squirrel groups talk about taking down the government, Jeff said. The Light Foots' mission is to be ready to help. Scenarios in which the militia might be called on include a meltdown of the US economy and ensuing chaos, invasion by foreign entities, natural disasters, and search-and-rescue missions. Operations that the Light Foots will not undertake are listed on the group's website: "We will NOT obey orders to blockade American cities, thus turning them into giant concentration camps."

Jeff walked me outside after the interview. The skies over Coeur d'Alene were deep blue. I said winter would be here soon, and he told me about a training mission nearby where he and his battalion had slept on a mountain peak in two feet of snow. It was fourteen degrees, and a canteen he kept inside his sleeping bag froze solid. In the morning they successfully neutralized their target, which was a pile of crates and cardboard boxes.

Something changed that afternoon. The landscape flattened. It looked like the northern plains, except there were mountains in the distance. The peaks on the Washington border weren't tall like those in Montana; they were low and forested like those in Maine. Five hundred miles from the Pacific, the landscapes of the northland were getting mixed up in my head.

Some light pushed through the clouds, and shadows ran across Spokane Valley. Two hours later a silhouette of the final obstacle between me and the ocean lifted off the horizon. The Cascade Mountains run north–south across Washington, from the Columbia River in the south to the US-Canada border in the north. The range makes up the northern backbone of the American Cordillera, a twelve-thousand-mile chain of peaks stretching from Chile to Alaska. The mountains were not an obstacle to Washington's early settlers. The last miles of the Oregon Trail passed through the Columbia River Gorge to the fertile, well-watered western slope of the Cascades. The first whites to follow Lewis and Clark were "Nor'wester" explorers, trappers, and businessmen. Protestant missionaries followed and sent out a call to their followers to join them. Around 1850, the first flood of homesteaders arrived on the Oregon Trail. One was George Washington Bush, one of the few multiracial pioneers of the era. Bush and five white families traveling with him had planned to settle in Oregon. After the provisional government there passed a discriminatory law forbidding blacks from owning land, they continued north to Washington.

Bush's father was born in India and was of African descent. His mother was an Irish maid who worked with Bush's father at the home of a wealthy Philadelphian named Stevenson. Stevenson left his fortune to the Bushes when he died, and they left it to their son when they passed. George Bush moved to Illinois in 1799 to start a cattle-ranching business, then moved the business to Missouri. He fought in the Battle of New Orleans for Andrew Jackson during the War of 1812. After the war, he trekked into the northland to try his hand as a voyageur with the Hudson's Bay Company.

At age fifty, Bush married a white woman in Missouri, despite antimiscegenation laws. The Bushes had five sons and brought them all on the trip to the Northwest. Bush had always been generous with his wealth and fronted the money for six wagons to make the two-thousand-mile journey. Rumor has it he built a false bottom into his and carried $2,000 in silver with him.

The family settled on Puget Sound near Tumwater, on a homestead they called Bush Prairie. They operated a free boardinghouse there and were influential in creating America's land claims north of the Columbia River. The British had a strong foothold in Oregon Country when American settlers began arriving. Overlapping land claims and hostilities between the two nations led to the Treaty of 1818, which mandated cohabitation of the region. The plan was unpopular from the start, and in 1844 James Polk was elected president on a promise to pursue manifest destiny and revoke the agreement.

When Britain refused an offer to draw the border along the forty-ninth parallel, Polk pursued a northern border of fifty-four degrees and forty minutes, near Alaska's current southern border. The boundary would have given America two-thirds of the continent and incited the rallying cry "Fifty-Four, Forty or Fight!" across America. Then war erupted with Mexico along the southern border, and Polk and Congress quietly walked their proposal back to the forty-ninth, again. The British agreed, and the official border was decided on in the 1846 Oregon Treaty.

It was forty-eight degrees and raining when I headed into the North Cascades to see the final leg of the northern border. Two women driving a Chevy Suburban stopped me as I turned off the Mount Baker Highway onto Forest Service Road 3065.

"Where you headed?" they asked.

"Twin Lakes," I said.

"Rain rutted out the road," she said. "We got high-sided and almost couldn't get out."

"How far up?"

"They're four feet deep," she said. "Your car will disappear."

The woman was right. My little sedan disappeared in the first gully. Luckily, the wheelbase was so short that the car scooted out the other side without getting stuck. I drove around the edge of the next ravine, then floored it through the third, bouncing up the other side. The dirt road worsened from there. Water rushed through the trenches so fast that I could feel it pushing the front tires. The grade turned vertical. I teetered along a five-hundred-foot cliff for the last half hour. Then the road flattened, and I coasted into the Twin Lakes campground in the half-light of dusk.

There was one campsite left on the shore of upper Twin Lake. I set up my tent in the dark, cooked a quick meal, then read by lamplight until I fell asleep. Six hours later, songbirds announced the second-to-last day of my journey.

Dawn put pieces of the sky back together. Clouds hugged the Nooksack River valley, and a few lingering stars were reflected in the Twin Lakes. Goat Mountain was a black cone. I could see the Skagit and Picket Ranges from my campsite. To the south was Mount Sefrit and the glaciers of Mount Shuksan. The mother of them all, Mount Baker, looked like an ice cream scoop dropped on the thick forests of northwestern Washington.

The sound of falling water was constant. There was a surprising amount of snow in the peaks for the middle of September. Dirty white streaks of it were tucked into north-facing couloirs and crags. The first light came from the west, not the east. Thick bands of blue and pink wrapped around the horizon. A few summits poked through the puffy ceiling below. The campsite was set at five thousand feet, but it felt like three times that.

I packed a few books, the cookstove, and a couple cans of food into my knapsack and headed out on the trail. It was just light enough to see bear grass and ladies' tresses growing between the trees. The sun crested the peaks, and yellow light painted the fields auburn and green. I was hoping to stay in a fire lookout that night on Winchester Mountain. I had read about fire lookouts in the North Cascades for years, specifically in John Suiter's book *Poets on the Peaks,* which documents Gary Snyder's, Phillip Whalen's, and Jack Kerouac's time as Forest Service lookouts in the Cascades. They spent months alone in the huts, practiced Buddhism there, and wrote some of their best work.

Private clubs have since restored many of the lookouts and rent them out. Guests can stay at the Winchester Lookout on a first-come, first-served basis, so I hiked quickly. Forty-five minutes in, I crossed the tree line on a loose gravel path. Bristle bladder ferns grew in the talus. The pitch was incredibly steep. The trail hugged a drop-off so sheer that I would fall a thousand feet if I lost my footing.

I was wearing running shoes and slipped a few times. The trail wrapped around a ledge and up the backside of Winchester. Then it passed through a few boulders to the summit. I scrambled on all fours the last fifty feet and made it to the top.

Out of nowhere, the lookout appeared on the highest point of the peak. Twenty paned windows — five to a side — wrapped around the square hut. A half-dozen wooden struts held up planked wooden shutters. A haze hung over five long ridgelines leading to Bellingham and Seattle. Valleys in between were choked with humidity and smog. North was the dark schist of the Picket Range. Sunlight bleached the scene white and pale blue.

A young couple had just left the hut, and a family was camped next to it. "It's all yours," an eleven-year-old from Spokane told me as his parents packed up and headed home. I rested on a long, green bench built into the southwest wall. A rough-hewn table in the corner held a stack of guidebooks. The walls were covered in green, horizontal planking. A small shelf in the opposite corner supported a two-burner propane stove. Below that, a steel locker held extra food, fuel, and a half-smoked joint left by another camper.

Two miles north of the lookout, the line I'd been following for two years ran between American Border Peak and Canadian Border Peak. The cut crossed over the pass, then dropped toward Tomyhoi Creek and the Fraser River. The segment was one of the most difficult to mark on the northern border. The Northwest Boundary Commission began the task in 1858. Nearly two hundred cooks, Indian guides, horsemen, laborers, and messengers were hired to do the job. Axe men cut ahead of the astronomers, and laborers followed, leaving iron markers and piles of stone along the forty-ninth.

When the commission hit the highest peaks of the North Cascades, they called on Swiss-born Henry Custer to explore them. Custer was an experienced mountaineer and trekked the Nooksack and Chilliwack River drainages, the Picket Range, and Ruby Creek for three years. He climbed dozens of unnamed peaks and ridges and paddled whitewater rivers in dugout canoes with guides from the local Stó:lō tribe.

James Alden was hired to follow Custer and sketch and paint watercolors of the range. While Alden painted, Custer recorded topography with three compasses, a barometer, a sextant, and prose: "No mortal pen could be found to describe this grand and glorious scenery properly and justly. This endless variety of shapes and forms, these thousands of different shades and colors."

Custer mapped a thousand square miles of mountain country that had never seen a white man before. No one would follow in his footsteps for a dozen years. His forty-seven-page account of the area was included in the boundary commission's final report, but the report was somehow lost before it could be published. In 1907, Congress commissioned a new survey, and another team started all over again.

At sunset, the sky turned dark blue. I tried to remember the color of the stones, the cool air, the auburn sunlight touching my forehead. I thought about the first day of the trip at West Quoddy Head in Maine and tried to memorize the dark spires, rounded massifs, and marshmallow flanks of Mount Baker's glaciers. I thought about all the parts of the northland — oceans, rivers, lakes, plains, cities, reservations, and towns — and how they linked from east to west. It was indeed its own territory: a forgotten belt of wild, old America delineated by iron monuments, rock piles, and clear-cuts.

The full moon rose quickly. The valleys filled with shadows. Then Mars appeared, and a deep-blue shell slid to the horizon. Straight down from the summit, I could see orange campfires burning in the Twin Lakes campground. A dull, pink glow marked Bellingham and, south of that, Seattle. An approaching storm filtered the starlight. I lay down on a cot and closed my eyes. When I opened them the next morning, the moon and stars were gone and a steady rain pelted the hut.

The weatherman said the storm was a hundred miles across when it boomeranged around Bellingham and headed for the North Cascades. It would drop a quarter inch of rain on Winchester Mountain before noon, he said. Another inch and a half would fall throughout the day, likely washing out the Forest Service road and much of the trail.

I packed quickly and started down. Rivulets of rainwater made the path slick. The downpour started near the tree line and didn't let up until I got to the car. Water hadn't filled the gullies yet, and it was easier driving down than up. I eventually pulled onto the Mount Baker Highway and followed the swelling Nooksack River west toward the end of the line.

The road twisted through old-growth Douglas fir and red cedar. Old-man's-beard lichens grew on west-facing limbs and trunks. The river was pale blue with sediment from the East Nooksack Glacier on Shuksan. I followed an old pickup truck onto I-5 just before Bellingham and headed north to the Peace Arch Border Crossing in Blaine. Illuminated signs announced how long the wait at the westernmost border check in the mainland Lower 48 would be: less than five minutes at 3:00 p.m. on a Thursday. The east side of the highway was thick with trees, broken every now and then by a meadow. The west side was layered with mackerel sky as the storm wandered onshore.

I parked near half a dozen picnic tables at Peace Arch Park. A path led west and then north, past a few sculptures and a rose garden. A border patrol agent wearing a bulletproof vest and a 9-millimeter pistol watched me. He did not look relaxed. Visitors are allowed to walk across the border in Peace Arch Park. That's why the park was created. You can lounge on the lawn with your feet in Canada and your knees in America, if you want. You can jog laps between the two countries, as the Blaine High School cross-country team was doing when I arrived. The original intention of the park was to show good faith between two friendly nations. In the modern era of high security it had become a giant headache to those in charge of policing it.

I walked into Canada, past three tourists taking pictures of themselves with one foot in either country. It felt strange crossing the forty-ninth — like I should explain myself. I did about two minutes later, to an agent standing nearby. I told him I had traveled the entire border from Maine to Washington. He listened politely, scanning the park.

"What are you looking for?" I asked.

"There's a guy that we are watching," he said.

I asked which one, and he didn't answer. A woman walked her poodle between two rose gardens. Another woman, in a business suit, sat on a bench. A lone, dark-skinned man wearing a suit that was too large for him walked in circles while he spoke on his phone. Little houses with carports and swinging deck chairs crowded the northern edge of the park. Anyone could feasibly walk across the border and into one of the houses if no one was looking.

I left the agent and passed the last border

monument on the western edge of the lawn. The continent ended at a rocky beach strewn with kelp and seaweed. Beyond that was the Pacific. I could see three or four islands, a red navigational buoy, the backside of the Blaine Harbor jetty. Streaks of light reached down to a small island on the Canadian side of the border. A fishing boat headed in from sea. Another steamed out through a bright circle of sunshine. I could see the boat's rig and a tall wake peeling off its stern.

I watched the water for a while, then walked to the car and drove south. Fifteen minutes later, a reporter on the radio said that the Peace Arch crossing had been shut down. A man had driven to the Canadian border check and told the agent his car was loaded with explosives. He demanded to be let through or else he would detonate the bomb. The Royal Canadian Mounted Police and border patrol evacuated the neighborhood and park. The border was closed for four hours, and the man was put in jail. By 10:00 p.m. it was open again, and lines on either side started to move.

I spotted a sign for the Lummi Reservation as I headed south on I-5. I turned off the highway and drove past a man selling wild salmon out of a pickup truck. A few miles later, the Nooksack River, now a hundred yards wide, rushed under a bridge. Down the road, a red sign with ten-foot-tall letters spelled "PLAY, DINE, SPA, HOTEL" on the side of the Lummi Silver Reef Casino.

I took a left at a gas station and picked up a young casino worker, named Gary, who was hitchhiking. He had been born on the reservation and lived down the street from Jewell James. He said he grew up somewhere else, after child services took him away from his parents and put him in a foster home. He made his way back as a teenager and ended up in jail after a few brushes with the law. "The elders in there yelled at me for screwing up, for not attending ceremony," he said. "They said I should know about my tribe. They took me under their wing, and I learned Lummi songs for the first time. I learned the tradition. Blacks, whites, Latinos, Asians all fought in the jail yard. If you were Indian, they left you alone."

Gary wore chinos, and his shirt had the casino logo on it. He was six feet and well over two hundred pounds, and wore a long braid down his back. He had a wide, cheery face, a little stubble on his upper lip. When he was young, he had dressed like a gangster. Now he wore slacks and a button-down. He was a painter, specializing in traditional Lummi art. He got into it after he was released from prison and took a drawing class. "From then on," he said, "all I could see was art. I drew every single day for five years."

Gary won every art competition that he entered, and he was awarded a scholarship to a college in Bellingham, where eventually he painted alongside artists like Jewell James. "I was lost before that," he said. "I had no identity. The artwork let me connect with who I was, let me know how I could help my people, where I should be. There is good energy and bad energy out there. And if you get hooked by the good energy, you do good things. You go out and find a mentor, and then you are a mentor to someone else. I have four kids now. I teach them these things. I was in foster care for ten years. The bad energy draws you in a different direction. At some point in your life you will have a chance to choose between them."

Gary pointed to a row of wooden stakes sticking out of the water. "Those are my father's nets," he said. "That's how we catch the salmon. The nets wrap around the stakes and leave an opening for fish to get in. Once they are in, the fisherman pulls the net closed and up onto his boat. When the water is high, that's when the crabs are eating. When it goes out, that's when the silvers come in. We are getting to the end of the season. That's when the dogfish come."

A man standing on a wooden dory a half mile away threw a net. A thin, black circle flew across the white silhouette of Mount Baker. A pink mooring buoy held the man's boat in place. The proposed site of the Cherry Point coal terminal, which Jewell James and northwestern tribes had beaten in court, was a few miles north. The facility would have loaded fifty-four million metric tons of coal annually to be burned in Asia. A handwritten sign stapled to a telephone pole nearby read: "You Deserve to be Loved." Another behind it: "Believe in Who You Are."

"I'm a father, brother, teacher, student, artist," Gary said. "I'm everything I wanted to be." Not all of Gary's family can say that. He was in a hotel room at the casino six months before with a younger cousin. The kid went to the bathroom and when he didn't come out, Gary went in to see what was wrong. The boy was dead on the floor. He had overdosed on heroin. "It took me a while to get through that," Gary said. "I didn't paint for months."

The ocean wasn't silver anymore. It had

turned dark gray. The ridgelines leading back to the North Cascades vanished one by one. Bellingham looked like a cluster of facades, set on the edge of a hill. "Eighty-five percent of the Lummi live below the poverty level," Gary said. "Over there in Bellingham, there are millionaires."

I dropped Gary off at his father's house and drove around the reservation. A pickup truck stacked with coolers drove in front of me. Two boys crossed the road, both wearing black hats, black jeans, and fishing boots. They had made a shelter out of driftwood on the shore. They sat beneath it and smoked and watched their nets. Another sign on a telephone pole read: "Keep Your Head Up."

Down the street, some of the houses were nicer, with less junk in the yard. One was a mansion with two stainless-steel salmon welded onto wrought-iron gates. White people lived there, Gary said. Forty-four percent of the population on the reservation was now white. When I asked Gary how whites had purchased Indian land, he shook his head and said, "They just did."

The road hugged the shore, then turned inland past a thirty-foot-tall mural that Gary had painted of a squid. The telephone poles running along the soft shoulder were brand-new. The road was freshly paved. "You Are Not Alone," a sign read. "Kindness Matters."

I drove past an open-sided lodge at the Lummi cultural learning center that held two dozen traditional Lummi canoes. Then I bought a five-dollar ticket to a Lummi High School football game and watched the Blackhawks dismantle the visiting team. The Lummi team had been to the state championships five times in the previous eight years. Families cheered, and a few women pounded small drums as the Blackhawks ran down the field. A Winnebago parked behind the bleachers had a "We Believe in Blackhawk Nation" sign taped to the side. In the windshield was another sign that read "COAL," with a slash through it.

It was raining hard now. The horizon line across the ocean was soft and white. Rain hitting the water made a thick fog. I continued inland until I reached a roundabout. A sculpture of two golden salmon crossing each other stood in the middle of the circle. Douglas fir crowded the road, moisture beading up on the needles.

I drove around a few times, looking for a sign. There was nothing, no opening in the trees, nothing down the road. I needed to get back to Seattle to catch a flight that night. It would cross the northland in five hours flat. There was no map in the glove box, no phone signal, no one to ask. I had no idea which way was north, south, west, or east. The last building I'd passed was twenty minutes behind me. I kept circling, waiting for another car to come, peering down each of the roads, the four points of the compass, looking for a way home.

ACKNOWLEDGMENTS

This book was born in 2014 during a lunch with editor Matt Weiland and agent Paul Lucas. We shaped the basic concept in less than an hour. Three years and four thousand miles later that idea became the book you are holding. I am grateful to Matt and Paul for the vision, talent, and blind faith they brought to that table.

I'd also like to thank the MacDowell Colony for offering early, enduring, and vital support for this book, with both a fellowship and a Calderwood Art of Nonfiction research grant. Icebound in the woods of northern New Hampshire, with temperatures dipping to minus-twenty degrees, hundreds of pages of notes coalesced into a story.

I can't thank enough the captains, guides, mushers, tribespeople, bartenders, and dozens of hapless northlanders I bumped into, tracked down, or downright stalked along the way — who opened their lives, jobs, and hometowns to a stranger. More than anything, I hope that I have told their stories well. The poet Christian Barter was invaluable in editing early drafts of this book, as were friends and colleagues Kim Stravers, Peter Kray, Margaret Brown, and Derek Loosvelt. Finally, big thanks to Em-J Staples who hunted down the most elusive facts in the book and made sure I didn't mess them up on the page.

Lastly, eternal thanks to Sara Fox — my wife, travel buddy, colleague, and personal photographer — who never says no to a trip and always makes it look better than it was.

A NOTE ON SOURCES

Finding source material on the history of America's northern border was an adventure. Early explorers spent more time surviving and navigating the wilderness than they did documenting their travels. Most accounts are secondhand, and no two chronicles about a subject are the same. There are some exceptions. Samuel de Champlain was devoted to keeping a journal. After facing off against an Indian army, he would sit back against a tree, draw meticulous sketches, and summarize the day's events. His journals, most of which can be found online now, are the greatest window into northland life before the border. David Hackett Fischer's excellent interpretation of Champlain's writings in his book *Champlain's Dream* (Simon & Schuster, 2008) is a close second to the real thing. Hackett gives context to the Frenchman's exploits with extensive detail pulled from the shores of Brittany, Acadia, and the Great Lakes.

It should be said that this book was researched and written from the perspective of an American looking north at the border, and that many Canadian figures and historical events have been omitted. This was not done out of bias, but merely because, having grown up in Maine, that was the path I took and the story I chose to tell. The story of America's forgotten border is a tale of early mistakes and more than two centuries of fixes. Which is to say that there is no definitive event, treaty, document, or history that sums up the US-Canada border. Much of the language in the flawed 1783 Treaty of Paris, which defined the first miles of the boundary, and a dozen subsequent treaties that attempted to clarify and amend it, can be found online. The language is dense and from another time. Jacques Poitras's *Imaginary Line: Life on an Unfinished Border* (Goose Lane Editions, 2011) helps unravel some of the first treaties and explain how the eastern section of the line took its current shape.

Champlain's journal, and those kept by fellow French explorers Gabriel Sagard and Jean de Brébeuf, are the best sources for Étienne Brûlé's mysterious life in the northland. Consul Wilshire Butterfield combined their accounts, with additional sources, in *Brûlé's Discoveries and Explorations* (Helman-Taylor, 1898). René-Robert Cavelier, Sieur de La Salle, left more of a paper trail on his adventures across the Great Lakes. Francis Parkman does an excellent job painting a picture of the man, his mission, and his manic mind in *La Salle and the Discovery of the Great West* (Little, Brown, 1888). As for the lakes themselves, Wayne Grady's *The Great Lakes: The Natural History of a Changing Region* (Greystone Books, 2007) offers a comprehensive resource for how, when, and why the sweetwater seas took the shape that they did. Dan Egan's study of the lakes in *The Death and Life of the Great Lakes* (W. W. Norton, 2017) is an eye-opening summary of commerce on the lakes and how invasive species, pollution, and climate change are irrevocably changing them.

A century and a half passed between the Treaty of Paris and the marking of the northern border through Minnesota's Boundary Waters. William E. Lass uncovers the long-forgotten story of the surveyors who finally penetrated the lake country in *Minnesota's Boundary with Canada: Its Evolution since 1783* (Minnesota Historical Society Press, 1980). Grace Lee Nute followed the French Canadian canoe men who carved the first path through the Boundary Waters — documenting songs they sang, their paddling style, and what they used for bug dope — in her book *The Voyageur* (Minnesota Historical Society Press, 1955).

Lack of information was not a problem at the Standing Rock Sioux Reservation. Joye Braun, Harold Frazier, and many others recited Sioux history and 150 years of treaty law from memory, as did many of the youth I interviewed at the camp. Investigative reporting by the *Intercept* was invaluable when I was comparing contradictory reports released by the Standing Rock Sioux tribe, pipeline officials, and North Dakota law enforcement. Sioux chief Red Cloud was the most relevant historical figure to the struggle at Standing Rock and was relatively unknown in contemporary America until Bob Drury and Tom Clavin documented his incredible life and victory over the US Army in *The Heart of Everything That Is: The Untold Story of Red Cloud, an American Legend* (Simon & Schuster, 2013).

Driving through North Dakota's northland, I found Ian Frazier's masterpiece *Great Plains* (Farrar, Straus & Giroux, 1989) useful for understanding the region's importance to Plains Indian nations and US history. *The Day the World Ended at Little Bighorn: A Lakota History* (Viking Adult, 2007), by Joseph M. Marshall III, was similarly helpful in explaining the backstory of the Lakota people and informed my decision to use the word "Indian" to describe American tribes. Beth LaDow homes in on the story of Montana's northern border and how it changed the northern plains in *The Medicine Line: Life and Death on a North American Borderland* (Psychology Press, 2002). Wallace Stegner's memoir, *Wolf Willow* (Viking, 1962), is a powerful personal history of growing up in Medicine Line country, as is Tony Rees's precise recounting of drawing the northern border along the forty-ninth parallel in *Arc of the Medicine Line: Mapping the World's Longest Undefended Border across the Western Plains* (University of Nebraska Press, 2008).

The boundary commissions that surveyed and cut the northern border have gone unheralded in American history. Anne P. Streeter recounts the first boundary survey in the Pacific Northwest in *Joseph S. Harris and the U.S. Northwest Boundary Survey, 1857–1861* (Trafford, 2012). *The Pacific Northwest: An Interpretive History,* by Carlos

Arnaldo Schwantes (University of Nebraska Press; revised, enlarged edition, 2000) is a must-read when touring the western extent of the northern border. Schwantes covers everything from James Cook's discovery of the region to David Lynch's *Twin Peaks.* Finally, John Suiter's *Poets on the Peaks: Gary Snyder, Philip Whalen and Jack Kerouac* (Counterpoint, 2003) is a deeply researched and unrivaled biography of the Beats and their time in the fire lookouts of the North Cascades.

ABOUT THE AUTHOR

Porter Fox is the editor of *Nowhere* and the author of *Deep.* His writing has appeared in the *New York Times, Outside, National Geographic Adventure,* and *The Best American Travel Writing.* Raised in Maine, he lives in New York.

The employees of Thorndike Press hope you have enjoyed this Large Print book. All our Thorndike, Wheeler, and Kennebec Large Print titles are designed for easy reading, and all our books are made to last. Other Thorndike Press Large Print books are available at your library, through selected bookstores, or directly from us.

For information about titles, please call:
  (800) 223-1244

or visit our website at:
  gale.com/thorndike

To share your comments, please write:
  Publisher
  Thorndike Press
  10 Water St., Suite 310
  Waterville, ME 04901